AF412426

MATTHEW C. EAMES

DICKON EAMES

An American sculptor in France

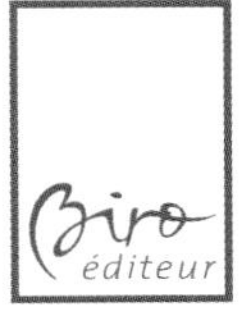

Biro
éditeur

© Biro éditeur 2007
www.biroediteur.com
ISBN 978-2-35119-034-0
© 2007 ADAGP for the works of Dickon Eames

Printed in the European Union

I dedicate this book to my dear mother who has been of inestimable help in my endeavours to memorialize my father and I also extend my gratitude to all members of the Eames family.

CONTENTS

DICKON EAMES, MY FATHER

I was barely twenty when my father died. It was only several years later that I came to understand the full import of his death - for me and for the rest of the world. Today I feel the time has come to place his life and work in their true perspective. Dickon Eames was in every way an independent. He belonged to no clique and followed no school. This is probably why little has been written about the man and his work.

This book is a tribute to Dickon. It is neither exhaustive nor totally objective. It is my personal vision of an artist, his family and his history, accompanied by the testimony of friends, the opinions of specialists and critics, and - most important - an overview of the work accomplished by my father during the twenty-five years of his life as a sculptor. It has not been an easy task to gather the material, track down the information, eliminate false trails and follow up authentic ones, then put it all together as simply and naturally as possible. No, it has not always been easy. But I hope you will agree with me that it was worth it.

Welcome to the life and work of my father, Dickon Eames.

CHRONOLOGY

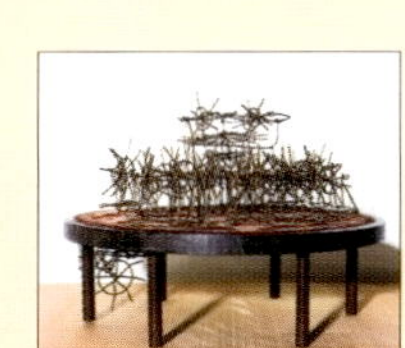

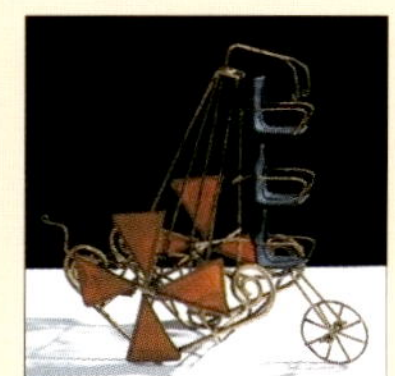

1945	Birth of Richard Comyn Eames (Dickon Eames) on 20 January in New York.
1959 - 1963	Art studies - Tabor Academy, Marion, Massachusetts (USA).
1963 -1965	Student at the "Art Students League" and the "New School for Social Research", New York.
1965	Dickon meets Mark Brusse for the first time in New York. Meets Del Geist at Philip Hourwich's home.
1966	First group show at the De Mena Gallery, New York. First small metal sculptures, first experiments with welding.
1967	First stay in Paris and first marriage (to a Frenchwoman).
1969	Lives for a while in Ibiza (Balearic Islands).
1970 - 1973	Lives in Corfu (Greece).
1972	Meets Carolyn Hartley, his future wife.
1972	3 solo exhibitions of his "small machines": Ora Gallery, Athens - Glyfada Gallery, Corfu (Greece) - Galerie Georges Moos, Geneva (Switzerland).
1973	Returns to Paris. Dickon and Carol take an apartment in rue Tiquetonne, in the historic "Halles" district.
1973	Marries Carol in England on 28 April.
1973	Further work on the "Machines" and a group show at the Galerie Georges Moos, Geneva (Switzerland).
1974	Meets Mark Brusse again in Paris.
1974	Buys the house in Freneuse, Normandy. Extensive works, addition of a studio. The family moves there permanently.
1975	First meets Anthony and Liliane Stone.
1977	Thierry Glaizot starts a country doctor's practice nearby.
1977	Birth of Matthew Comyn Eames on 9 September.
1977	Solo exhibition, "Ball Machines & Balloons", at the Galerie Balans, Amsterdam (Holland).
1977	Group show - Museum der Stadt, Recklinghausen (Germany), on the theme "To fly - a dream".

1977	Meets Peter Woodd, John Wolff, Peter Townsend.
1978	Group show - Museum der Stadt, Münster (Germany).
1978	Peter Woodd introduces Dickon Eames to Anton Furst and at their instigation Dickon starts making holograms.
1979	Solo exhibition around the "Crankshaft Series" - Galerie d'Theeboom, Amsterdam (Holland).
1979	Exhibition with Mark Brusse and Klaas Gubbels - Galerie Sisu Ontwerp Centrum, Nijmegen (Holland).
1980	Solo exhibition - Galerie d'Theeboom, Amsterdam (Holland).
1981	Group show - Galerie d'Theeboom, Amsterdam (Holland).
1982	Holograms by Dickon Eames are presented in a group show - Light Fantastic Gallery, London (Great Britain).
1984	A new hologram exhibition: group show at the Light Fantastic Gallery, London (Great Britain).
1986	Start of a collaboration with Jean-Claude Riedel. First solo exhibition at the Galerie Riedel, Paris (France), on the theme "Tuyaux" (Pipes).
1987	Solo exhibition - "Recent sculptures" - Galerie Riedel, Paris (France).
1988	Solo exhibition - "Colors" - Galerie Riedel, Paris (France).
1989	Solo exhibition - "Série Grise" (Grey Series) - Galerie Riedel, Paris (France).
1991	Solo exhibition - "The Aviary" - Galerie Riedel, Paris (France).
1991	Group show - Art Forum Yanaka, Tokyo (Japan).
1993	Solo exhibiton - "Hard & Soft" - Galerie Riedel, Paris (France)
1994	Solo exhibition - "Les Fontaines" (Fountains) - Galerie Riedel, Paris (France).
1996	Solo exhibition - "Les Guerriers Orientaux" (Oriental Warriors) - Galerie Riedel, Paris (France).
1997	Dickon Eames dies suddenly on 14 February.
1997	Memorial Exhibition on the initiative of Mark Brusse - Galerie Eric Le Gallo, Espace 061 - Rouen (Normandy).

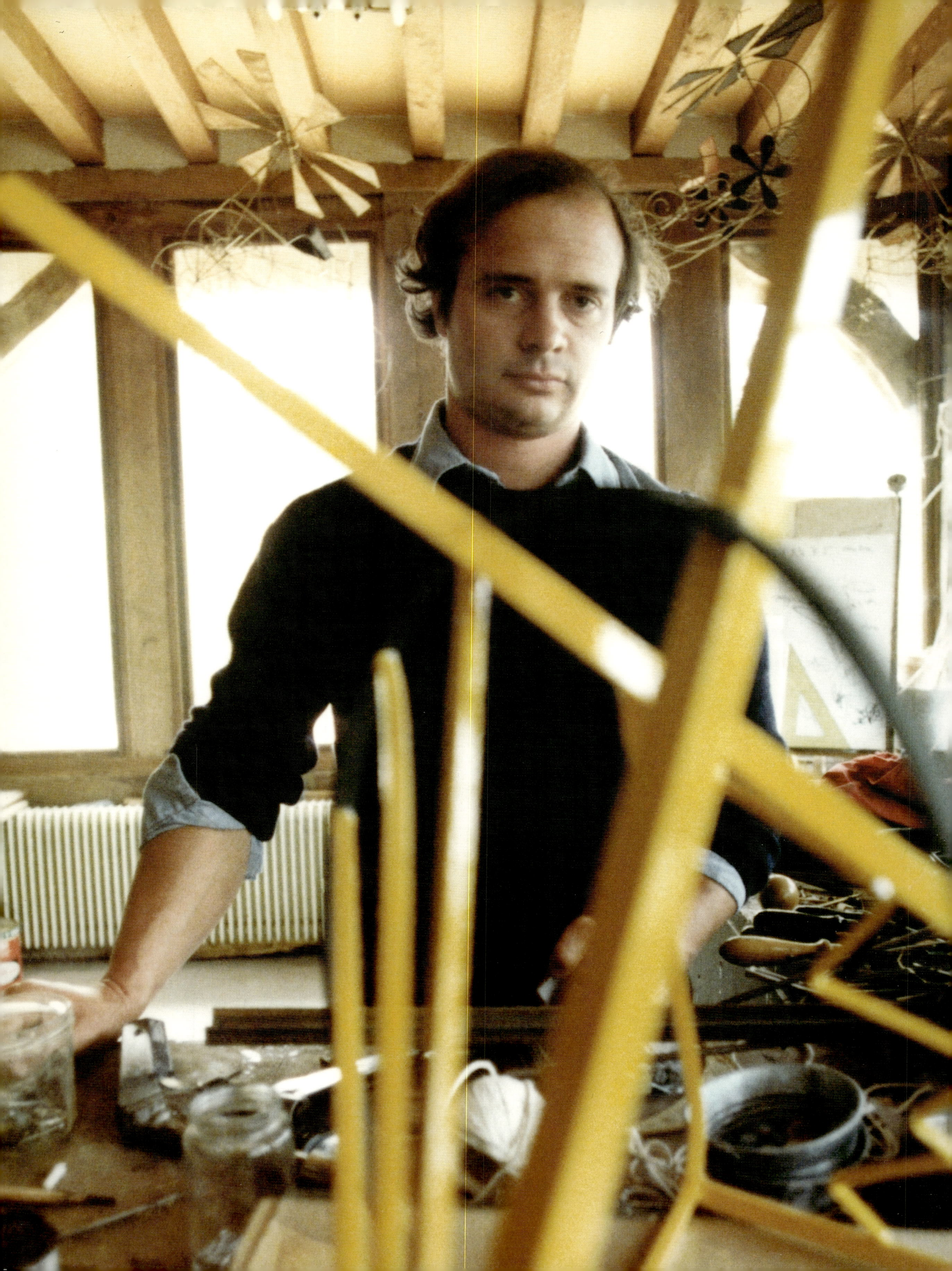

1 AN AMERICAN IN FRANCE

The smell of hot metal was everywhere in our house. It was a pungent, mineral smell - powerful but not overpowering, thrilling and at the same time reassuring. If I close my eyes I can smell it now. It hung in the air, got into the closets and into our clothes. It stayed on our skin and clung to our hair. When we went outside, we took it with us. I realize now how much it was part of my life.

When I say the house smelled of hot metal, I'm over-simplifying. It was more complex than that. To my child's nose, the smells of steel, copper, brass, iron and zinc were constantly changing, depending on whether they were being heated, hammered, cut, sanded, flattened or bent. Then there were odors of paint, varnish, wood, glue, sawdust. And then there were cooking smells from the kitchen, and earthy, organic smells from neighboring farms, all mingling with the workshop smells to create a uniquely potent and soothing whole.

In quiet moments I recall our house and I inhale these memories. My father is there, very close. I see him welding two pieces of metal together in a cascade of white sparks. It's very hot. There's a low, throaty roaring sound backed by a plaintive, high-pitched whine. The metal puts up some resistance but in the end it always gives in. My father is getting pieces together for a show in Paris. It's a big event but he seems curiously unconcerned. Sometimes he just stops what he's doing, switches off the torch, takes off his

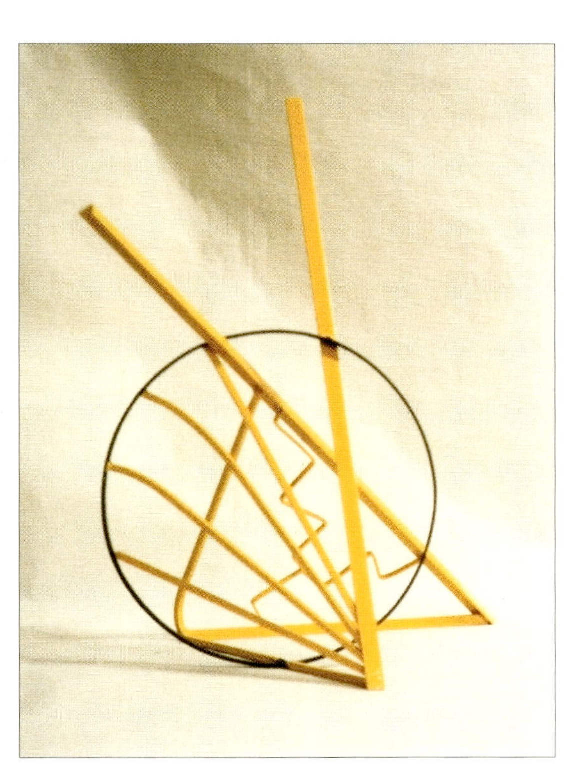

My father created this sculpture
to celebrate my arrival into the world.

mask, goggles and gloves. Then he sits down, lights a cigarette and screws up his eyes in that special way of his. He's looking at what he's just done, and yet he isn't looking. It's more a feeling, an internal thing. The studio is suddenly a lot quieter, but the heat and the smell linger in the air, on my father's clothes, on my father's skin.

Then my mother comes in, bringing other scents that take their chances with the muscular scents of the studio. It ought to be a losing battle and yet - they also have their part to play. Like when a painter mixes his colors. Sometimes one of the colors is so strong and intense you don't think it has changed at all. And yet it has. My mother brings scents of the garden, the countryside, horses and dogs. She brings scents of soap and lotions, linen, pastry, apples, butter. These gentler scents somehow hold their own, expanding and weaving themselves into the complex fabric of odors that suffuse my childhood home.

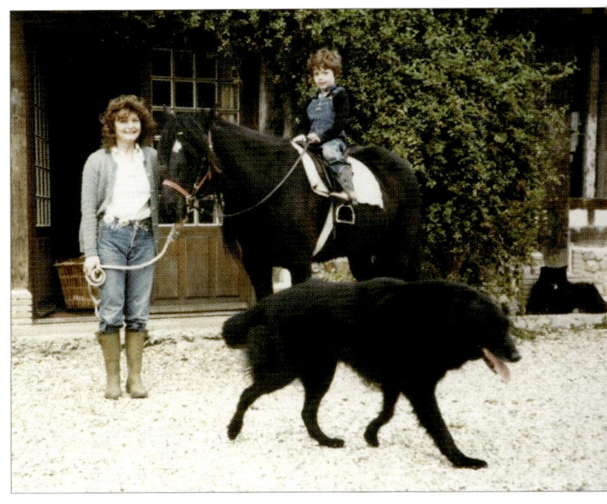

I learned to love riding thanks to my mother, an excellent horsewoman. Here I am with Carol, in front of our house in Freneuse, on one of her Dale ponies.

My mother always arrives with two or three of our dogs behind her, and very often with friends who have come to lunch, to dine or to stop off for a few days at our house in the fields. All at once the place is noisier, merrier, there's a lot of laughing, joking, talking. Bottles are uncorked, dishes handed round. The conversation quickens, I don't understand much of what's being said but I'm one of the party and having fun. The people who come through Normandy to see my parents are as different as can be: Parisian, American, English, Dutch, Japanese, Greek. They chatter away in all these languages and I bask in a delicious sense of freedom. Nobody notices it's way past my bedtime.

My father leaves his studio to join us on these occasions, but he'll go back there in an hour or two, probably when everyone is napping under the apple trees. Or sooner, or later, or whenever he decides. In any case, part of him is always there.

The studio is Ali Baba's cave. It's a scientist's laboratory, a mechanic's workshop, a garden shed, a utility room, a scrap dealer's yard, a kitchen gone wild ... it's all of these, and it's also unlike anyplace else on earth. There are gas cylinders lined up like soldiers, for welding and cutting. There are tools everywhere - pliers, hammers, electric saws, planes, drills, shears - all lying in fabulous disorder, as if instantly dropped there after use. Everything is familiar, yet every day I find something new, something different. It's here that an artist's work was born. That artist was my father, Dickon Eames.

Dickon Eames: 1945-1997. A short life. A work so intensely concentrated it might have been touched with a sense of premonition. On February 14, the day of my father's death, this work began a new life without him. Ten years later, the edge of grief is softened, the sense of injustice appeased. Ten years later, after false starts and wrong turnings, attempts to erase certain memories, to reject, circumvent and transcend the work itself - the better to remember the man himself - the two of them come together again. But today they co-exist differently, organized into a new logic. Seen in this new light, everything becomes clear: it is time for me to accept history, and to share it.

When I was very small, I didn't really know what my father did for a living. Does a child ever ask himself that? It's usually other people who ask. Especially when you start school: "What does your Dad do?"

For a long time, I thought my Dad was a magician. (That doesn't necessarily mean I've changed my mind today!)

He would spend long hours in his studio where we could hear the metallic whine of metal being cut, smell the curious smell of heated metal and glimpse the flickering glow of a supernatural blue light. When my father came to join us, he sometimes brought me a metal object - a train, a car, a boat. These toys were for me and my friends - made by my Dad the magician. They were admired by everyone I played with and they gave me a special status. But I couldn't just "commission" a toy from my father. I had to wait patiently for the next miracle to be produced. If I insisted, I was sure to get the short, sharp answer that my friends and I still recall: "I'm not a toymaker!" He could have fooled us! These toys were truly beautiful. They stayed with me throughout my childhood and beyond. They intrigued and astonished my friends and, most important, they were the "props" that allowed me to act out epic adventures. Thanks to them, I took off alone or with my accomplices to distant lands where dangers lurked at every turn. Thanks to them, I came back miraculously unscathed from braving malicious Martians, hostile pygmies, wicked wizards, earthquakes, floods and werewolves.

As soon as I went to school I made a whole houseful of friends. They would come to our home for the after-school snack the French call "goûter". We had heaps of room, and my parents always had time for them. I was an only child and they didn't want me to be a loner in an adult world.

The boys in my class were intrigued by these foreigners who didn't do things quite the way other people did: "Monsieur" who didn't have a real job, the beautiful "Madame" who bred unusual horses and rode so well, a boy who called his parents by their first name ... and all these pets and favorite animals around. It was country living, but not as they knew it. Then there were the games - with plenty of space and imagination to keep up the momentum.

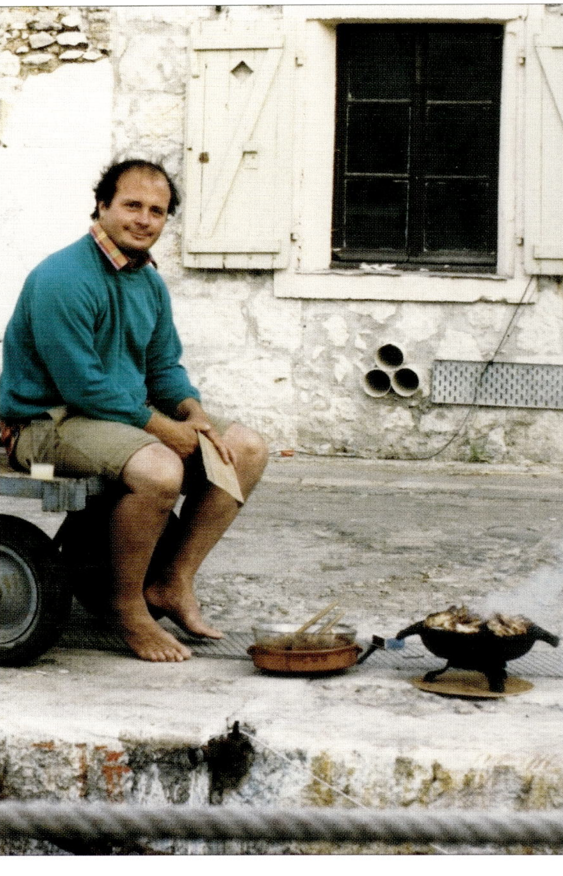

Dickon on vacation in Villefranche, on the Côte d'Azur.

The whole family pitched in, even my Grandad from New York who built me a tree-house during one of his stays.

My best friends were the Glaizot brothers. Henri was a little older than me, Louis a little younger. We were soon inseparable - a gang of three. Our parents encouraged this allegiance and became friends in the process. At the time, Glaizot *père* was a young doctor who had set up his practice in the region. Soon all the Eames had been to see Dr. Glaizot. And thanks to Henri, Louis and me, the family doctor quickly became a family friend. The Glaizot family became my own "French family" - and has remained so ever since. The distances between us have widened, our lives have branched in different directions, but we still meet with the same delight, aware of the treasure that underpins our relationship - an entire childhood closely shared.

Throughout my childhood, the Glaizot children were my brothers and sisters. They introduced me to French life, and more specifically, to French family life. With them, I imbibed values and traditions they themselves took for granted. In their company, I immersed myself in the culture, the language and the rituals that made up the Glaizot lifestyle. My parents were pleased to see my "French side" developing in such happy circumstances. It was natural for them to want their son to be perfectly assimilated into their adoptive country and culture. And after all, I was born in France! With the Glaizot family, I discovered provincial life in the heart of Normandy. With my parents, I explored yet more realms: poetry, art, a love of animals, a talent for hospitality. I thank both families for opening these doors. And for making my childhood magical.

For my childhood was indeed full of magic. Not just because my father was a magician, but because I lived in

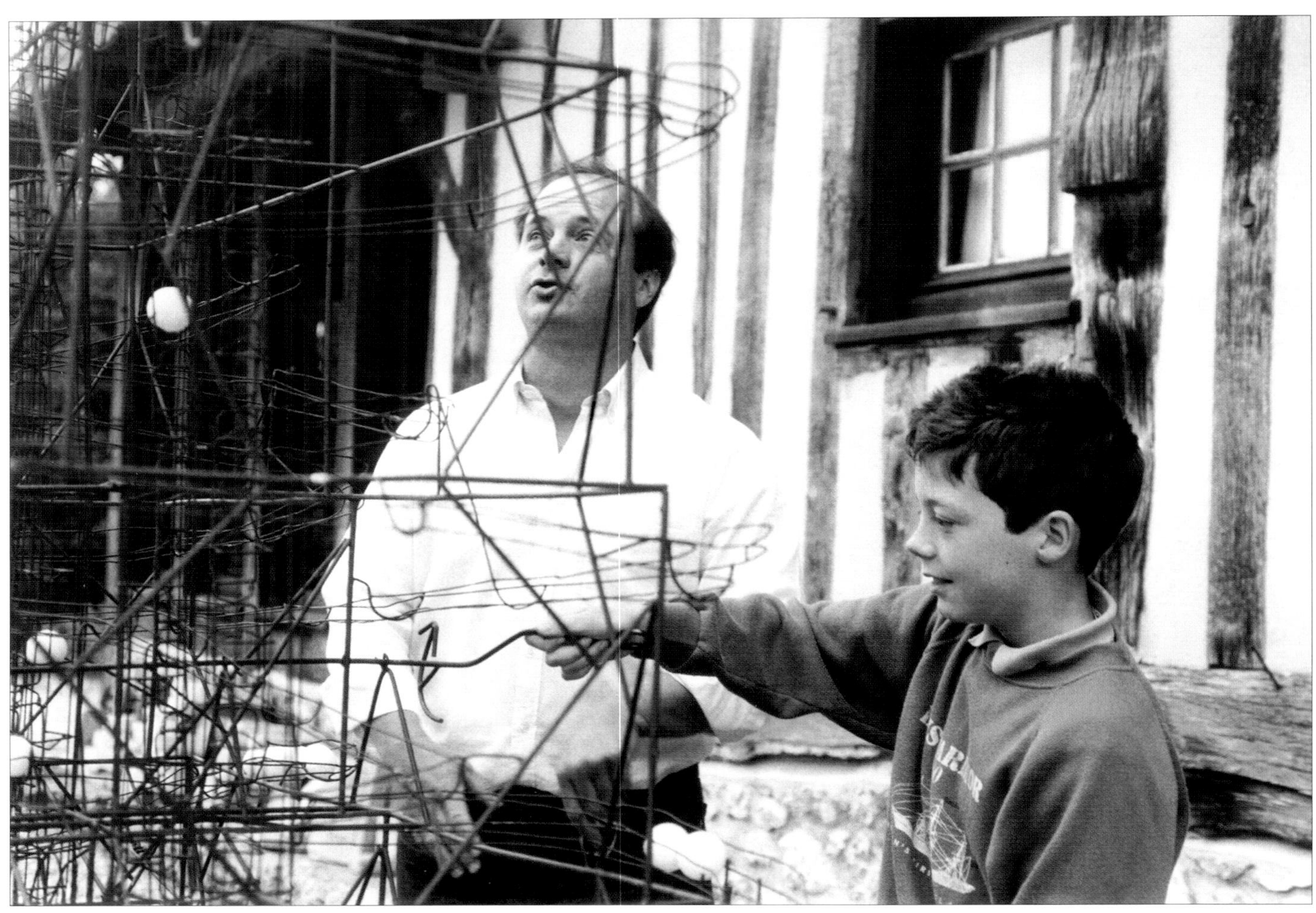

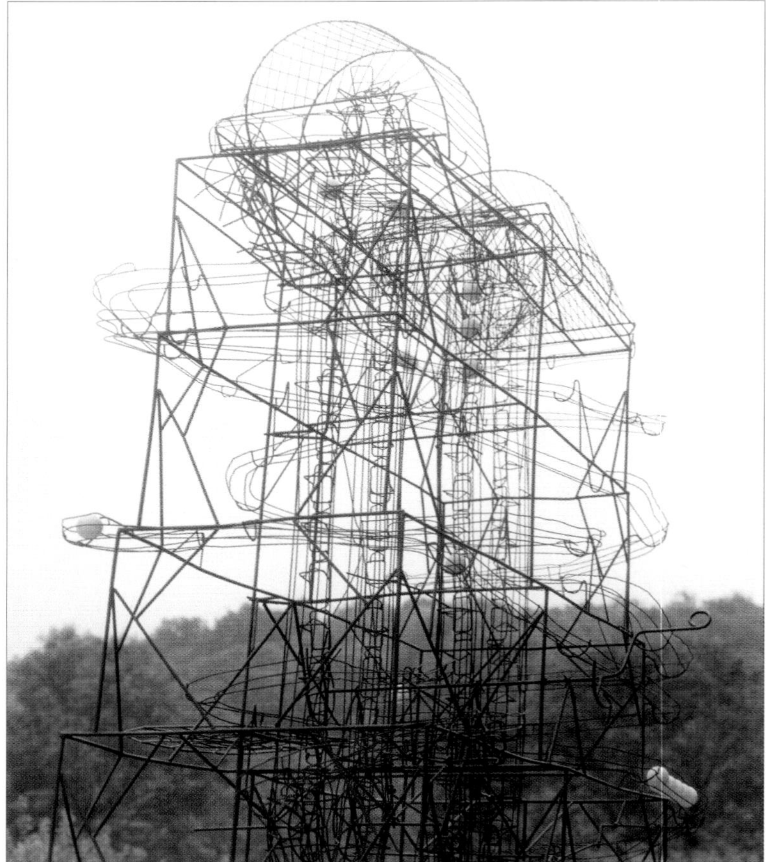

Dickon and myself next to the "Ping-pong Ball Machine". One of a magnificent series that Dickon created in 1977, the year I was born.

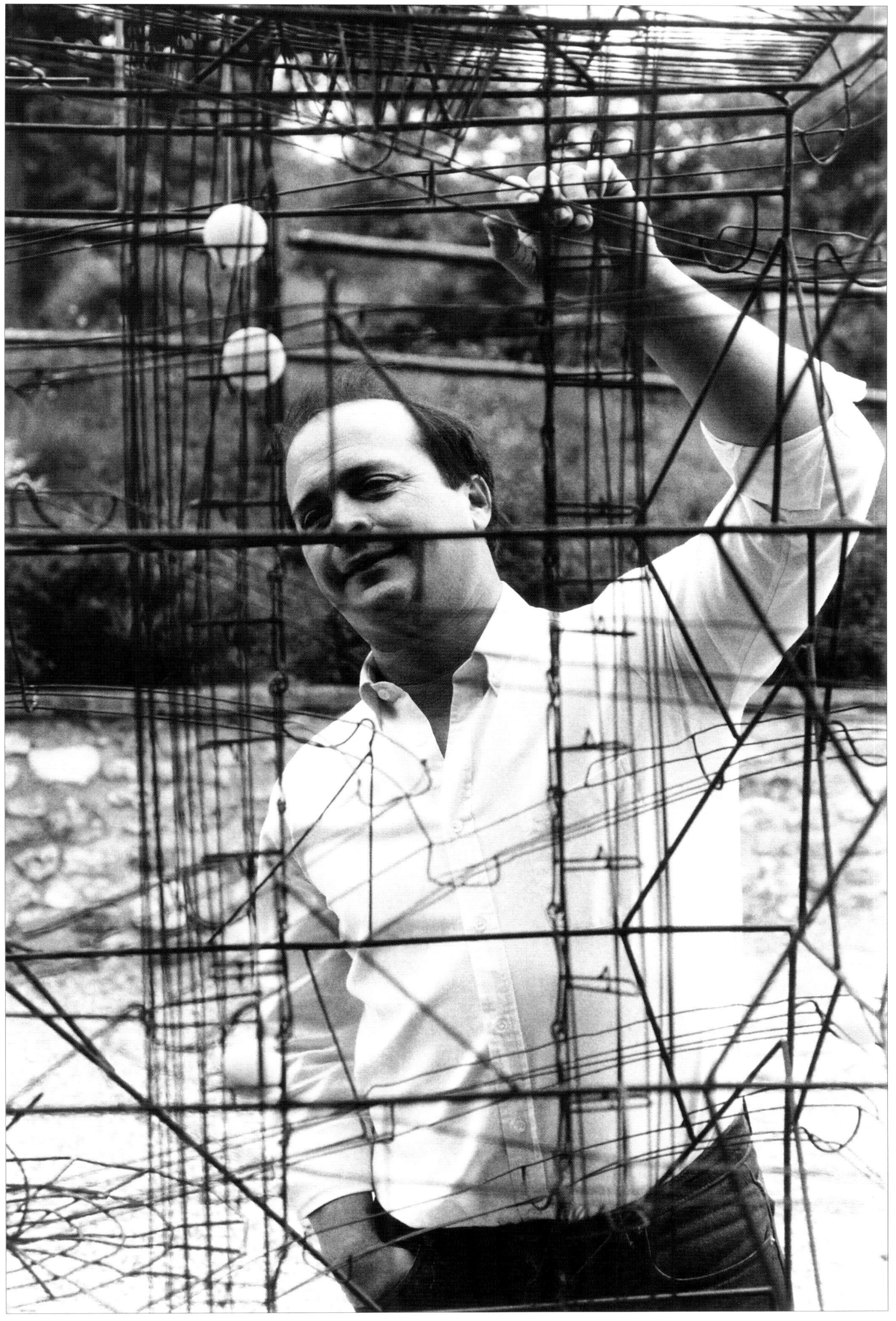

an environment anyone would have envied. A commodious house crowned with a massive thatch roof that overhung the windows like inquiring eyebrows; nooks and crannies everywhere; stairs to leap down three, four, five at a time; a vast garden; stables, horses, carts, tack, dogs ... my parents gave me the run of it all. I was allowed to ride, cycle, shout, play noisy games, sleep late if I felt like it. It was as permissive a life as a child could wish. Even today, I marvel at my parents' wisdom and generosity in offering me a world whose only boundaries were what I made them.

Dickon was my model. He was idolized by my friends. He never talked down to us, and let us do all sorts of things that would have horrified my friends' parents. With Dickon we were free to disagree and express our opinions, even if he always had the last word. In any case, his last word always gave us plenty to think about.

Sometimes he drove us to see his scrap merchant in Brionne - a treat I shared only with the Glaizot brothers. We piled into the pickup and set off in search of treasure. We followed Dickon as he rummaged through unstable mountains of scrap iron - girders, steel tubing, crankshafts, bathtubs, hubcaps, nuts, bolts, cogs, chains. We watched as he fingered, examined, weighed up the potential of each find. He could tell at a glance what metal it was, what alloy, what part it had played in what machine or system. He was usually on the lookout for triangular shapes and tubes, but sometimes he discovered something wonderful, like the nose of an old Boeing that he took home just because it was beautiful and astonishing.

Life was a game, with its mishaps and misfortunes, not to be taken too seriously. One of our family jokes was my father's propensity for "shipwrecks". He was something of a specialist in this field. Whether he inherited his nautical leanings from my grandfather, a respected member of the

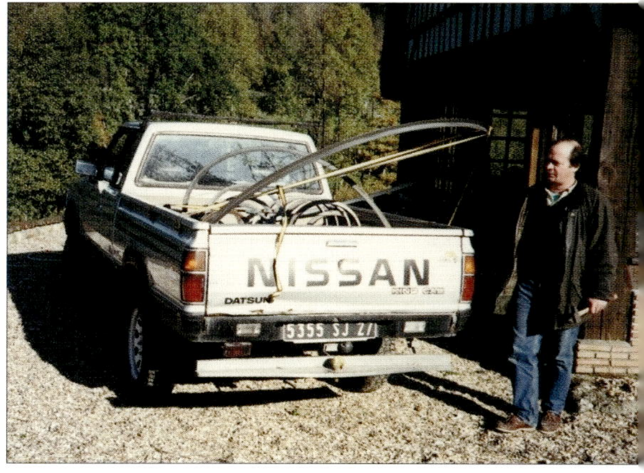

My father and his famous pickup, full of precious scrap that will one day be art ...

New York Yacht Club, I can't say. Grandfather Eames was something of an artist too: he once came all the way from New York to Normandy aboard his own yacht. It couldn't have been plain sailing either: my father subsequently took the boat out for a short sail and nearly sank. The boat was shipping water fast!

As for my father's cruises on our local river, the Risle, they were always a big adventure. He had his own craft, a kind of canoe with a sail, and he loved to take it out. But if he spotted something interesting on the bank, in his excitement he forgot all notions of good seamanship. Many are the times he swam to shore, the canoe was recovered downstream, and its sail and contents dried out ready for the next outing.

Dickon never dramatized. Even my deepest soul-searchings got an answer that was concise and at the same time opened vast horizons. "Choose your life" was his motto, a simple idea that could have seemed immensely complicated for a young boy raised on more traditional lines.

Here I am in my father's studio, making my first incursions in a vast and complicated world that never fails to fascinate me. Tubular contraptions propped on the workbench, scraps of metal beneath my feet, tools all about me, and here and there a battered object waiting to be given new life. I'm five or six - old enough by Dickon's reckoning to explore this territory in my own way. Everything draws me here - the smells, the lights, the sounds, the curious artefacts that have been part and parcel of my earliest years. Now I am old enough to add this den of treasures to my other playgrounds. My father watches me out of the corner of his eye - a sorcerer and his apprentice, both absorbed by metal's infinite possibilities. He lets me roam at will in this unforbidden land, lets me touch, feel and handle each discovery, but he also teaches me to wear goggles when I watch him weld, to be careful of rusty nails, sharp points and jagged edges, to respect the forces of flame and fire. By the age of nine, things have taken a more serious turn. I'm old enough to help my father, to hand him a tool, a piece of metal tubing, a can of spray paint. Dickon is the surgeon, I'm his assistant. An operation can take hours. We lose all notion of time. I get my first lessons in welding and soldering. And I start tinkering with objects of my own making. How could I not? It all looks so easy when my father does it. It's a time of happy trial and error, but my first real "work" is a tribute to Dickon.

I remember this sculpture - my first (and I have to say, last) serious attempt at welding. I made the piece in copper, because it is the easiest metal for a ten-year-old to work with. I had decided to make a gift for my father. Maybe it was his birthday, or Father's Day, or Christmas, I don't remember. Or maybe it was for no special occasion, just an idea that took hold. What I do remember is my determination to make a sculpture, a sculpture called "Dickon". Of course I couldn't keep the project a secret: I needed my father's workshop, his tools, and most of all, his advice and assistance. The welding apparatus fascinated me and I was impatient to put it to my own personal use. My father's input in the project was heroic. He stayed totally focussed on my concept, never letting his own ideas intrude. He showed me how best to arrange my pieces to get the shape I wanted, how to handle the blowtorch, adjust the flame, count the seconds. For the rest, he gave me free rein. He kept a close but discreet eye on me, and no doubt my mother did too. She wouldn't have been far away. But together they gave me the freedom to take a "grown-up" project from concept to finished work.

I make no great claims as to the result. The child's hand is there to see, there are lumps and bumps where the welding torch went a little haywire, but as a memory it's perfect! The best part was working alongside my father. To impose my will on fire and metal, like him. To create, like him, the curling smoke and sparkling clusters that tell you an object is about to be born. I stuck out my tongue more than really necessary, hammered my thumb once in a while, snagged my shirt and singed a few hairs. But at the end of it all, I had never felt happier or prouder. My father was my model. I would have walked a highwire or straddled a lion if such had been his business in life. Instead, I tamed fire and metal, because Dickon was a sculptor.

When I finally handed him my gift, he seemed so moved and delighted I was elated for weeks afterwards. I wore my pride like a badge and recounted my "exploit" to anyone benevolent enough to listen.

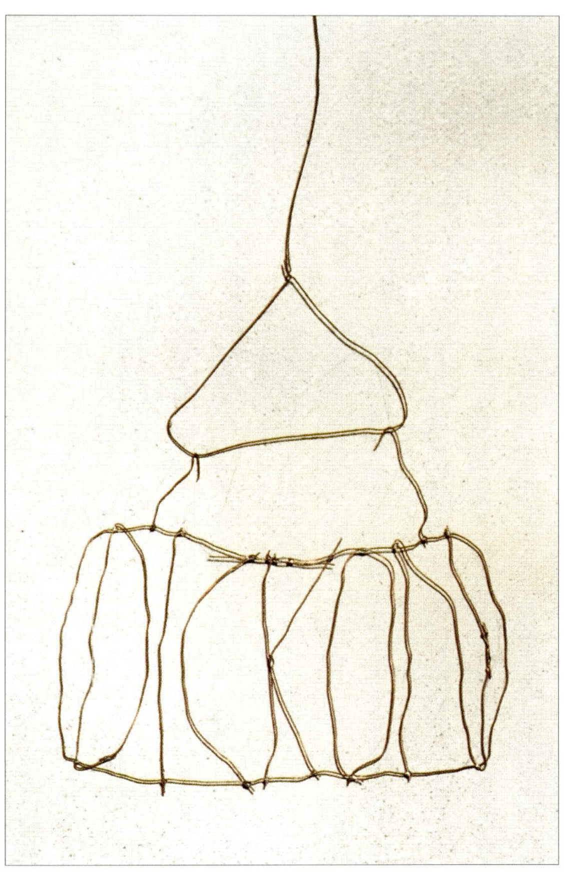

My first sculpture, dedicated to Dickon. A son's tribute to his father.

The studio is never far from my thoughts. I can be thinking of something else and it's there - a beating heart, a background music. It's the canvas on which ideas are projected and plans are made. I can cross an ocean and take it with me. I can exchange the streets of New York for the shores of the Caribbean and it is with me still. Is it the studio that haunts me, or is a part of me still there in the studio? In my mind's eye I revisit every corner, every sound, every odor, every texture of my childhood. It takes only a small mental step for the

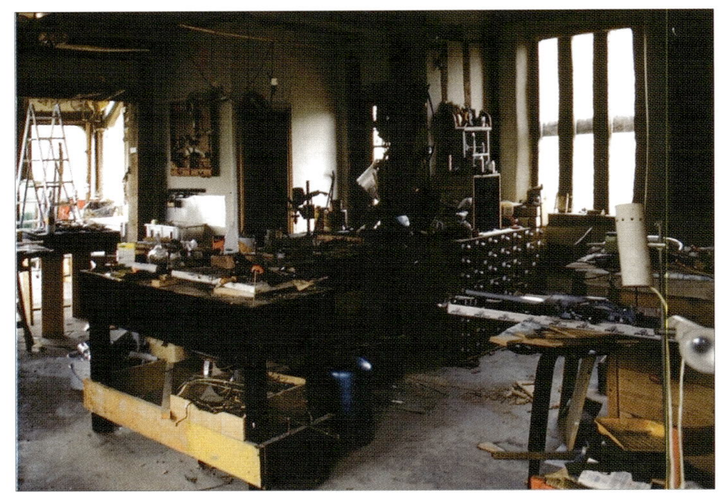

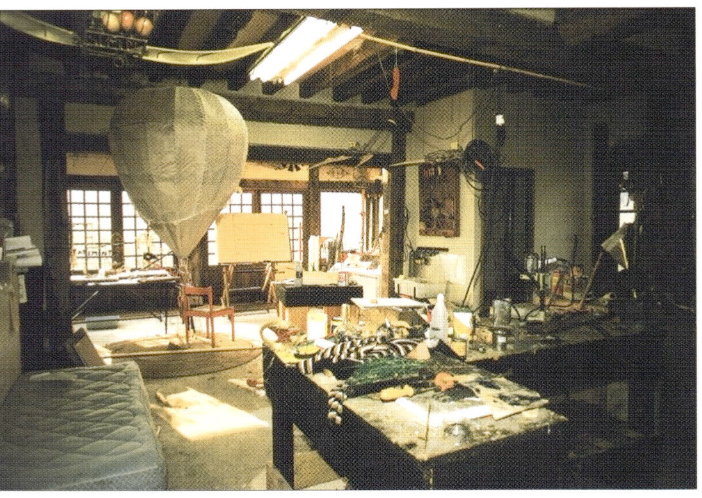

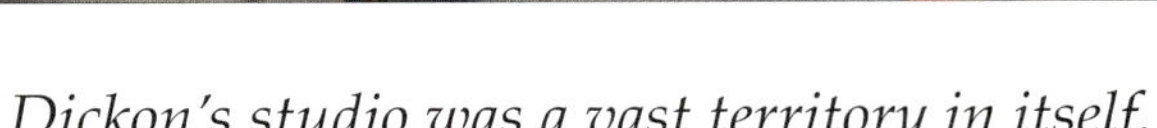

Dickon's studio was a vast territory in itself.

A balloon from the series "Ball Machines & Balloons".

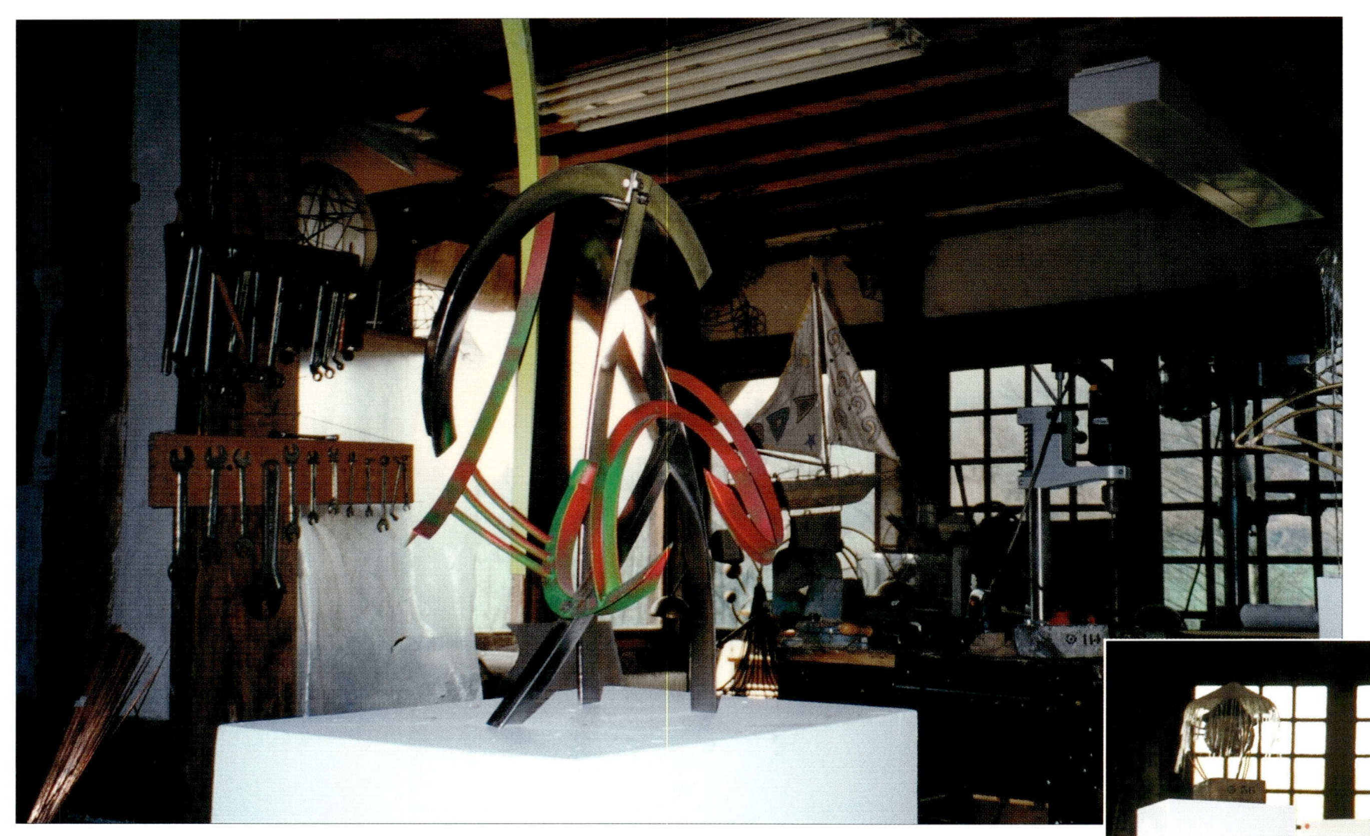

A tribute to Humphrey B. from the "Hard & Soft" series.

"Guerrier Oriental" (Oriental
Warrior), one of Dickon Eames'
very last works.

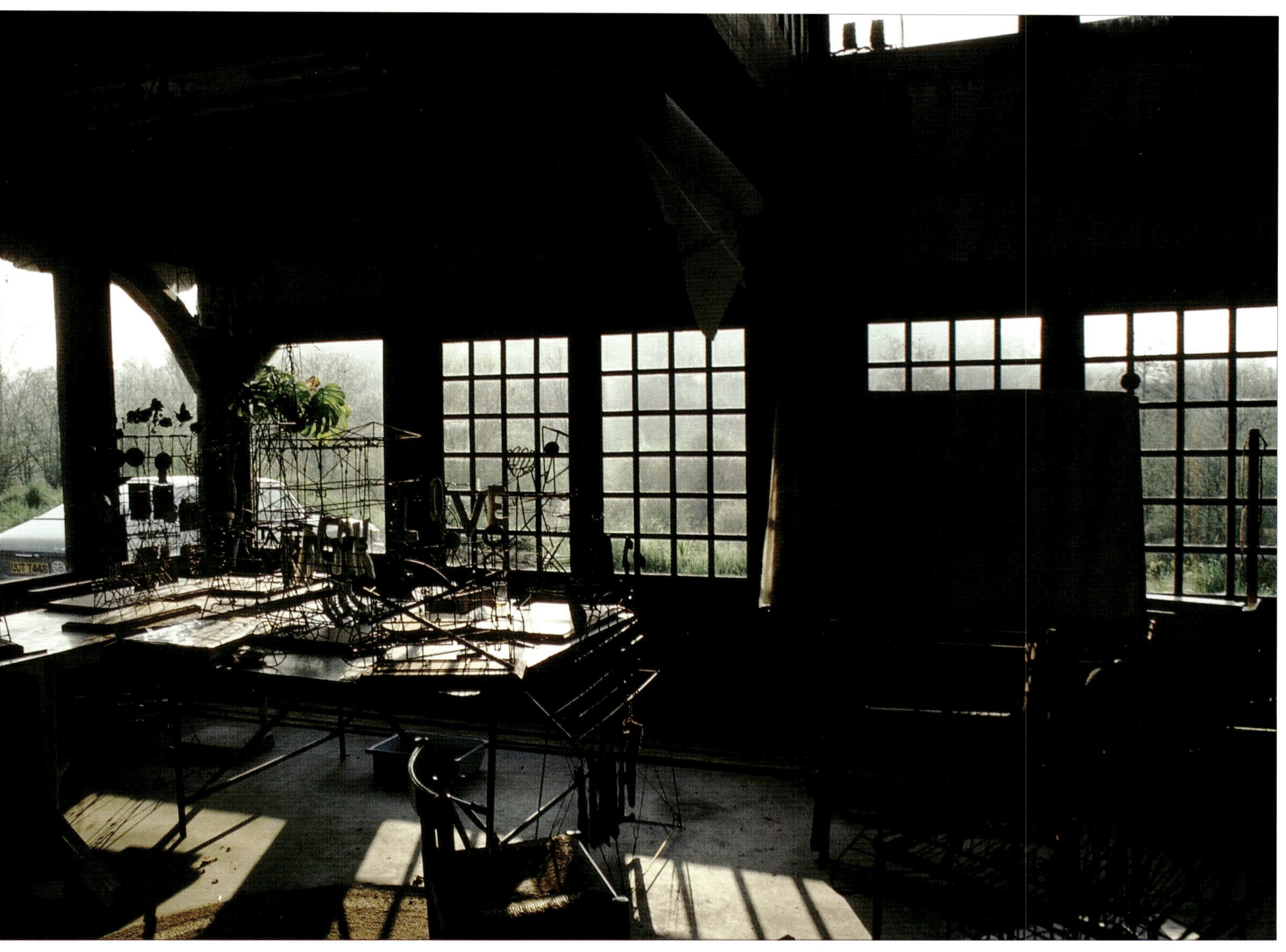

Light poured in from the windows on each side.

shapes to become sculpture, for the sculpture to become a man's work, for that work to become the life of an artist ... my father.

Dickon's studio adjoined the kitchen of our house in Normandy. People naturally congregated in the large, friendly living and dining area, and were just as naturally drawn to the studio, intrigued but never repelled by the acrid smell of molten metal. When my father closed his studio door, it was only to have a moment's peace to think something out, or to protect us from a particularly risky welding operation. Apart from those times, we were free to come in, watch him work and ask him questions.

I could always confide in my father. He gave me all his attention, his eyes looking straight into mine with no hint of judgment or reprobation. Little problems were listened to as seriously as big ones. Anxieties became challenges to be met, doubts were treated with respect. He taught me to question accepted ideas and recognize the value of uncertainty. He never made long speeches or waxed philosophical. But his ideas were apparent in the way he worked and lived, in the way he talked to fellow artists, to local tradesmen, to the scrap merchant. He never insisted, never laid down the law, yet things always seemed to go the way he intended. He knew how to listen, gave his opinion without being opinionated, took a positive approach to each situation.

Dickon was a popular man - friendly and outgoing, treating people with a warmth and directness that cut through bourgeois niceties. Our neighbors were first surprised and then captivated by my father's easy ways.

In photos, Dickon has an absent, pensive look, a smile hovering faintly on his lips as if his thoughts were elsewhere. These images are deceptive. My father was a vibrant presence. He was enterprising, energetic, available for others. He meditated deeply about things, but this was simply part of life, not an exercise in self-indulgence. He was totally unconceited, always ready to laugh at himself, to turn people's conception of an artist upside down. He fashioned his life and his art on his own individual principles - but discreetly. Discretion, in fact, was the essence of his style. He never burdened others with his problems or doubts. But he was not the gentle dreamer the photos would have you believe.

Dickon grew up in an affluent, cultured family whose relations and influence could have opened many doors. His parents would not have frowned on an artistic career. His mother was herself a respected New York artist. But

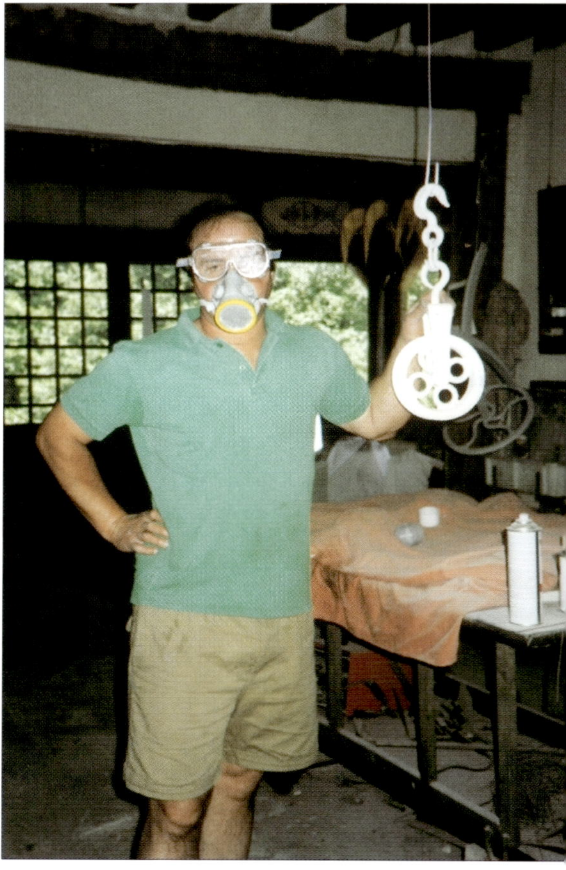

Dickon Eames in his studio. The piece he is working on is called "Wheels in a Wheel" and is part of the Série Grise (1989).

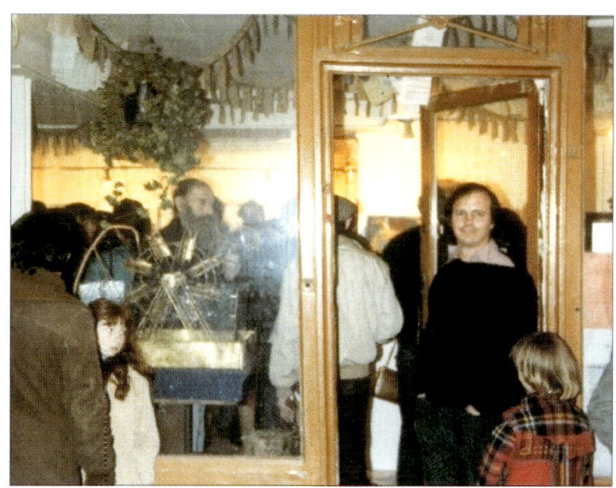

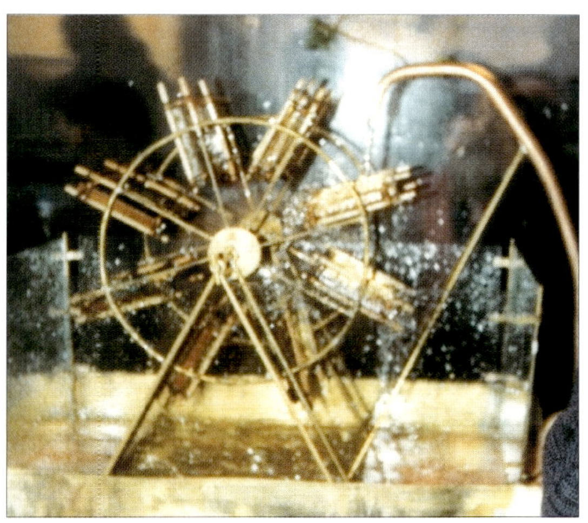

"Lettres de mon Moulin"
at the Bar de l'Aventure
(Paris, April 1980).

Dickon had other ideas. Very early on he left the family home and set out to see Europe. The Sixties were in full swing, and in the atmosphere of liberation that swept up a whole generation, Dickon traveled, made friends, experimented, celebrated, took jobs, moved on ... questing in every direction for a direction he could call his own.

Today, with a score of major exhibitions and three hundred art works to his name, we can safely say that he found it. And having found it, he no longer needed a whole continent to bring his dream to fruition. He narrowed his choice to a house in Normandy, or, to be more precise, to the four walls of a Normandy studio. It is here that my thoughts return again and again.

The studio is in the house - a natural part of its architecture. It is flooded with daylight on three sides, as my father intended when he designed it. The volumes are well thought out, like the rest of the house, also designed by Dickon. It is a large, rather imposing house which - unlike the studio - has a sense of order about it. From outside it looks vast, peaceful and comfortable. On the inside, it feels friendly, protective and welcoming, far from the hustle and bustle but not cut off from the world. Our house is in Freneuse-sur-Risle, a village in Normandy only a hundred miles northwest of Paris - convenient for my father when he has an exhibition in the capital. We live all year round in the quiet green valley that surrounds our picture-postcard village. We are not the only "Americans" (as the locals call us) living in the area. Another American often comes to Freneuse - his French wife's family has a house here. They soon become our friends.

When we haven't any visitors, the house hums along quietly. My mother tends the garden, rides, looks after the horses and the dogs. My father works at his own pace and keeps his own hours. In the daytime, when he is not

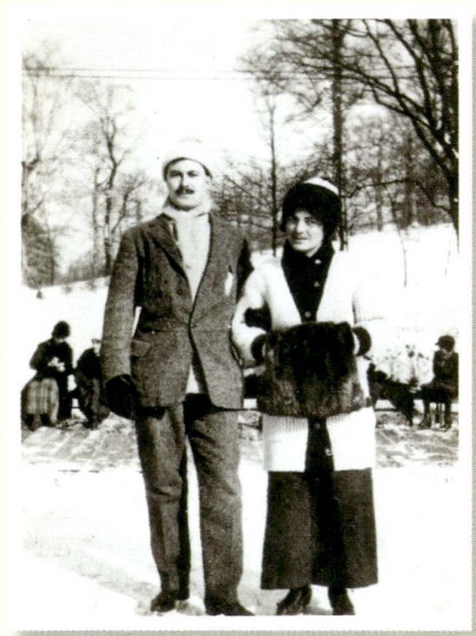

*Alaister C. Eames,
Dickon's paternal
grandfather, seen here with
his second wife, Naomi.*

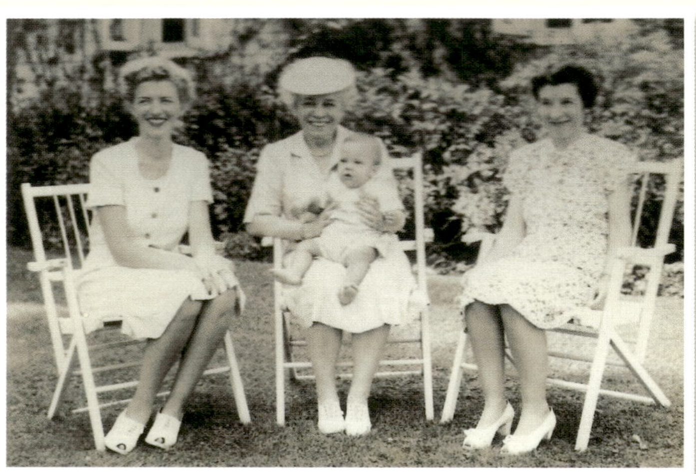

*The baby in the middle is Dickon, sitting
in the lap of his aunt, Helen Roebling.*

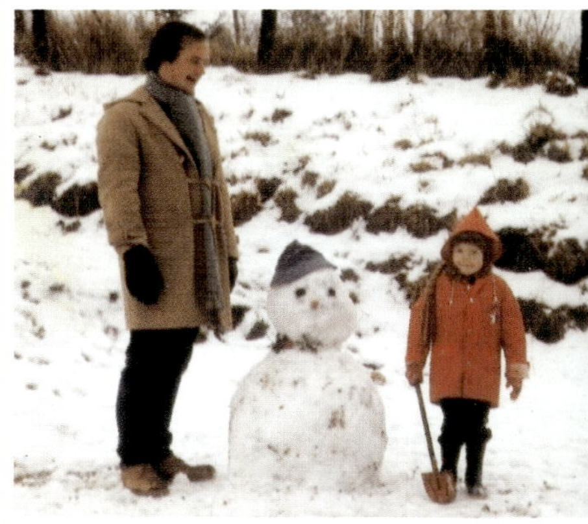

*My father, me, and a snowman.
We are in Freneuse, in the early
1980s, enjoying the kind of winter
rarely seen in Normandy.*

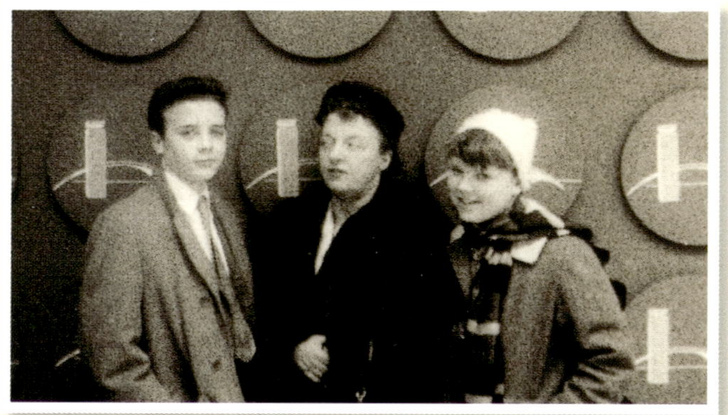

*Dickon with his mother, Betty Waldo Parish,
and his sister, my Aunt Lizi.
This photo was taken in New York in December 1959.*

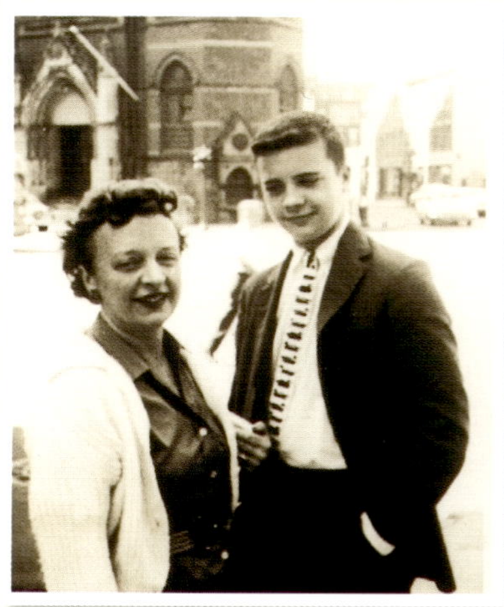

*My grandmother,
Betty Waldo Parish, with
Dickon in New York.*

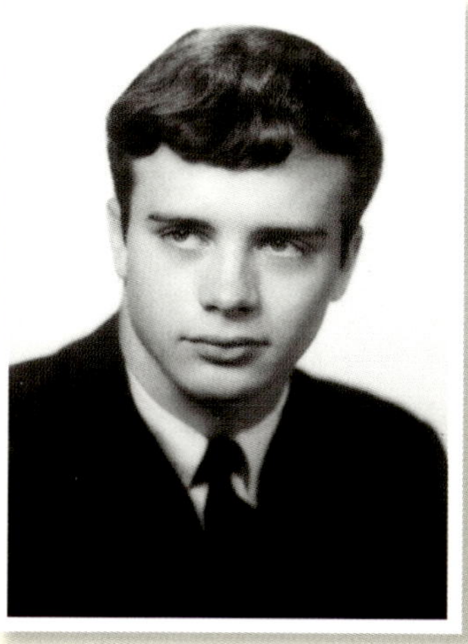

Dickon Eames at 17.

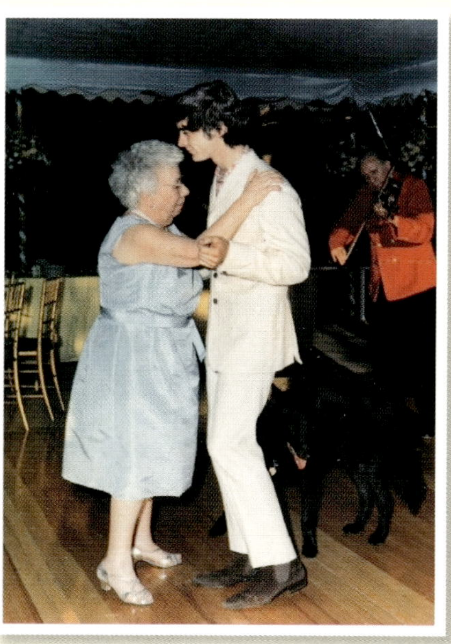

*Dickon, aged 18, dancing with
his aunt, Helen Roebling.*

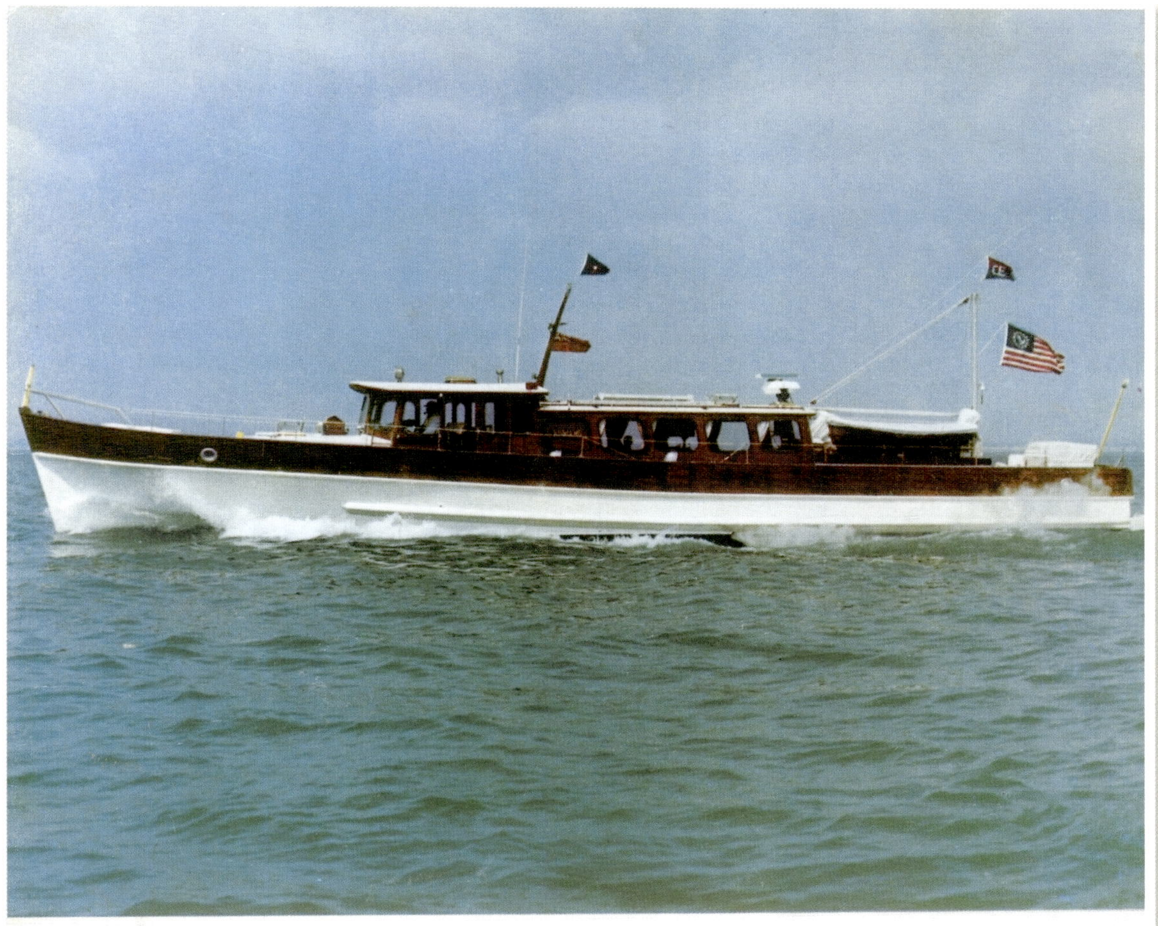

Andiamo

Length - 73 ft.   **Beam - 13 ft. 6 in.**   **Draft - 4 ft. 6 in.**
Now painted white with varnished trim.

A BOAT TO CRUISE EUROPE

From Helsinki to the Isle of Skye — from Tangiers to Istanbul — and all the rivers and canals between the Mediterranean and the Baltic, literally several thousand miles of fascinating inland cruising. This is a boat that has done it all, over thirty six thousand miles of cruising in European waters. She has carried her crew safely and comfortably all over Western Europe for the past ten years and is ready to start all over again. This is a family cruising boat, a sailing man's power boat with a character appearance that has brought favourable comment wherever she has gone.

Delivery will be made to virtually any port in Western Europe.

Offered Through

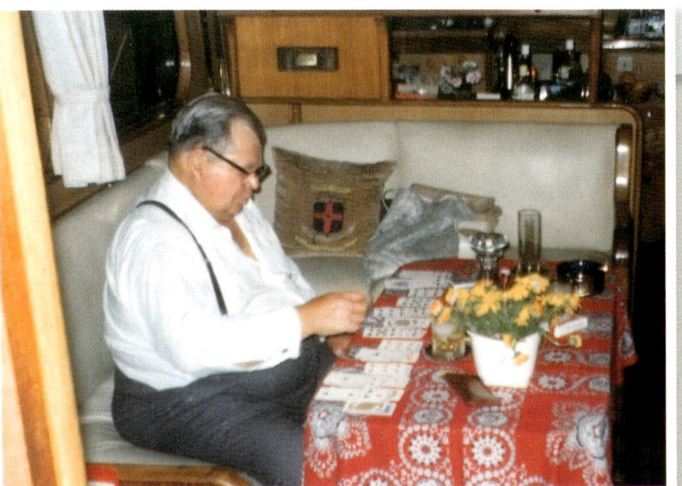

It was on this yacht, the Andiamo, that my grandfather Eames crossed the Atlantic. Looking at this picture, I still find it hard to believe.

My grandfather Eames, on his famous yacht, the Andiamo.

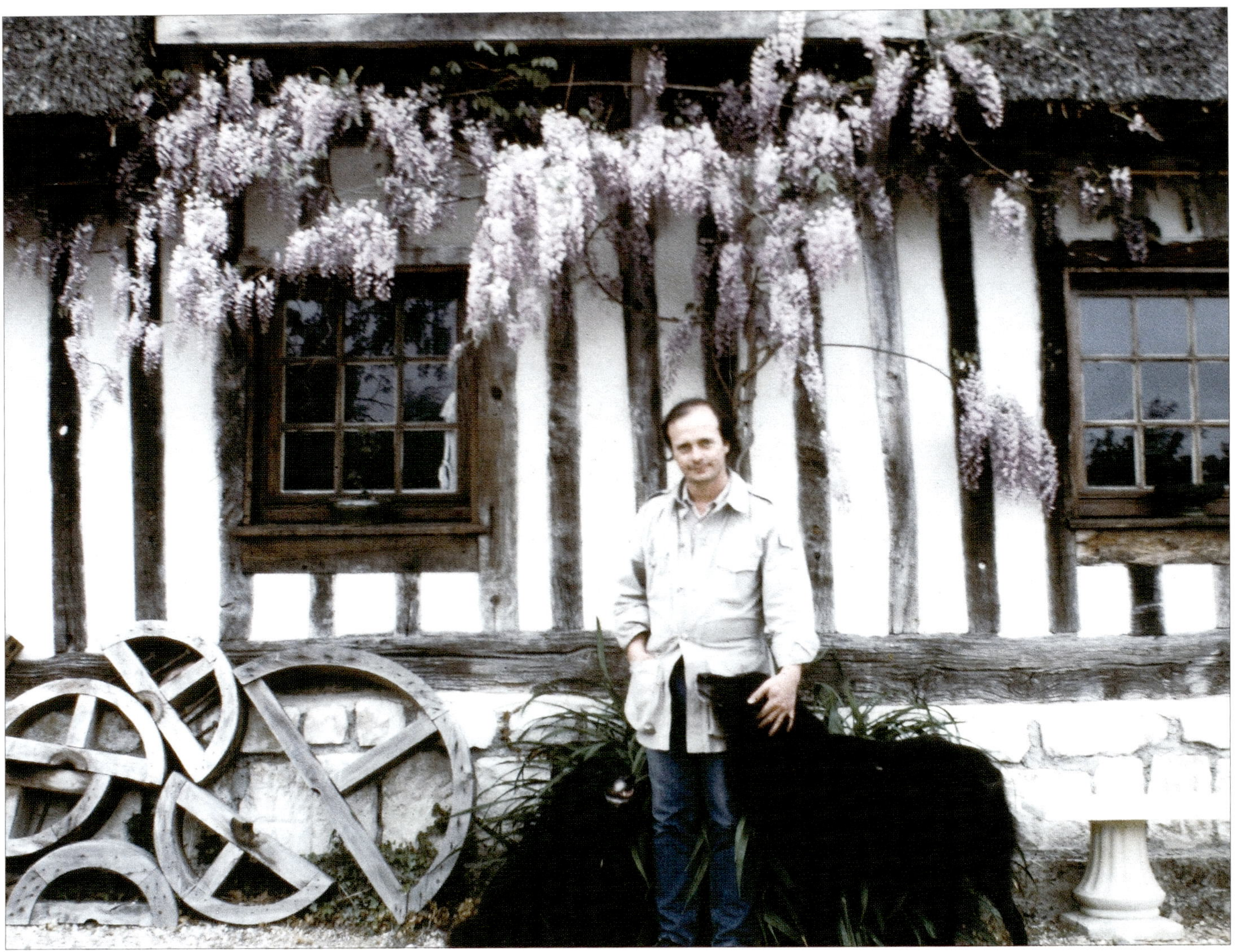

Dickon Eames and his beloved dogs in front of our house in Freneuse.

welding, he may be off hunting for scrap or doing things about the house. Daytime is practical. Nighttime is creative. It is at night that he plans future projects and notes the various materials he will have to find.

Our house has a history. First there are the stories from before the day my father bought it. Then there are the stories of how my father brought a virtual ruin back to life. The house is a dream that my father fulfilled. It is also my story and fills my own dreams. To tell the story of the house is to approach Dickon's art as he himself lived it.

2 FROM THE HUDSON TO THE SEINE

Apart from a love of dogs, nothing seemed to predestine my father for country life. He was a genuine New Yorker, like his parents, and grew up in an atmosphere buzzing with creative energy. While his father was a banker, Dickon could also count among his relatives the Roebling family - the famous engineers who built the Brooklyn and Niagara Falls suspension bridges. His mother, Betty Waldo Parish, was a famous painter and a charismatic figure in the Village, always surrounded by artists and writers. This was the heyday of the Beat Generation, of Kerouac, Burroughs and Ginsberg. My grandmother was also an accomplished printmaker: today her works are on permanent display at the Susan Teller Gallery on Broadway.

In her youth, my grandmother observed the usual rites of aspiring American artists, which of course included a spell of Bohemian life in Paris. She got to know all the favorite haunts of the Montparnasse district, home to painters and writers in the 1930's. A famous sketch by Guy Pène Du Bois shows her sitting at the Café du Dôme in 1929.

Dickon Eames grew up steeped in the arts, surrounded by artists, artists' materials, conversations about art,

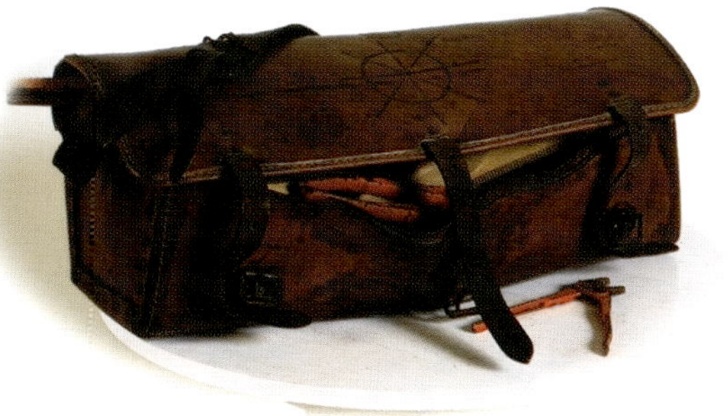

Dickon's bag - an item that rarely left his side.

books on art. He showed a creative talent early on, as well as a fascination for things technical. According to my aunt Lizi, he made his first "piece" when he was about 15. It was a plastic box with two rows of lights that blinked in a random pattern. A friend of the family had someone rebuild this box in metal and fit it with a handle. Dickon and friend would take it to Longchamps, the restaurant on 5th avenue and 12th street where the family tended to congregate, put it on the table and wait for people to come over and ask about it. The answer was always: "Sorry. That is classified information." As Aunt Lizi recalls: "This was at a time during the Cold War when we were all waiting to be blown to smithereens by a nuclear bomb, so people would just back away from the table."

But art wasn't just a game for Dickon. He developed his talent at the Tabor Academy in Marion, Massachusetts, famous for its encouragement of the arts and its international diversity. When I look at photos of this school, with its pale stone buildings, its high gables, its verdant grounds, its surrounding woodlands and its gentle perspectives, I can't help but think that in Freneuse, Normandy, my father sought to create something of the same atmosphere. Dickon graduated in 1963 at the age of 18. His life at Tabor had been a full one: a regular contributor to the school magazine, The Log, during his four years there, he became editor-in-chief in his final year. He obviously made a brilliant job of it, because that year The Log carried off first prize in the annual Columbia Scholastic Press Association awards.

Dickon continued his studies, attending classes at the Art Students League, as my grandmother had done, and also at the New School of Social Research, a crucible for progressive thinking and a magnet for a wide spectrum of artists and intellectuals. John Cage gave classes here, not only to musicians but also to artists such as Al Hansen, the Fluxus artist famous for his happenings and an habitué of Andy Warhol's Factory. Many years later, Al Hansen and Dickon Eames would meet and form a friendship in Europe.

Dickon Eames' first real exhibition came two years later, in New York. The year was 1965. I have very few records of this event, and only one piece from the show. It is a strange construction: a kind of pedestal table supports a procession of curious wheels made of brass and copper wire, not quite round and with overgrown spokes, rather like a child's drawing of suns. It is obviously the work of a young, untried artist, but in many ways it pre-figures his later creations. The intentions are there, a project is materializing. Time will allow the ideas to mature, practice will hone the technique.

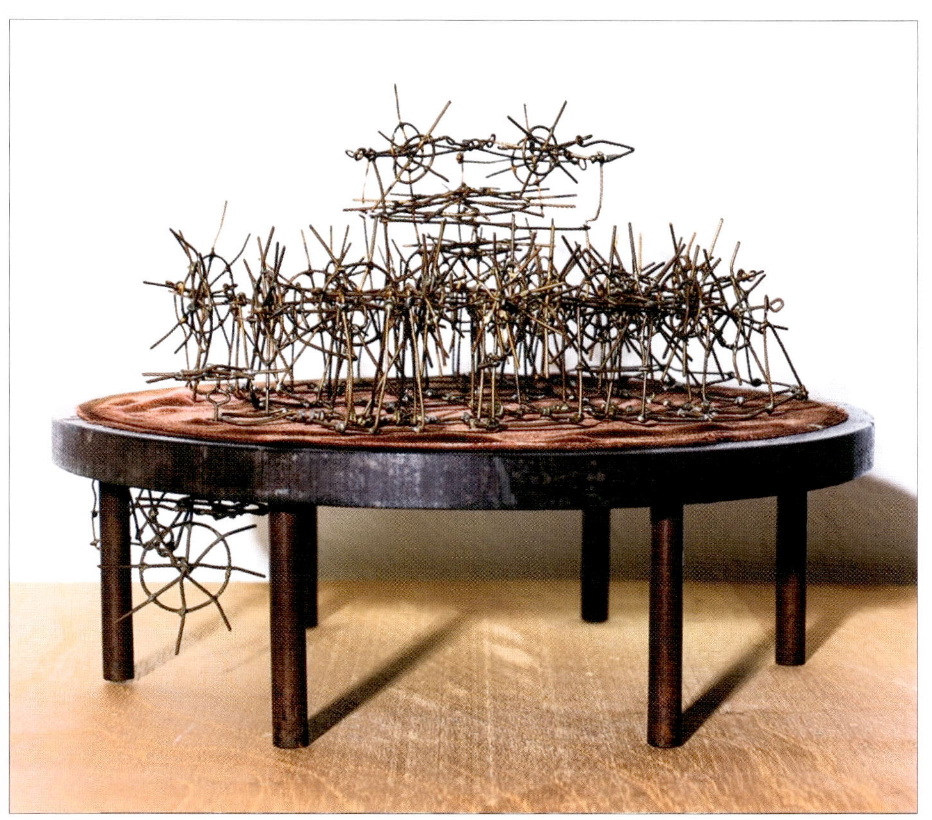

A work presented by Dickon at his very first exhibition, at the De Mena gallery in New York, 1966.

It was many years before my father's work was seen in an exhibition again. These were years of travel, encounters, working and learning. They began, as any artist's itinerary should, in Paris. But Dickon approached this traditional American rite of passage in his own individual way.

Ah, Paris! Betty Waldo Parish sometimes talked about the city, but Dickon tended to take his mother's stories with the proverbial grain of salt. For one thing, he suspected that they were less related to reality than to Betty's nostalgia for those carefree bohemian days. He also thought that Betty's Paris was probably not the Paris he would find. It was part of another era, forever lost. However, like any educated New Yorker, he knew about the great monuments and the little bistrots, the picturesque streets, the Latin Quarter, the booksellers along the Seine - all the ingredients of American tourist folklore - and he was attracted to them as one might be attracted by an entertainment, a recreational interlude. But once there, he quickly responded to the sense of profusion and freedom, the meaning behind the apparent disorder, the openness of mind, the convergence of eras and civilizations that give Paris its special status among capitals.

Why did my father leave his family, his friends and his country so young - first to pursue a nomadic life and then a settled existence in an environment so far removed from New York? Why all those miles and all those searchings before choosing the house in Freneuse, cupped in a hollow in the heart of the Normandy countryside, on the fringe of a scattered village with hardly a store and no main street to its name?

The reasons my father left New York are complex. I often wonder about this aspect of his life and his personality. The years we spent together hold very few clues. He was so pleased with his house in Freneuse, so happy to be living there - and to be frank, so much of a homebody - that it is hard to imagine what triggered the sudden departure, the years of roaming and finally the decision to make France his adoptive country. The easy answer would be that in Freneuse he found what he had always been looking for - a place to build in, a place to start a family, a place to practise his art. But that would be confusing cause and effect. Like the atmosphere of my childhood home, my father's journey is an intricate construction.

History of course had its part to play. My grandmother grew up in the Thirties - a paradoxical era full of hopes and fears for the future. Dickon's youth was marked by the war in Vietnam and the "Flower Power" counter-culture. In France, deep stirrings of resistance were working up to the explosion of May 68. Alternative lifestyles were emerging simultaneously on both sides of the Atlantic.

When my father set off for Europe, he made for places that captured the imagination of young Americans: Paris, Ibiza, Corfu. Did these modern-day utopias influence my father? I doubt that he rallied to any specific cause, or compromised in his determination to be a free agent. He was not, as far as I know, attracted to any ideology. He hated labels. He couldn't be described as a hippie or a beatnik, yet like them, he gravitated naturally to places where ideas could be explored and experienced beyond the pale of traditional authority. He brought with him a lively curiosity and an open mind, and besides - he had all the time in the world. He may even have thought about spending several years abroad, in the manner of 19th-century intellectuals.

Probably a major factor in Dickon's early wanderlust was the escalating war in Vietnam. Like so many of his compatriots deeply opposed to this conflict, he did not wait to be drafted. He boarded a cargo ship - I like to think it was some rusty, superannuated ocean-plodder, but we'll probably never know - and sailed for Europe. He arrived in Paris, the first stage of his European travels, at the age of 23. The year was 1968.

In France, growing resentment at what were perceived to be repressive measures suddenly burgeoned into a full-scale revolt by students, workers and intellectuals. Street battles, strikes and massive demonstrations brought the country to a standstill. The *mai 68* movement died out almost as quickly as it had grown, but for a whole generation the world had changed forever. Dickon happened to be there at the right time, as was often the case.

So began a nomadic life that was to last several years, interspersed with frequent return trips to New York. He may sometimes have felt the need to put down roots. For example, he decided to marry. She was French. The marriage was of short duration, and Dickon moved on, first to Ibiza. In the 1960s, the island exerted a magical pull on hippies, beatniks and bohemians of every persuasion. Officially part of Franco's Spain, it was paradoxically a symbol of sexual liberation, freedom and brotherhood. In those days it was not the seething tourist destination it is today, but rather a peaceable if lively paradise for young people, on a par with its near neighbor, Formentera, or its more distant cousins - Mykonos, Goa or Katmandu. These were places where you could dream of living, maybe for years, in a state of idyllic suspension.

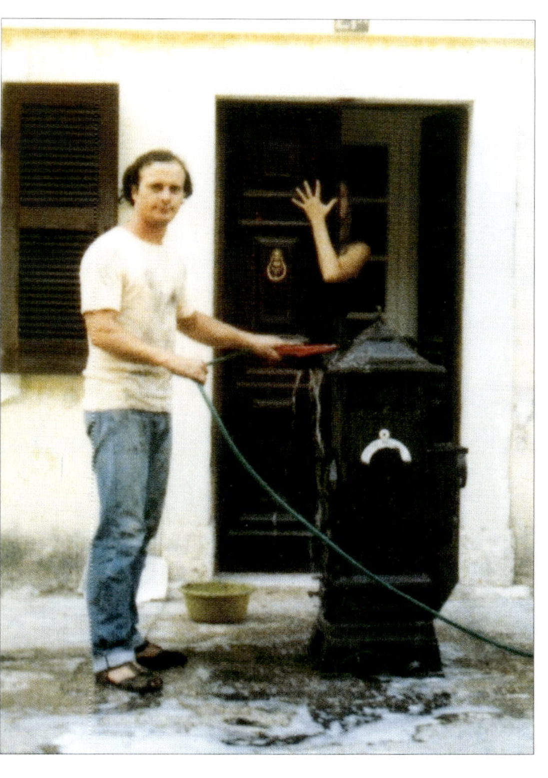

Dickon in Corfu.

But Dickon didn't remain in Ibiza long. He had tasted this brand of paradise and it was time to move on. The big vacation was over; the real search was about to begin. His route was mapped out, with Corfu at the end of it. Dickon was to stay three years, and it was here, I believe, that his life took a turn that determined all the rest. It was in Corfu that he began making art in earnest and laid the foundations for the work to come. And it was in Corfu that he met Carol Hartley, my mother, with whom he would spend the rest of his days. Corfu was a watershed in the life of Dickon Eames.

Just for a moment, imagine Corfu as a workplace. Imagine my father in the shade of the olive trees. The sea is sometimes blue, sometimes green, the breeze gentle, the air warm, winter practically non-existent. The "Colonels" have been in power for two or three years, tourists are few and far between.

Dickon has settled in, he is learning Greek and is not afraid to use it, unabashed by his sparse vocabulary and impossible accent. His life is beginning to assume a pattern: periods of research and reflexion, hours of thoughtful, unhurried work, and an enthusiastic immersion in local life. Congenial, cool evenings in the village café, early mornings at the port waiting for the boats to come in ... Dickon is not a tourist and the villagers know it. They not only accept him, they adopt him. He helps repair their nets, lends a hand repainting the *caiques,* is always ready to fix something broken. It is only a matter of time before he has a soldering iron in his hand again. Soldering! And then welding! In Corfu, Dickon's fascination with metal becomes an essential part of his life.

Metal was to be his medium. From then on he would devote himself to his art with a constancy and generosity that never wavered. His creativity had found its natural outlet. It was an exhilarating time for Dickon.

In 1972, at the age of 27, he had been living in Corfu for two years and was entering a very productive period, with three exhibitions in the same year. Two of these were in Greece - one in Corfu at the Glyfada Gallery and the other in Athens at the Ora Gallery - while the third was at the reputed Galerie Georges Moos in Geneva.

This last show, on the theme of imaginary machines, was enthusiastically received by critics and connoisseurs. His work showed the influence of Calder in his "circus" period: thin wires like light armatures tracing small, unlikely objects in space. These were his "machines for dreaming", made more of poetry than of metal, their very ungainliness seeming to work in their favor, if we are to believe the article by Rainer Michael Mason.

The Moos family is an impressive dynasty of art dealers. Records of their first gallery in Germany go back to 1899. At the time of Dickon's exhibition, the Geneva gallery was run by Maryam Ansari-Rodari, Georges Moos' daughter-in-law. Dickon and she met in Corfu, introduced by a mutual friend, the sculptor Kosta Alex. She admired the inventiveness and charm of Dickon's work and decided to arrange an exhibition, the first of two that the gallery organized. Thus Dickon's name features in the list of great artists - to mention only Matisse and Picasso - whose works have been exhibited in this prestigious gallery.

Life in Corfu was varied and sociable. Besides Kosta Alex and Maryam Ansari, the painter André du Besset, Peter Marcasiano and his wife Denise also came to Corfu and spent time with Dickon. I imagine that these visits took place mainly in the summer, and that Corfu was on its way to being "discovered" by holiday travelers. But whatever the time of year, Corfu was never monotonous. Dickon embraced island life and his art with equal energy.

1972 was a full year for Dickon, both professionally and personally. He was making a name for himself in art circles, he had projects in progress, and best of all, he was in love! He had just met Carol, my mother.

Carolyn Hartley was an attractive English girl, not only beautiful, but with a natural class and elegance that my parents' friends never failed to admire. She was sporty, an excellent rider, she worked as a model and in TV, and was thoroughly at home in the world of fashion, design and ... horses. This encounter would change both their worlds. They would head north, leaving the warmth of the Mediterranean for a more bracing climate, there to marry and build a life together until the day Dickon was suddenly called from us.

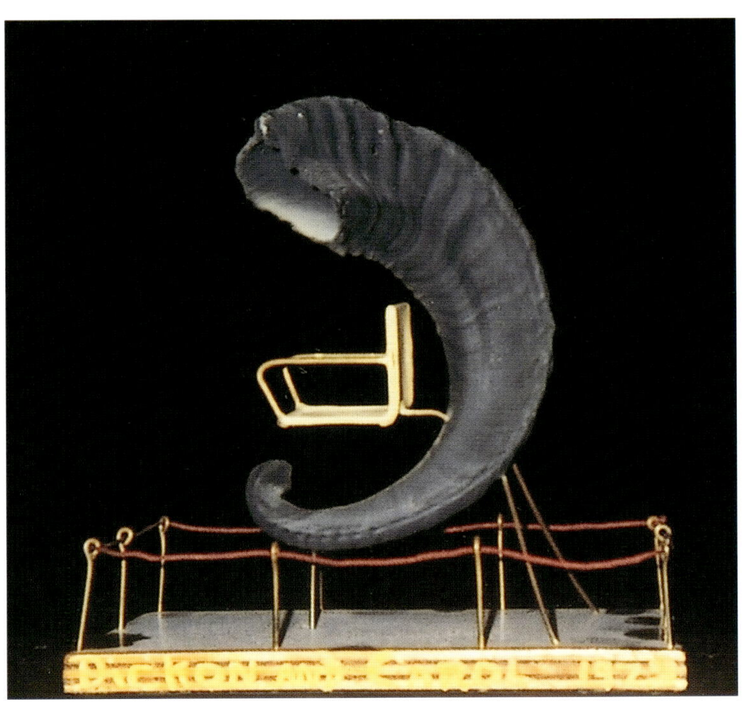

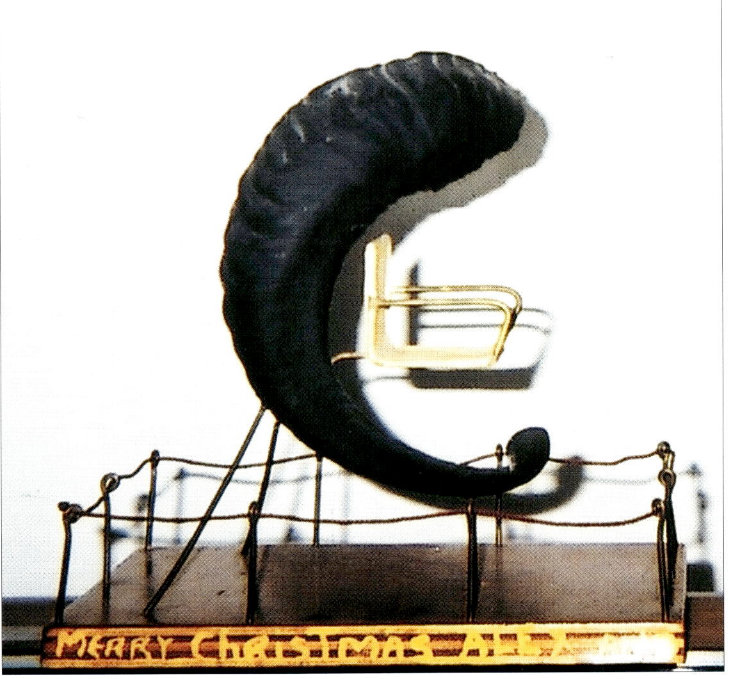

"Horny". This sculpture was made for Maryam Ansari-Rodari and Kosta Alex as a Christmas gift in 1972. An animal horn, canvas, rope, wood: Dickon was inspired by many materials besides metal.

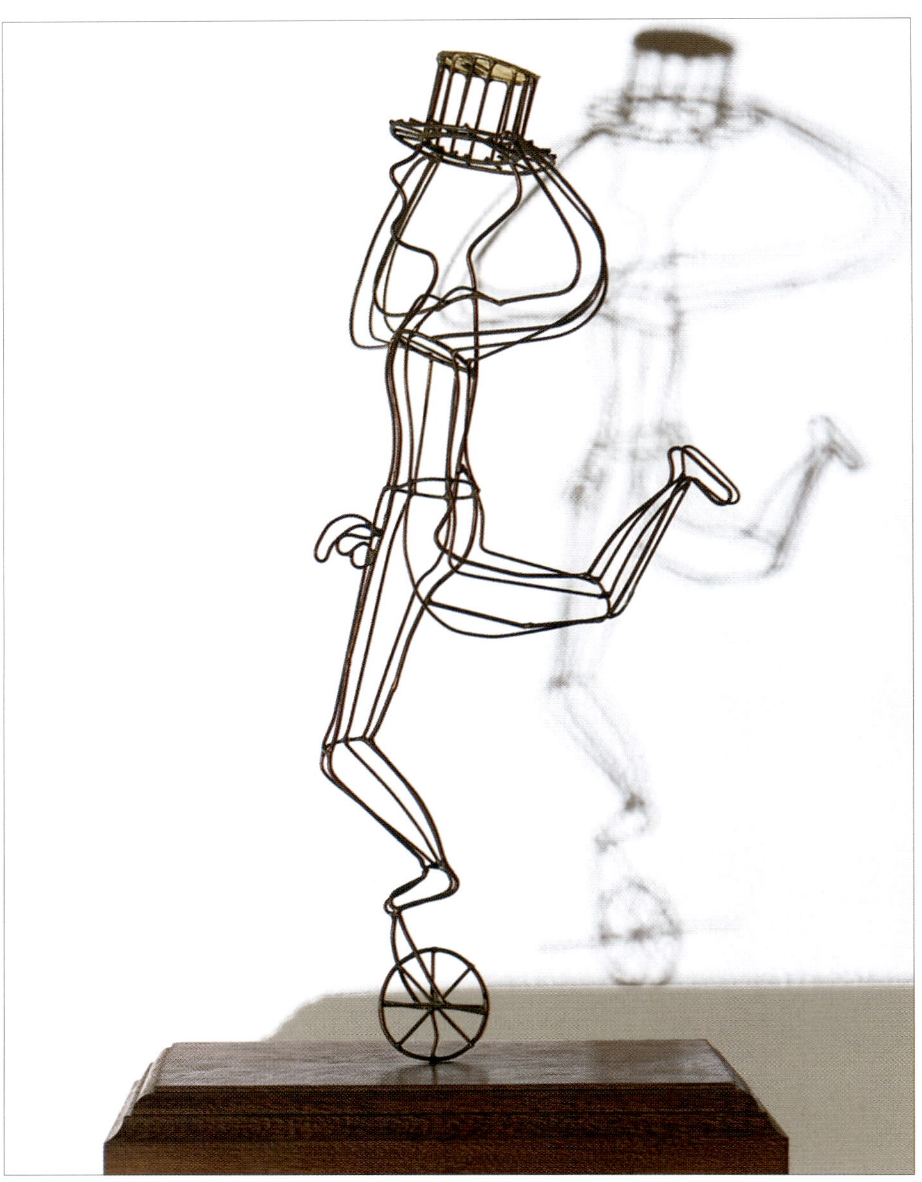

This playful allusion to Calder was a gift from Dickon to Carol
when they were living on the rue Tiquetonne in Paris.

Dickon and Carol left Corfu, made a detour to Avoriaz and were married in England. Soon they were back on the Continent - in Paris this time. These were blissful days for the young couple. They were in love, had plans galore, and were living a cosmopolitan life on the quaintly named rue Tiquetonne. They would not stay long however: the house in Freneuse was waiting, silent and as yet undiscovered.

My parents had set up home in the central district called "Les Halles". Here again, Dickon had managed to be in the right place at the right time. It was the time of the controversial *"trou des Halles"*. This was an immense, quarry-like excavation surrounded by high fencing, marking the demise of the famous *pavillons de Baltard,* the superb *art nouveau* temples of glass and steel that had housed the vast wholesale food market of the capital. The removal of the market to the outskirts of Paris, and the dismantling of these architectural masterpieces, incurred much wrath among Paris residents, and the unfilled "hole" was seen as a visible sign of the authorities' embarrassment at the mismanagement of a colossal redevelopment scheme. The destruction of the *pavillons* led to the creation of the first local residents' associations and to the first protest movements against developments undertaken without prior concertation. People wanted their market and their *pavillons* back. They didn't get them, but they did manage, almost unwittingly, to do something else. Thanks to their actions, the district began to attract elements of the counter-culture, and the area filled up with peaceable rebels who set about creating their own concept of city living.

In this lively neighborhood, Dickon and Carol were familiar figures, just as my grandmother had been in Greenwich Village. People knew them and hailed them as part of the "tribe". With their two big dogs trotting alongside, they felt at home here among artists, inventors, iconoclasts and dreamers. It was a congenial cocktail spiced with a spirit of artistic rivalry that suited Dickon's temperament.

While the "hole" stood empty, the folklore flourished. The lifestyle was a little reminiscent of Ibiza, with art galleries and museums thrown in. But like Ibiza, it was not a place you stayed in forever. Dickon's reasons for leaving Paris are easier to explain than his reasons for leaving New York. Carol was nostalgic for country life, Dickon needed space to work and create. Conditions in the rue Tiquetonne were just the opposite: a tiny studio in a cramped apartment, a checkerboard of narrow streets and dusty avenues, unkempt courtyards behind heavy street doors, rickety staircases, overflowing trashcans, the noise of bulldozers working in the "hole", the drone of traffic, the babble of people living on top of each other - all the

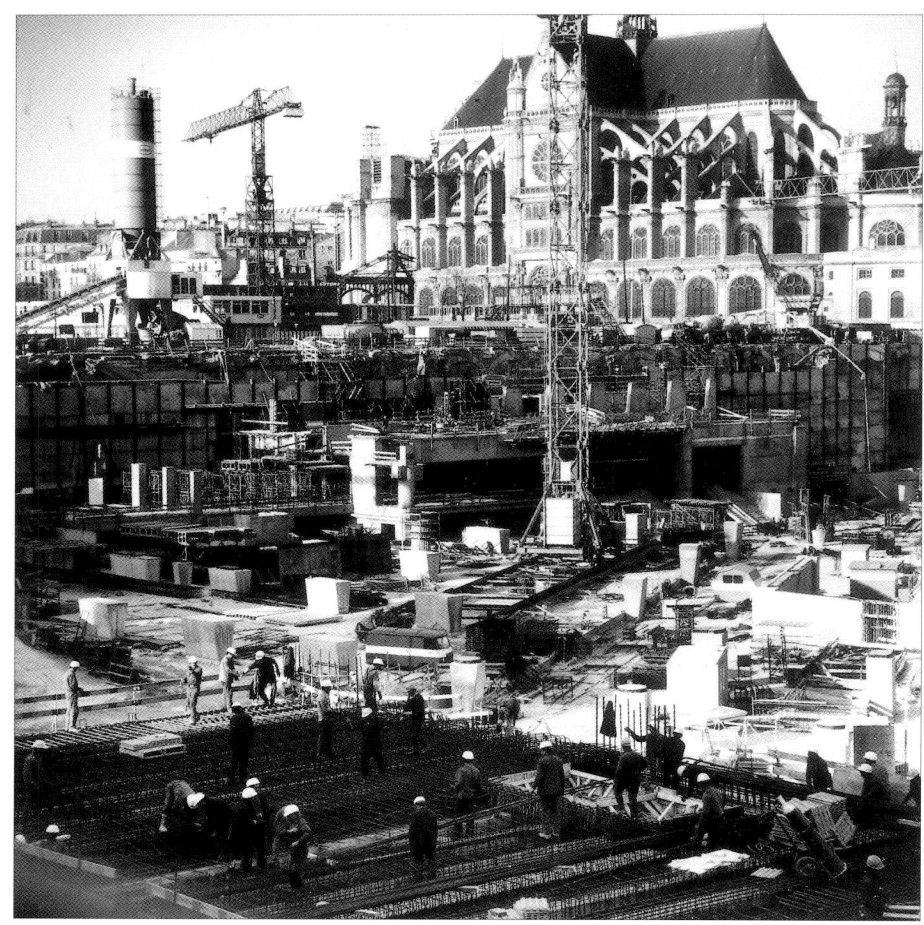

In the foreground, the controversial "trou des Halles".
In the background, the church of Saint Eustache.
This was how the district looked when Dickon and Carol moved there,
together with many other artists and musicians in the 70s.

charm of bohemian life in the big city! It had been fun, but in the hustle of those carefree days Dickon never lost sight of his inner ambitions. It was time to move on.

Dickon's friendships tended to be remarkably resistant to the erosion of time and distance. My parents' friends deserve a special section in this book and I shall come to them later. But at this point in the story two personalities come instantly to mind: Del Geist and Mark Brusse.

Dickon's friendship with these two artists goes back to his early days as an artist in New York. Del Geist, a renowned exponent of earth art and environmental art, is a natural New Yorker whose works have made their marks - or landmarks - all over the U.S. and beyond. My father and he used to meet up whenever Dickon came to New York. Mark Brusse is from Holland. After years of traveling and working abroad, he came to live in Paris. As I mentioned before, Mark and Dickon first met in New York. They subsequently lost touch with each other before meeting again years later in the following circumstances.

One evening in 1974, Dickon happened to be in Mother Earth's, a popular haunt of young Americans in Paris, just a stone's throw from the rue Tiquetonne. Suddenly he found himself face to face with his acquaintance from his New York days. They took up the conversation as if it had been only yesterday. It was the beginning of a friendship that lasted till Dickon's death.

Mark's star was rising fast in the art firmament. His work was widely publicized, he was the recipient of grants, commissions and critical recognition, and his work was exhibited regularly in major galleries on several continents. He would sometimes badger my father to show more commitment to his work. "You're an artist, but to be a great artist you have to work more seriously, Dickon. You have to give it all you've got, do nothing else, think of nothing else." On these occasions Dickon would nod and say nothing.

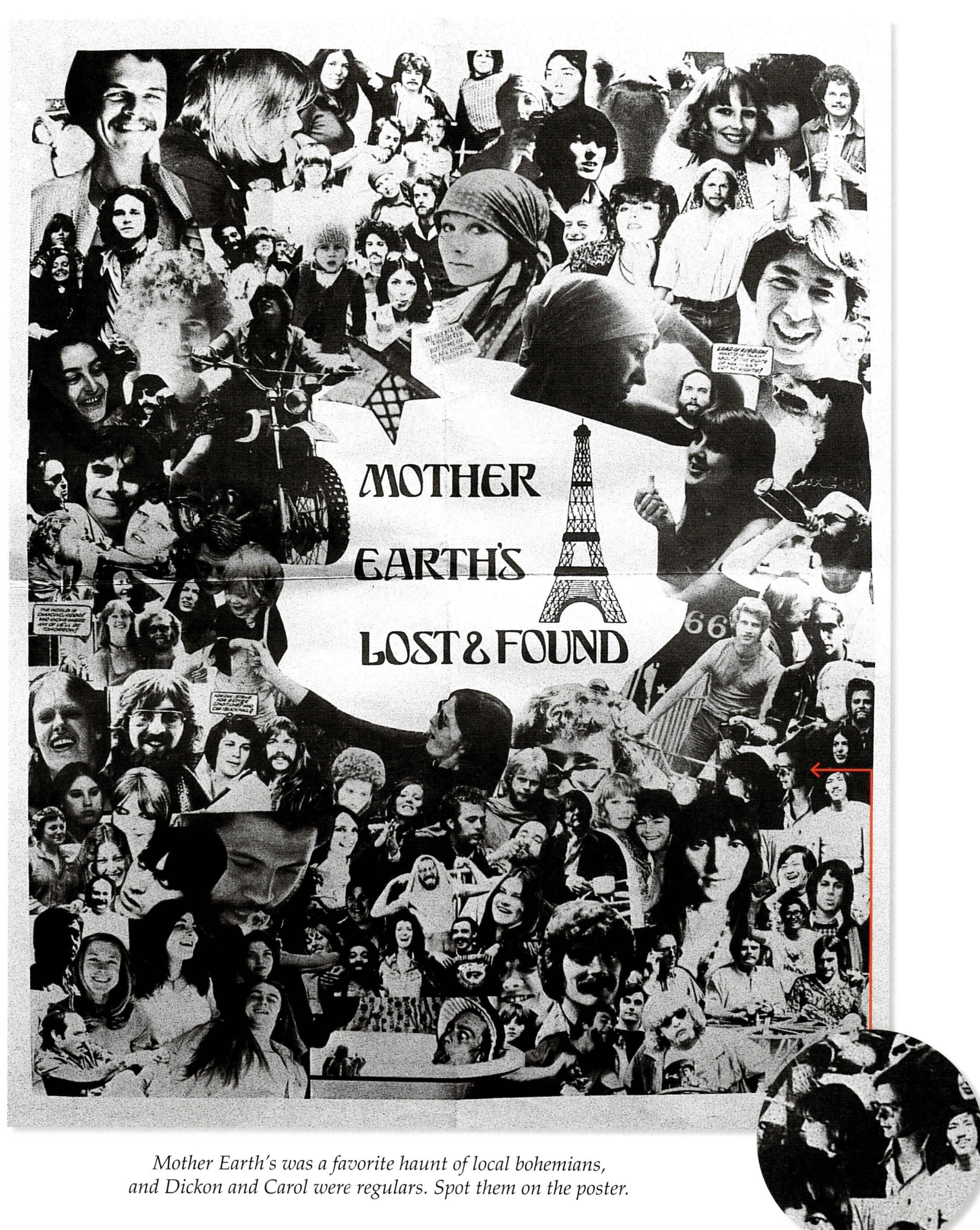

Mother Earth's was a favorite haunt of local bohemians,
and Dickon and Carol were regulars. Spot them on the poster.

Dickon was diffident, not to say a little secretive, about his art. He hardly ever spoke of it, and when he did he tended to play it down, calling it his "amusement". It was a very different approach from Mark's. The pieces Dickon created in the rue Tiquetonne during his "wire" period still showed Calder's influence. They were small, lightweight pieces, as befitted the limited working area, designed in continuity with the "machines" he had exhibited at the Galerie Georges Moos two years earlier.

Dickon had his own individual approach to work, characterized by the style and discretion that were his hallmark. Even close friends, to whom he opened up most, knew only a fraction of what he was really doing or planned to do. Dickon was the great guy, the pal you dropped in on, or went out with, always ready to listen, talking relatively little, and rarely about himself. And because he was known for his dry sense of humor and his self-deprecating style, many took this as a sign of dilettantism. I spent enough time with my father to know differently.

At this period a lot of things were changing for Dickon. A new chapter in his life was beginning. He had reached a new stage of artistic accomplishment and he was not yet thirty. The young artist from New York had already come far: from the post-war years of urban America to new utopias under southern skies, from hippie movements to underground culture, from fiestas under the sun to fêtes in Paris bistrots ... a continuous process of looking, listening and learning.

What was remarkable was that once he had finally settled down to his art, he never turned his back on those exuberant years. He continued to love life, celebrations, friends, informal get-togethers and discussions that went on into the small hours. The kaleidoscope of experiences became part of his art. Each experience and each project was a continuation of the previous one: the construction of a life and an art, step by step.

This ability to weave past experiences into the living present made Dickon a wonderful father and teacher. He encouraged me to experiment, and was unjudgmental in his attitude to me, remembering only too well his own youthful doubts and blunders. In the sadly brief years that we shared together, what I remember most vividly is his quiet but unstinting affection.

Dickon's sculpture was taking more and more of his time, and Mark Brusse had plenty of ideas as to possible galleries and exhibitions. The talent and the opportunities were there. Now only the space was missing. My mother needed the countryside, my father enough room to work, the dogs a vaster domain for exercise. Everything pointed to a new departure - to somewhere not too far from Paris. Normandy seemed to offer the ideal combination: less than two hours from Paris, a region of attractive towns and villages, rich pastures and gentle valleys, the heartland of pedigree cattle and horse breeding. Here my mother could indulge her love of riding and gardening. Here Dickon could stake out a territory for his many projects.

The idea took hold fast. First my parents made some excursions to the Risle valley, where friends of theirs had a house. They discovered a peaceful, untouched landscape dotted with little villages and isolated houses. They were impressed with the sense of authenticity and tranquility, with the unpretentious beauty of everything they saw. All they had to do was find the right house and surroundings. My father wasted no time. Taking his trusty mobylette, he rode all around the region, up and down highways, down dirt tracks and into farmyards, asking questions in his direct, matter-of-fact way. He soon found what he was looking for: a very large, imposing old building, well hidden from passers-by. It was in Freneuse-sur-Risle, and as he found out later, was one of the region's old tithe barns.

This barn was typical of the kind of property that could then be bought in the Norman countryside: a deserted building, dilapidated but basically sound, with, in this case, an unsightly corrugated roof. All the original beams and some of the half-timbering were still intact, and even better, it was beautifully situated. Standing outside the scattered village, it could only be reached by a narrow winding road. It lay below road level, hidden from view by thick hedgerows, and it was big, very big. For two Parisians accustomed to the proportions of the rue Tiquetonne, it was a world in itself, complete with outbuildings, surrounding meadows and woods. A deal was swiftly closed.

This is where my father's story truly begins. Out of a deserted barn my father brought his dream house to life. He liked to say that he built it with his own two hands. That's true of course, but he also called on the know-how of highly skilled professionals, starting with his close friend the architect Max Lyons.

The house was like a laboratory - a prototype of his creative process. In the construction of this house his art found its full expression. He was able to apply his methods on a grand scale - developing the concept, planning, gathering the materials, deciding the structure, constructing, adding, completing. In building this house, he freed himself of all mental barriers and let the artist in him take over.

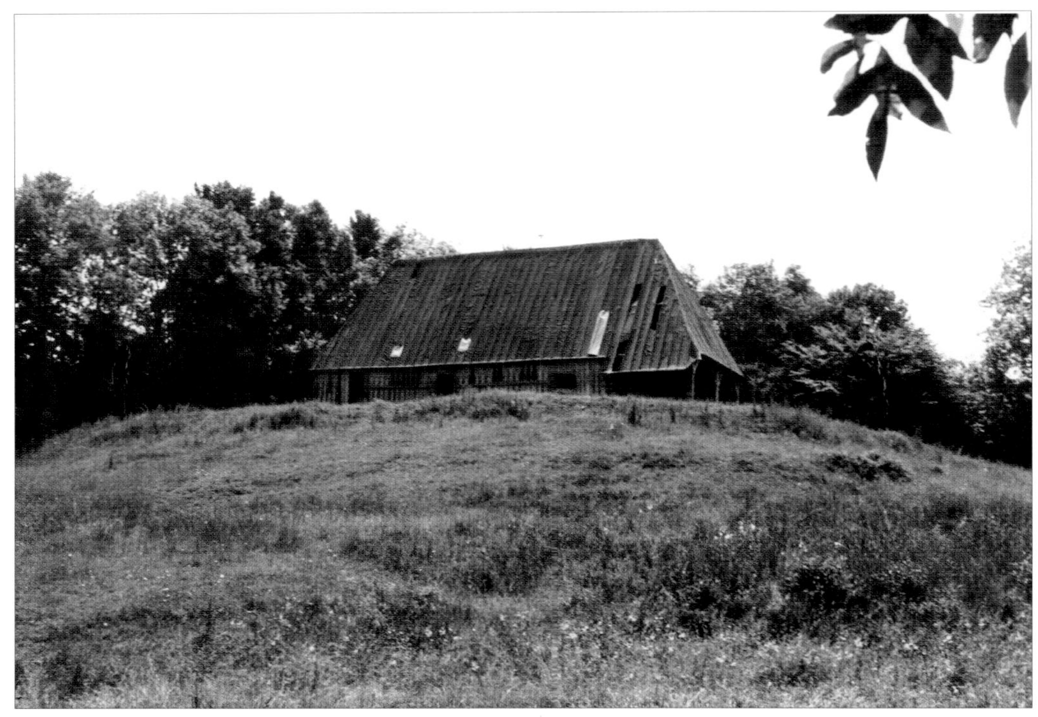

The tithe barn as it was when Dickon and Carol discovered it.

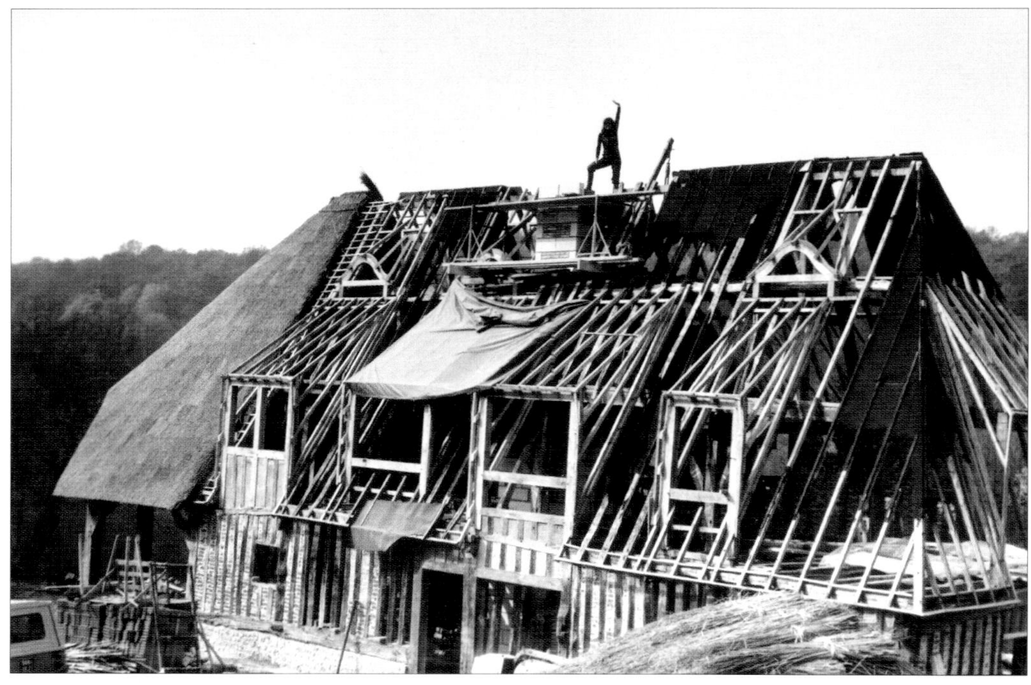

Carol stands triumphant on a ridge beam. The new roof is taking shape.

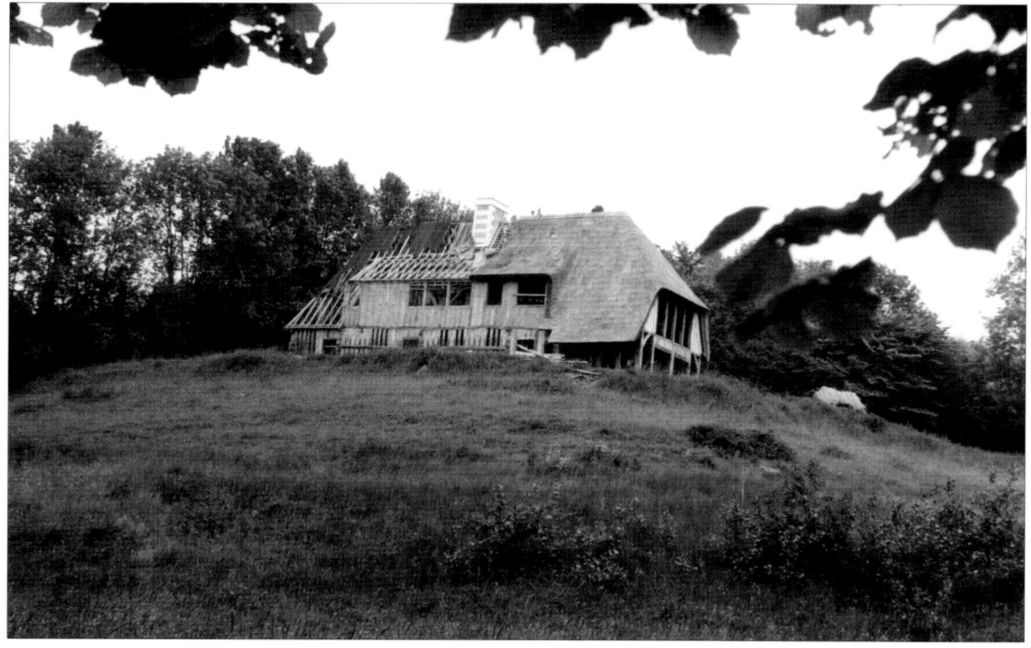

In just a few months, the house has adopted its own distinctive style ...

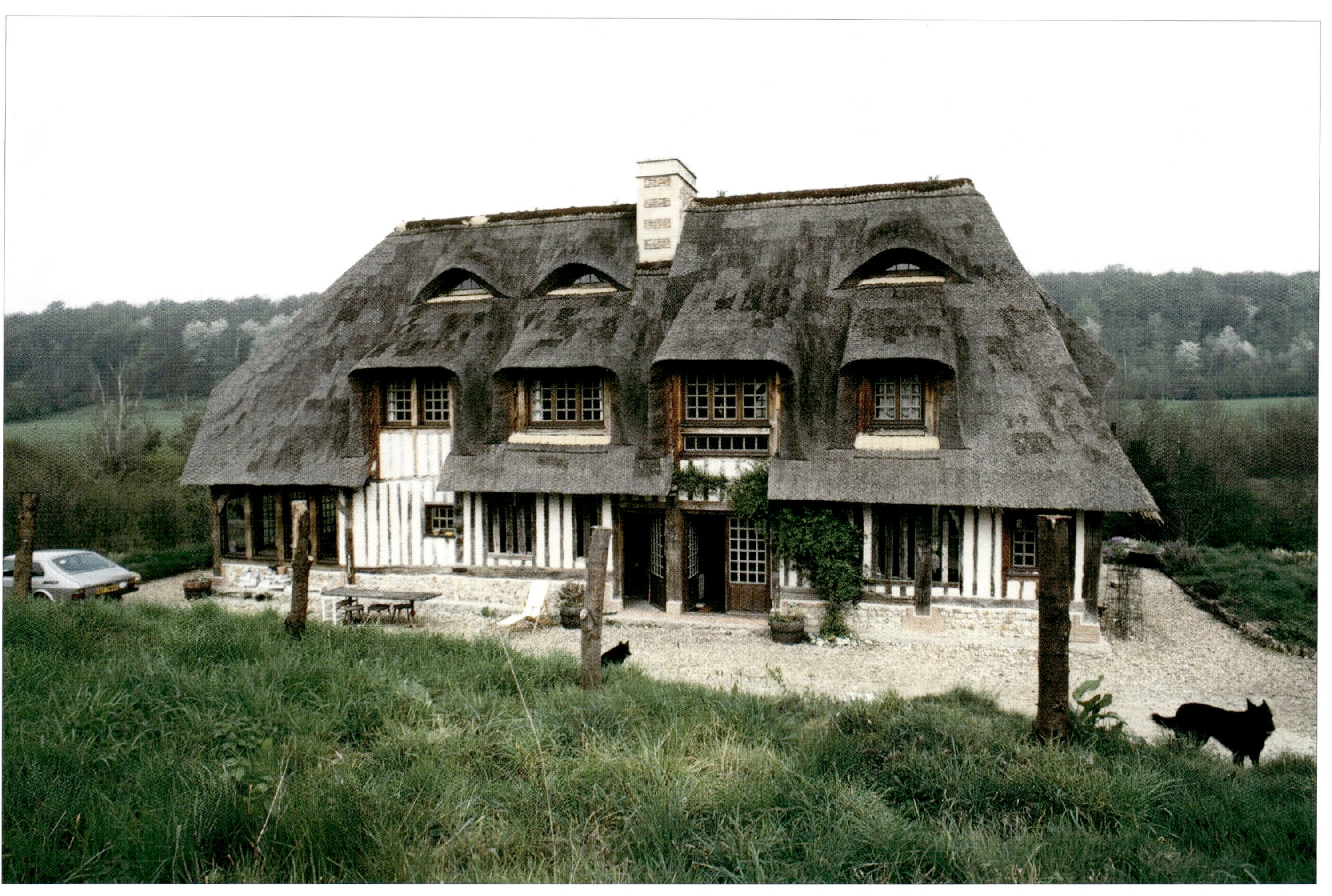

*... from the massive thatched roof to the half-timbered façade and many-paned windows.
This was the house I knew and loved.*

He divided the ground level of the barn into two roughly equal parts: one for everyday living, including a large kitchen area where people could congregate, and the other for his studio. The upper floors were for the bedrooms and the various connecting passages. He invented a whole system of wooden beams, overhanging indoor balconies and dark wood staircases that gave the entire ground floor area a sense of vertical volumes. He brought light into every part of the building, even glazing between the timbering of the ground floor walls. It was a house unlike any other, and he built it in just one year.

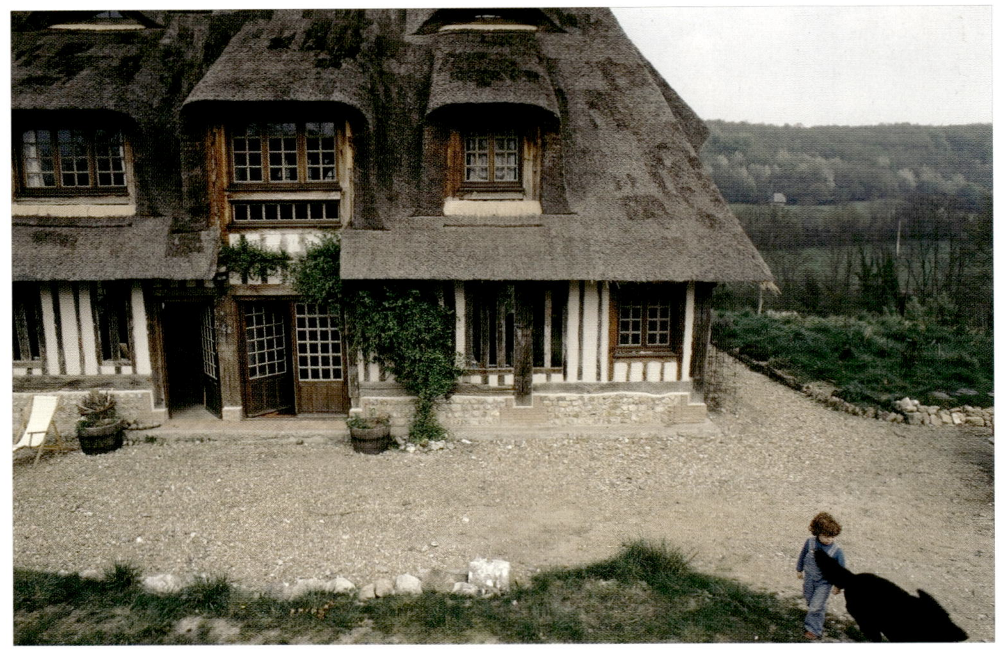

This is where I grew up. That's me, the little guy with the big dog, down there on the right. I'm going on 3.

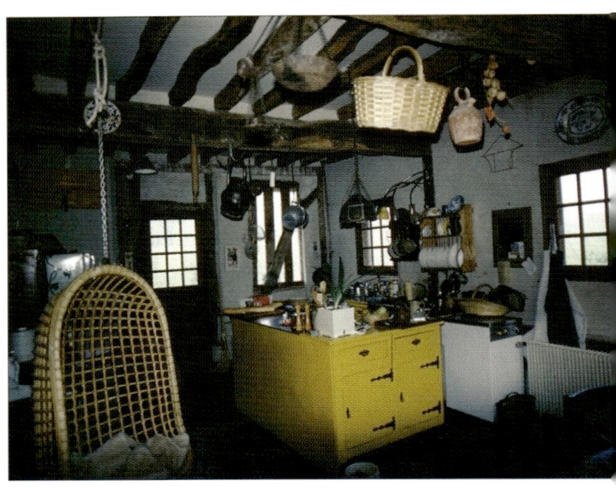

The kitchen was where everyone gathered - family, friends, neighbors ...

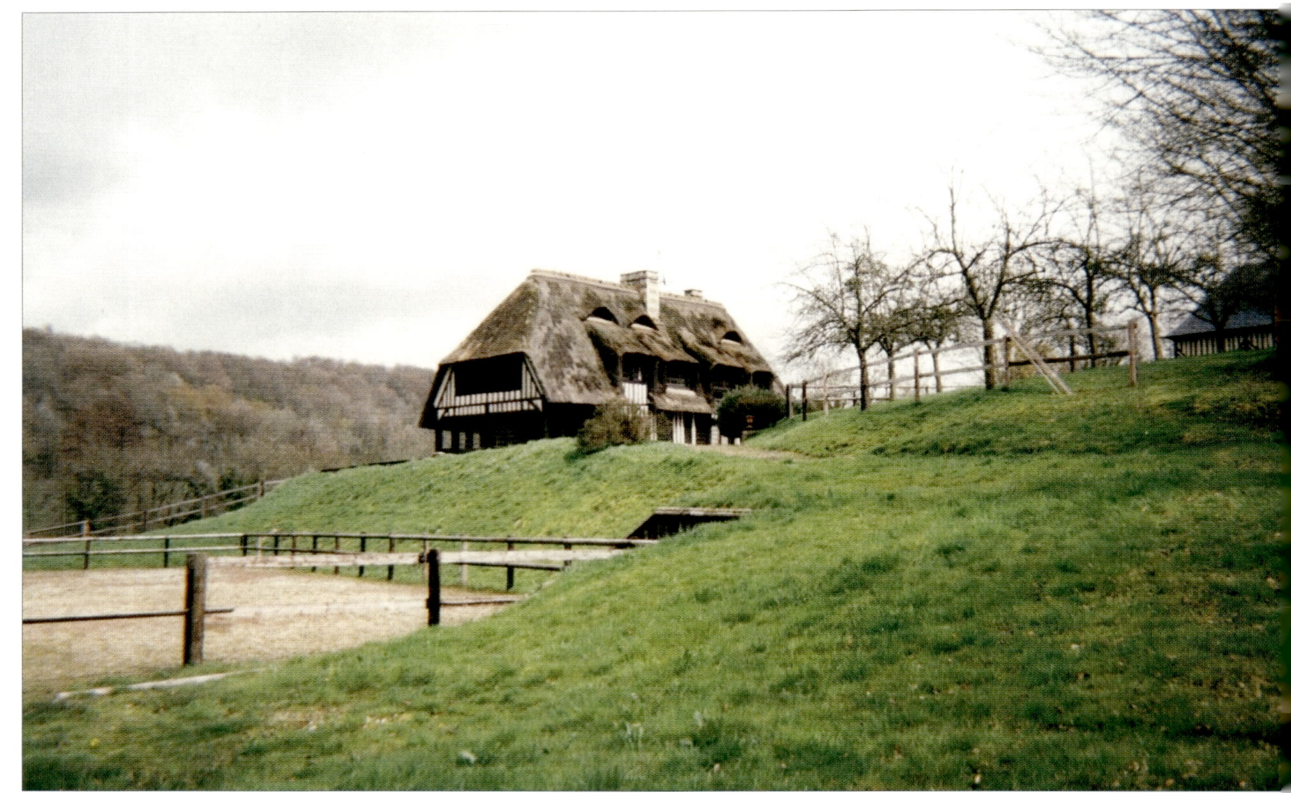

The vast, friendly house was full of surprising features and secret corners where a boy could play for hours at a time.

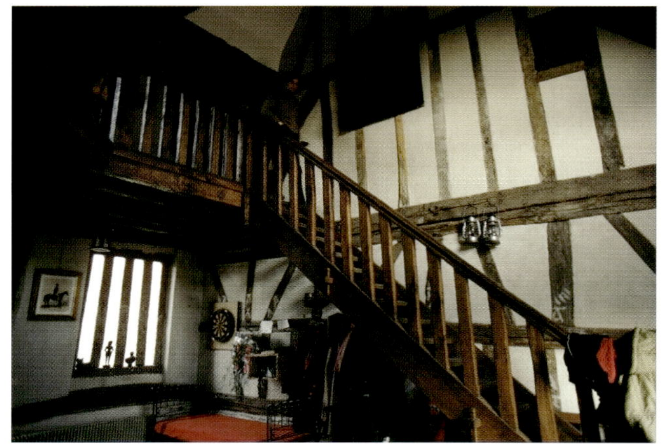

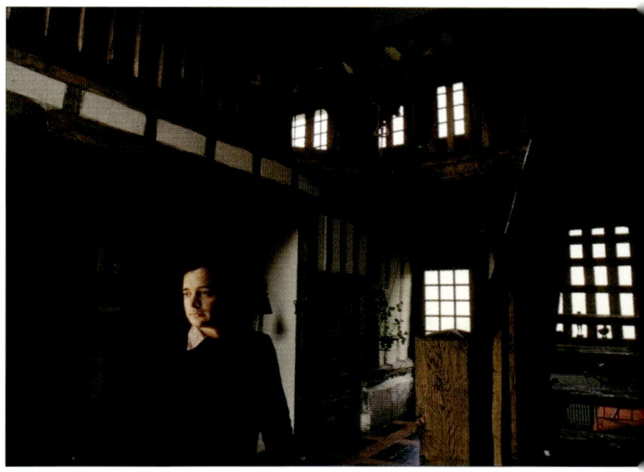

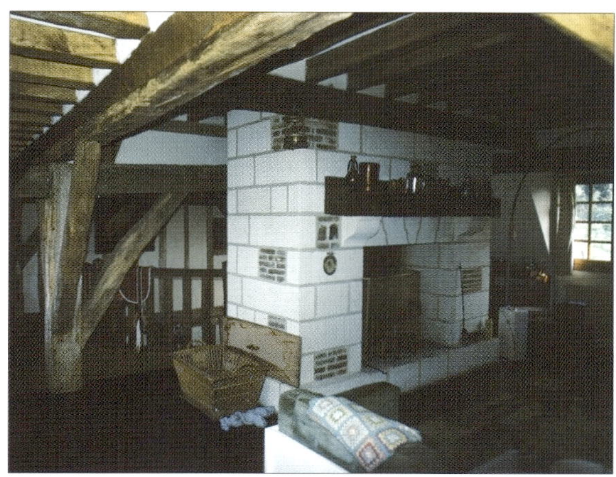

This fireplace, like all the others in the house, was designed by Del Geist.

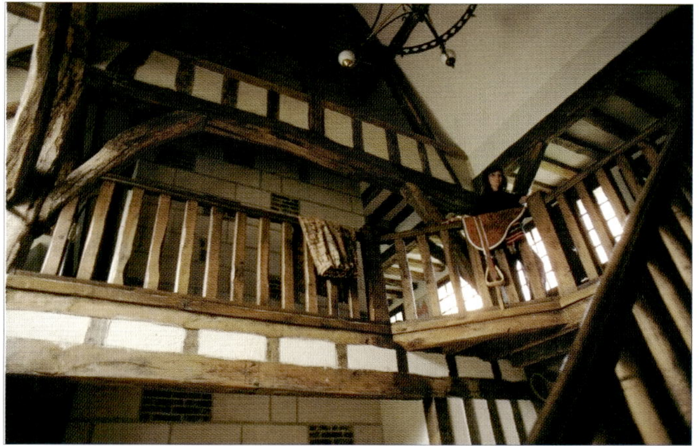

The floorplan and contrasting volumes were created by Dickon, with the precious assistance of his architect friend, Maximilian Lyons.

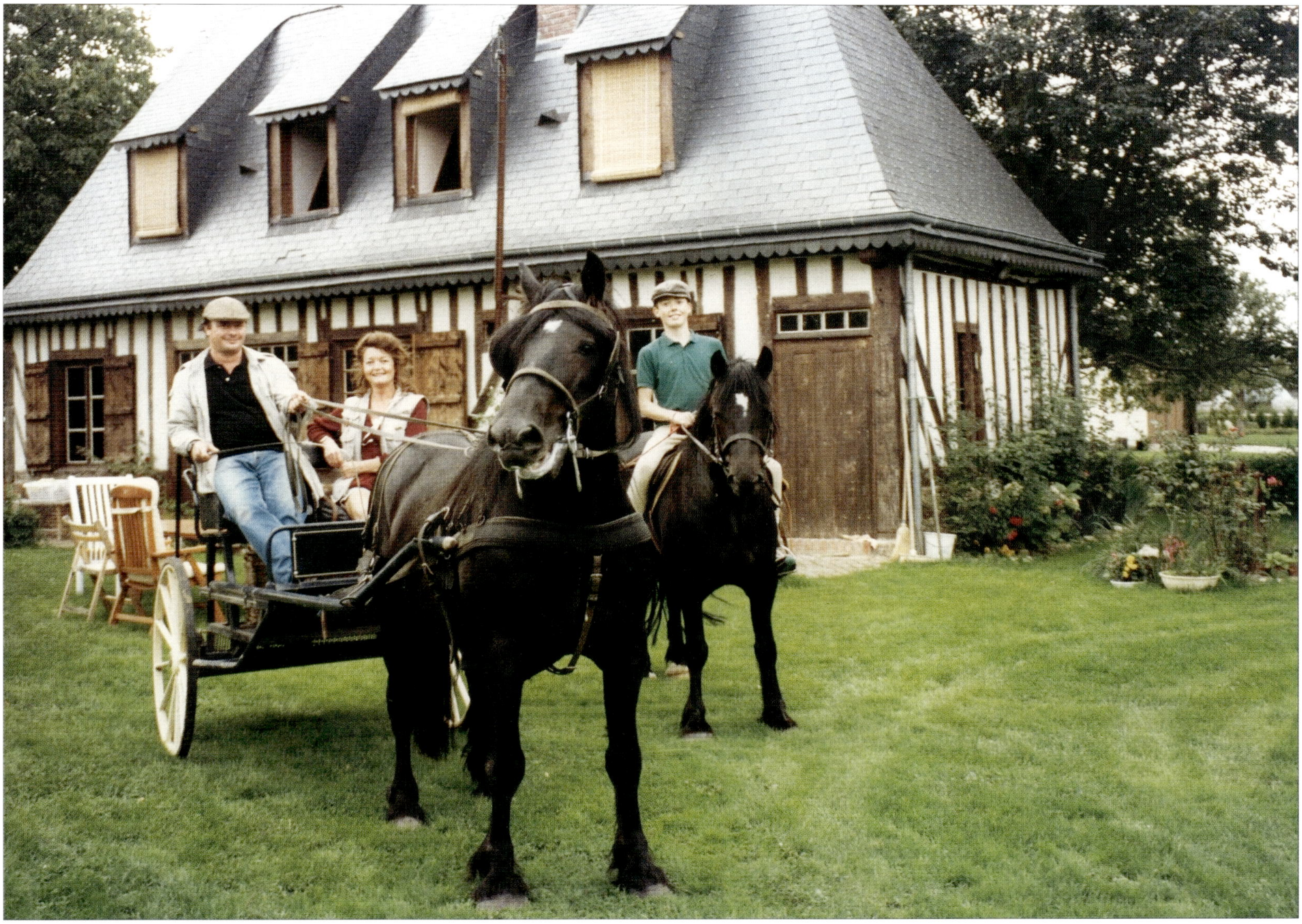

Dickon and Carol driving a carriage drawn by our stallion, Star, one of my mother's finest Dale ponies. I am riding my own pony, Smoky, son of Star. Smoky's coat never turned completely black, so I used to feel I owned the world's only gray Dale.

Dickon and Carol moved in. My mother set about organizing the garden. The stables received their first Dale ponies. This ancient breed was practically unknown in France, even in Normandy with its countless stud farms and riding schools. It was my mother who introduced this handsome breed to the region. For as far back as I can remember, there were Dale ponies in our home in Freneuse. We all became riders and carriage drivers under Carol's guidance. We had our own carriage that my father loved to drive at local competitions. While his French companions were re-living the days of horsedrawn travel, Dickon was possibly remembering the covered wagons that crossed the plains of America!

My parents's new life in Normandy began in 1975. It would last a little over twenty years, during which time Dickon Eames produced nearly three hundred sculptures. He worked quietly, without fuss or publicity. There were always pieces in progress, but in general his work remained practically unseen until he had an exhibition. Then he would become slightly more communicative, although he was never fond of being photographed or interviewed. He left the publicity to the galleries, stayed in the background, attended the opening, met the right people, then quickly returned to the studio in Normandy where other projects were waiting. When his pieces sold well, he was proud and delighted. Recognition was important to him, as for any artist. He had a very individual method of working. Each idea took shape through a process of mental construction. He rarely made sketches. He noted down details, sizes, materials and colors, but only for the purpose of ordering what he needed. He hardly ever drew plans, rarely made models,

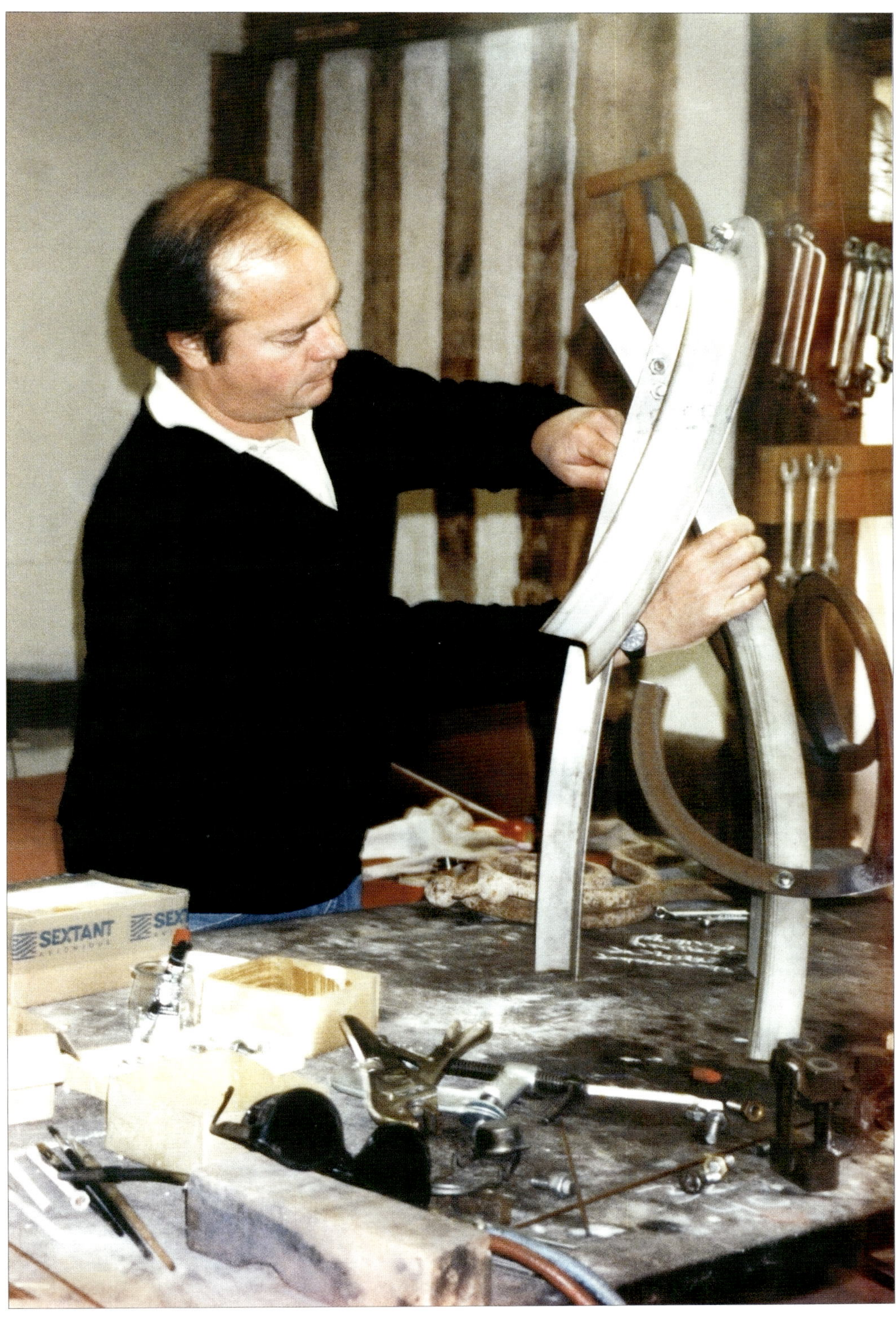

*Dickon at work in his studio. The sculpture, part of
the "Hard and Soft" series, is a tribute to Humphrey B.   .*

and didn't seem concerned with the details of the assemblage. Even for complex operations, he never made trial runs. It was always right first time. The volumes, the lines, the contours and the movement were already there in his head. He had the ability to think in three dimensions and could mentally see the object from every angle. It was an artistic approach based on geometry and mathematics, and heightened by color. The color factor might seem paradoxical for an artist working in the steely grays of metal, but for Dickon color was life.

There was nothing static about Dickon or his art. His enthusiasm was all-encompassing, as powerful when he was inspecting scrap at the dealer's yard as when he was engrossed in welding two pieces of a sculpture. Ideas followed one another in a kind of productive turmoil. This was evident from the state of his studio, and from the way he would switch from one register to another: from small sculptures in slender metal wire to monumental pieces, from complex constructions to something close to *art brut*. Everything was always evolving - colors, materials, techniques, formats, ambiences. While he was a great admirer of Calder and Matisse, his method of exploring and experimenting was pure Eames.

When he drove back from the scrapyard with everything he needed in the back of his pickup, he considered that the work was practically done. And if he was disappointed with the end result, he might take it all apart, leave it for a few weeks or months, then start something else using the same bits over again. He never put down his tools, because there were always other works waiting. He went from one to the other in a continuous process of creation. It was work, it was life, it was art.

Was the finished result exactly what he had imagined? I think the materials sometimes took him further than he had originally planned. In handling a specific material or component, he could be seized with a new inspiration.

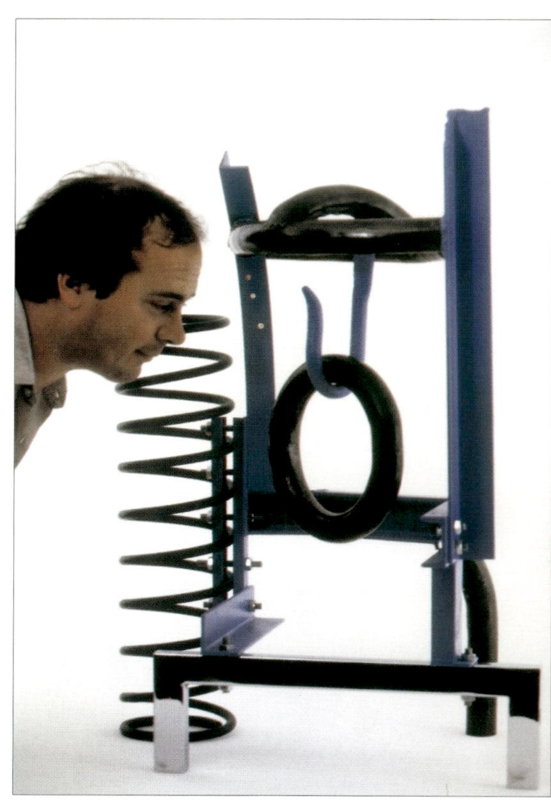

Dickon Eames and "Black Ring"
("Sculptures récentes", Paris, 1987).

You can see it in some of the photos of Dickon in his studio. He is standing, looking determined and yet meditative, among tubes, springs, wires, tools and bric-a-brac like a schoolboy let loose in a candy store. So much to choose from, so many ways to go! It's a rare and wonderful feeling, made all the more delicious because he doesn't know yet how it will end. He is ready to be surprised, even to be a little overwhelmed by what might happen. He is ready to yield to unexpected emotions and push the limits. That is what his sculpture is all about.

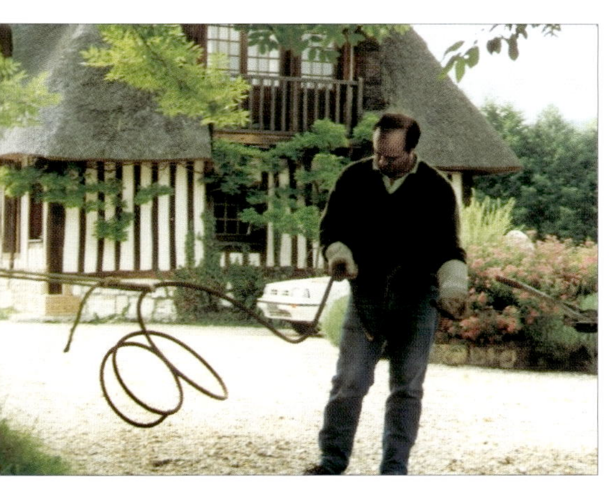

Dickon Eames working on his "Fontaines" series (1994).

Dickon often spent hours contemplating something that looked to me like a botched Meccano construction. He would turn the pieces this way and that, look at them from every angle, fiddle with a nut, hum a tune ... in fact, do nothing in particular. Then all at once, like a calligrapher finally tracing the perfect character, he would organize the different parts into an object that suddenly took full possession of the space it occupied.

These periods of reflexion were occasionally very long. Sometimes, when dusk crept over the garden, my mother would put her head around the studio door and suggest a break at the big kitchen table. Then Dickon might put his thoughts away for the night and start again the next morning. These apparently "blank" periods were not very frequent or long-lasting. As a general rule my father took a simple, light-hearted pleasure in his work. He was as natural in his art as in everyday life.

There were days when he didn't work in the studio at all. But he never went far. There were things to buy in the nearby towns, in Pont-Authou, Le Bec-Hellouin, Saint-Philbert or Brionne. And he never went empty-handed. Wherever he went, he always carried somewhere on his person a pair of pliers. I never saw my father without his pliers.

Wherever he was - in the house, the garden, or the out-buildings - there was always something to be fixed, a nail to be pulled out, a wire to be tweaked. Whatever the job, Dickon had the pliers for it! He was famous for his collection: cutting pliers, long-nose pliers, flat-nose pliers, lockjaw pliers, Z-bend pliers ... pliers were Dickon's talisman.

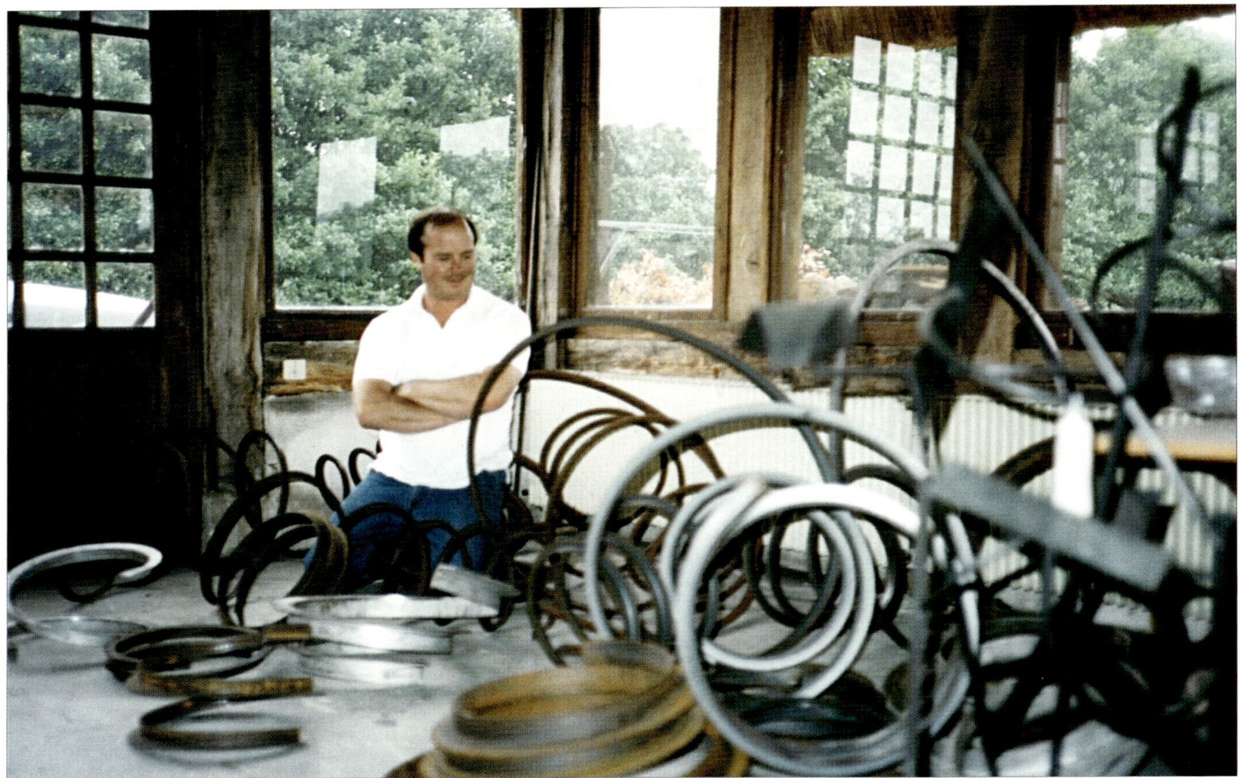

Dickon back from a successful foray at the local scrapdealer's. His look of delight still brings a smile to my face all these years later.

In 1977, the year I was born, everything was falling into place. The house was finished, friends and relations had already visited. The garden was maturing, the ponies were in their stables. And the young sculptor Eames was starting to attract serious interest in the art world. It was the beginning of an intense sequence of exhibitions.

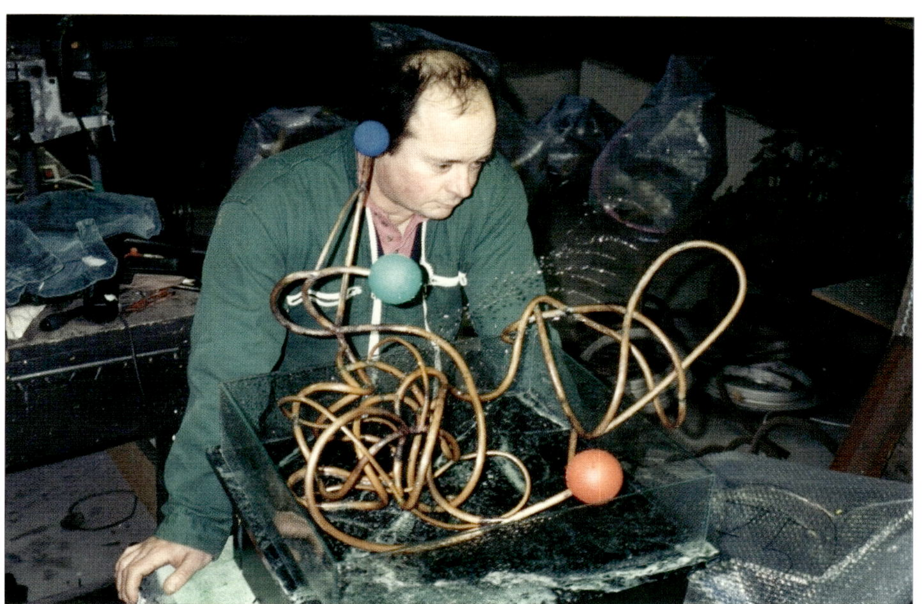

Dickon loved tackling new challenges and stretching the limits. With his "Fontaines" series, real water became part of the sculpture.

From 1977 to 1981 - five years - Dickon had seven exhibitions, either solo or group shows, in Holland and Germany.

In 1977 he had a solo exhibition at the Galerie Balans in Amsterdam, and a group show at the Municipal Museum of Recklinghausen, Germany. The theme of the German show, "To fly - a dream" brought together one hundred artists, from rising talents to past masters. The young Dickon found himself among the greats - Gustave Doré, Dürer, Goya, Odilon Redon - or, closer to our time, Max Beckman, Marc Chagall, Robert and Sonia Delaunay, Otto Dix, Max Ernst, Fernand Léger, René Magritte, Henry Moore and Robert Rauschenberg. In Recklinghausen he presented the first of his large sculptures - a giant balloon. Freneuse, with its infinite space, was proving to be an inspired move.

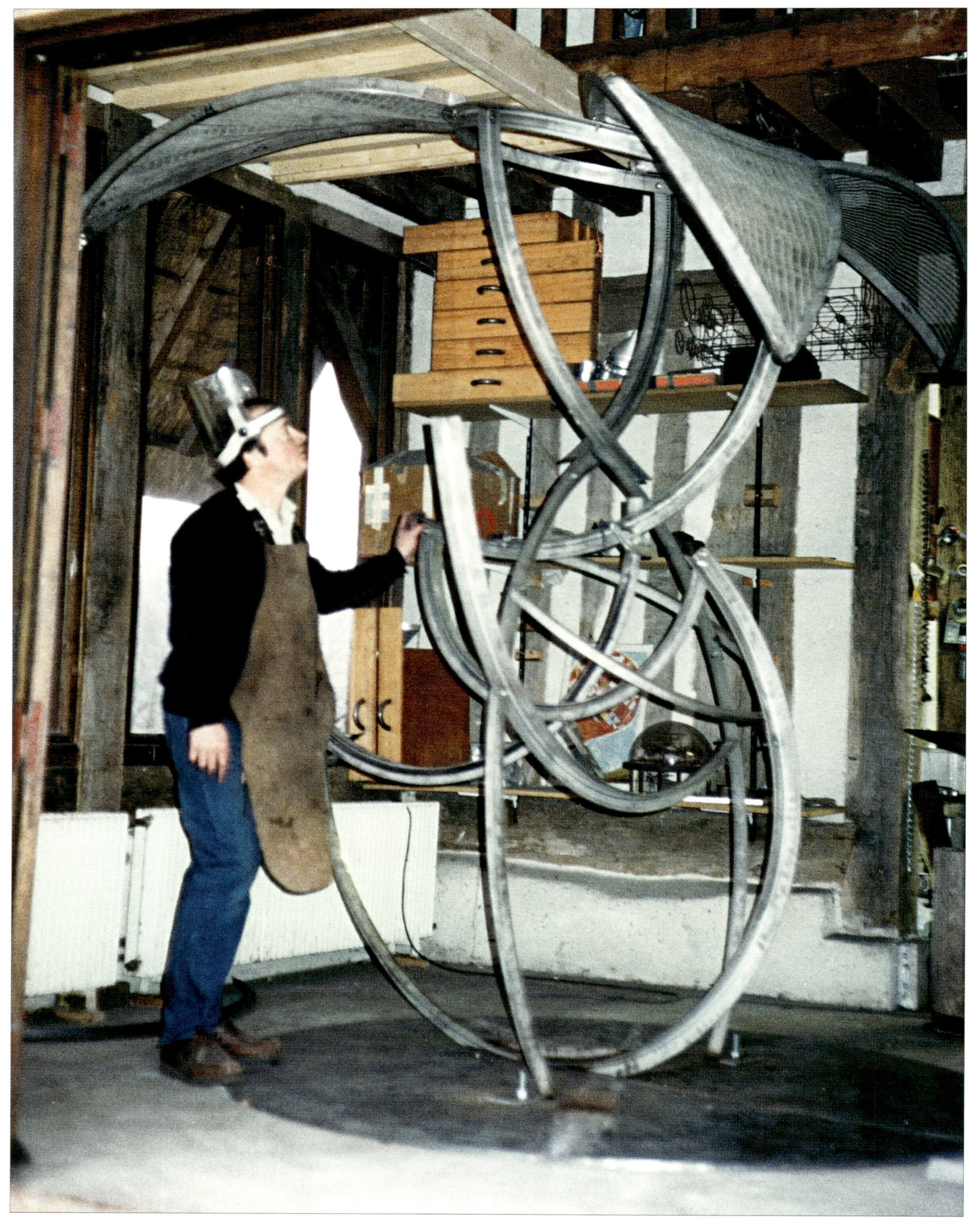

Here Dickon is constructing his large-scale sculpture, "Le palmier",
a work involving difficult techniques required by the chosen material: stainless steel.

This was the beginning of the "Flying Machines" period. It followed the "Birds" period, begun in Greece with Dickon's first exhibitions in 1972. There was a visible continuity between these two themes, a fact confirmed by Dickon in a text he wrote for the Recklinghausen museum, to be included in the catalogue of the show. The original text in English has been lost, but fortunately the German version has survived, allowing us a glimpse of Dickon's quiet wit and engaging simplicity. An English translation is provided in the next chapter.

The "Flying Machines" continued their travels in Germany and Holland, to be followed by the "Crankshafts". This was a series of seemingly simple constructions, which, when animated by turning a handle, delivered a message in images or words.

The time had come for Dickon to explore other avenues. A new medium was currently emerging - the hologram. It fired Dickon's imagination and led to a four-year period of intense production. Several of Dickon's holographic works are now in the collections of prestigious museums in Paris, Cologne, Stockholm and New York.

Review of an exhibition of Dickon's work at the Galerie George Moos. Tribune de Genève, 16 October, 1972.

The cover of the catalogue produced for a major show in Recklinghausen, Germany, entitled "To fly - a dream". Dickon contributed three works to this show.

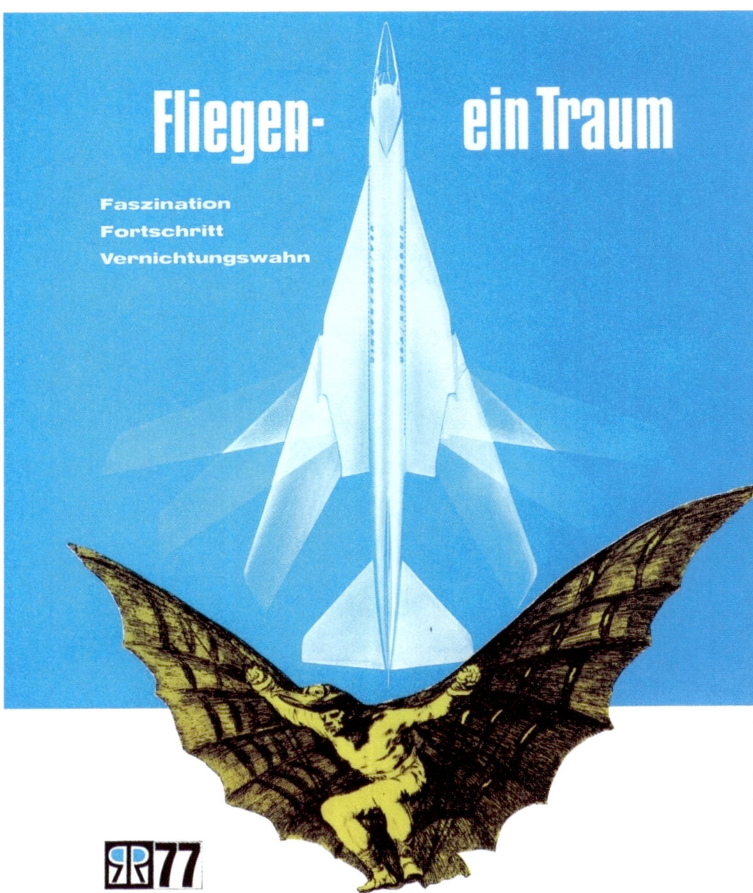

For this catalogue, Dickon wrote the text that follows the captions describing his pieces. His text can be found in the appendix to this book.

g, dort gestorben 1528.
ledewerkstatt des Vaters,
mut. 1490–1494 Wander-
Basel. 1495 erste, 1505/06
. 1520–1521 Reise nach
schöpferische Auseinander-
ens erbrachte die Klarheit
ke. Dürers internationale
m auf seinen Holzschnit-
er in Technik, Inhalt und
maligen Stand hinaus ent-

Nemesis, 1501/02

onogramm
nd Museum Ludwig, Köln

er niederländischen Reise
als »großes Glück« be-
n großen Flügeln, den weit-
en, den Pokal in der aus-
riesiges Ornament hebt
Grund, abstrakt dekorativ
seiner erstaunlichen Na-
gotischen Figurenalpha-
pfinden unschön, obwohl
Kopf ¹/₈ der Gesamtlänge,
liegt. Die Nemesis ist

Blick hinab auf die Erde.
lend, wahrscheinlich nach
der ersten italienischen

daß das Thema des
Gedicht von Polizian zu-
mütigen Glücksgöttin ver-
bunden wird. Ihre Attribute sind Pokal und Zügel
als Zeichen für Lohn und Züchtigung.
Hans Mielke, Albrecht Dürer / Druckgraphik, Kat. Königlicher
Palast Antwerpen, 1970

Eames, Dickon
geboren 1945 in New York, lebt in Freneuse-sur-
Risle. Studium der Bildhauerei an der New School
for Social Research, New York.

71 Flying machine for a small man, 1973
    (Flugmaschine für einen kleinen Mann)
    Messing, Seide, Leder, 100 x 100 x 50
    monogrammiert
    im Besitz des Künstlers

72 Tiger bay, 1973
    Messing, Seide, Leder, 80 x 80 x 50
    monogrammiert
    im Besitz des Künstlers

73 Balloon fulled by 4 birds, 1977
    (Ballon, von 4 Vögeln gezogen)
    Messing, Seide, Tuch, Seil, Ø 120, Länge 550
    monogrammiert
    im Besitz des Künstlers

---

encore plus rentables.
Pour cela il faut que les produits s'usent plus vite afin que les gens en achètent toujours plus, ce qui permettra de faire tourner plus vite l'appareil de production, lequel sera ensuite relayé par un complexe plus puissant qui, etc... La simple question produire tendant au virage. Eh bien, le voici ce « programme » :

Des nouvelles divertissantes

1) Un taux de natalité égal au taux de mortalité dès 1975 ; les couples sont dissuadés d'avoir plus de deux enfants ;

La machine structure de rêve

Si à la Renaissance un Léonard de Vinci inventait des machines (tel le fameux hélicoptère à rotor hélicoïdal), c'est parce qu'il était dans la tradition du temps que l'artiste fût aussi une sorte d'ingénieur. Ainsi, dans la peinture, science expérimentale alors, on avait éprouvé des solutions architecturales et perspectives réalisées dans les villes.

Au vingtième siècle, où elle connaît une existence souveraine ressentie comme une extraordinaire possibilité de libération et comme facteur d'oppression, l'artiste s'intéresse également à la machine. Pour un Duchamp, un Moholy-Nagy, elle met en évidence des qualités cinétiques et optiques ; pour un Calder elle engendre un espace plastique. Et ce ne sont pas les seuls : des créateurs d'une plus jeune génération se servent de la machine, mais presque à rebours, ils la dévoient de ses habituels buts utilitaires. Tinguely la tourne en dérision et l'extrait du cycle de la fonctionnalité. Scarpitta construit des bolides réels mais inutilisables, Panamarenko des aéroplanes presque conceptuels, Piacentino des véhicules de luxe purs objets de contemplation. Le mythe social, la fascination technologique, la domestication de l'énergie mécanique, la vitesse et le mouvement trouvent leur expression en tant qu'œuvres d'art dans les machines créées par les artistes.

Dickon Eames, né à New York en 1945, mais vivant à Paris et Corfou, présente pour sa part des constructions qu'il nomme « fantastiques ». Il veut peut-être dire par là que la machine est pour lui une splendide utopie, une structure de rêve.

Eames fabrique des oiseaux mécaniques, des voitures, des éléments labyrinthiques où circulent des billes. Ces appareils (faut-il parler de sculptures ?) sont le plus souvent actionnés par des manivelles, de sorte que l'amateur peut les faire fonctionner comme un enfant un jouet.

En effet, il y a une évidente naïveté dans ces véhicules faits de minces tiges de laiton. La transmission de l'énergie motrice est loin d'être parfaite, on reste dans le domaine d'un habile bricolage, et qui se veut tel. La forme générale des constructions, leurs mouvements aussi, restent assez schématiques, sans mystère ni complication particulièrement captivante.

Il faut vraiment toute la bonté de l'imagination et de la simplicité de caractère pour partir durablement en voyage avec Dickon Eames. Tant sur le plan poétique, intellectuel, que

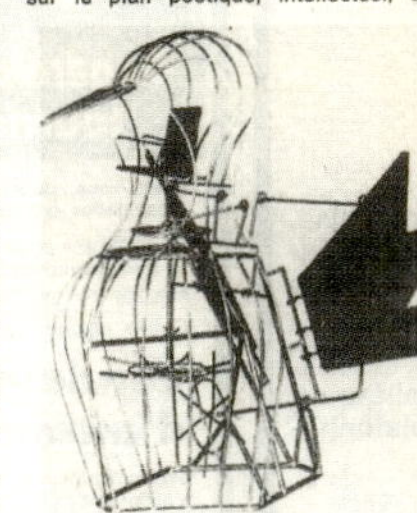

Peut-on partir durablement en voyage avec le « Canard » de Dickon Eames (1970) ?

mécanique, il manque un certain « dépassement » — peut-être surréaliste — une conception formelle qui matérialise une véritable interprétation ou signification particulière de la machine. *(Galerie Georges Moos).*

Rainer Michael MASON.

Associés contr...
est notre affaire...
tions du Masque...
lumes d'un se...
Christie qui con...
velles dans le g...
vres où sont ra...
Sherlock Holmes...
Beresford, repre...
tective privé d'u...
brouille de la f...
les nombreux p...
soumis. Ces no...
tissantes, et l'o...
plus la féconde...
niosité de l'aute...
pourtant les rom...
tel Hercule Po...
cellules grises...
che.

Un vrai cercle

A mesure qu'c...
(Editions des P...
Bill Turner on s...
s'est trouvé un...
livre aussi insip...
semblable, le r...
personnages so...
sistants.

Exbrayat et

Après avoir...
d'une petite vi...
Belle Véronaise...
Exbrayat décrit...
çais dans *Pourq*...
tions du Masque...
disparaît, et l'o...
sassiné. Sa suc...
mort, pose un p...
grands biens. Le...
jalousies et les...
nent, la tension...
nalement tout...
monde. Beaucou...
personnages tr...
(entre autres u...
gaffes sur gaff...
tuer le Pépé?...
sant.

Maîtrise psych...
d'une femme...

Voici mainten...
man policier, *La*...
tions Calmann-Lé...
grand talent, Pat...
jet peut se rés...
un détraqué vo...
couple et réclam...
paie, mais n'obt...
jeune policier pl...
prudent s'intéres...
ne lui attire qu...
tricia Highsmith...
simple avec un...

Dickon Eames: Paris, Frühjahr 1977. Peter Marcasiano und ich gehen am Seineufer spazieren zwischen Blumenständen und Ständen, an denen Tiere verkauft werden. Ich schaue mir die Hähne an, denn ich brauche einen neuen Hahn für meine Hennen, mein alter ist im Winter gestorben. Peter plädiert für einen »roten Rode-Island-Hahn«, aber ich möchte lieber einen schönen bunt gesprenkelten und einen solchen kaufe ich auch. Wir packen den Hahn in einen Pappkarton und gehen in ein Bistro, um einen Drink zu nehmen. Ich erzähle Peter von meiner Arbeit und daß ich bei den Ruhrfestspielen in Recklinghausen ausstelle, daß man dort einen Text von mir für den Katalog erwartet und daß ich gar nicht weiß, was ich schreiben soll. Denn wenn man so in eine Arbeit vertieft ist wie ich zur Zeit, dann hat man einfach nicht den nötigen Abstand, um darüber zu schreiben. »Ja«, sagt Peter, »aber ein solcher Text ist wichtig, denn eine Ausstellung ist ja so etwas wie eine Theaterinszenierung, nicht das einzelne Kunstwerk natürlich, aber eine Ausstellung.«
Ich erzähle Peter, daß die Ausstellung den Titel hat »Fliegen -- ein Traum«, ein Thema, mit dem ich mich seit längerer Zeit in meinen Arbeiten beschäftige.
»Fliegen«, sagt Peter, »das ist unendliche Ausdehnung, ein Über-Sich-Hinauswachsen. Der faustische Mensch. Den Deutschen muß dieses Thema liegen, denn sie sind ja besonders ›faustisch‹. Christus wäre zu erwähnen, der Vogel und der apollinische Traum. Du mußt vor allem auf eines hinweisen: daß Deine Flugobjekte nicht gemacht werden mit dem Ziel, damit auch fliegen zu wollen, ich meine, es darf nicht der Sinn von Kunst sein, daß sie in die Falle tappt, ›Nutzobjekte‹ schaffen zu wollen. Kunst sollte dazu da sein, unsere geheimsten Sehnsüchte auszudrücken. Den apollinischen Traum, emporzuschweben ins Unendliche! Schau Dir doch Deine Ballons an! Fliegzeuge, die etwas von diesem Traum an sich haben, vom Traum des Fliegens ins Unendliche. Du mußt einmal Nietzsche lesen: Apollo ist die Verkörperung des Traums vom Fliegen, Dionysos, das ist der Saft, der aus der Erde kommt, der Mann der Praxis. Das Apollinische und das Dionysische ergeben zusammen das Faustische mit seiner Bindung an das Unendliche, verstehst Du?« Ich nickte -- das schien mir in diesem Augenblick die intelligenteste Antwort, die ich geben konnte. »Du mußt etwas schreiben, was bei den Lesern sofort zündet«, sagt Peter. »Irgendetwas ganz Tolles muß Dir einfallen -- wie z. B. Du habest geträumt, man könne für Geld nichts mehr kaufen. Ich hoffe, daß Dir eine solche Idee für Deinen Text kommt.«
Dann standen wir auf und gingen weiter am Fluß entlang, Peter, ich und der Hahn.

Eddy, Donald
geboren 1944 in Long Beach, California, lebt in Santa Barbara, California. 1967–1969 Studium am Fullerton Junior College, Fullerton, California; an der University of Hawaii, Honolulu; 1969–1970 Studium an der University of California, Santa Barbara; 1971 Dozent an der University of California, College of Creative Studies, Santa Barbara. Don Eddy gehört zu jenen amerikanischen Realisten, die mit dem Hilfsmittel der Fotografie arbeiten. Er benutzt das Foto, weil es »einem Objekt die plastische Qualität nimmt und es in eine Fläche verwandelt«. Er macht seine Fotos selbst, weil es ihm auf ganz bestimmte formale ›Probleme‹ ankommt. Ob er Autos, Flugzeuge oder Schaufenster malt, immer

The introductory text for the Galerie d'Theeboom invitation was written by Jan Kuijper, poet and editor of a Dutch literary publication. The invitation was hand-set in lead type by the Joh. Enschedé company, the oldest printing company in the Netherlands, founded in 1703. The typeface chosen was "Romanée", designed in 1928 by the renowned Dutch designer Jan van Krimpen (1892-1958).

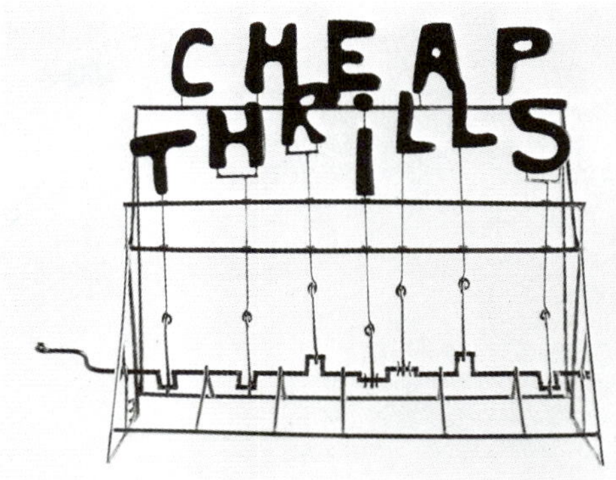

DICKON EAMES

Dickon Eames is in 1945 geboren in New York. Hij houdt zich sinds 1965 voornamelijk bezig met draadconstructies van messing. In 1968 ging hij naar Parijs; een paar jaar later heeft hij zich in de Normandische provincie gevestigd. Daar maakt hij ballenmachines, vliegtuigen, vogels, lucht-ballonnen, en de laatste tijd 'crankshafts', machines welker onderdelen door middel van een krukas kunnen worden bewogen. Die onderdelen dienen natuurlijk om een ander uiterlijk te geven aan het geheel waartoe ze behoren, zo gauw de krukas van stand verandert. Maar vaak hebben ze ook een betekenis op zichzelf, lijken het wel zonnen, manen, pruimen en bananen, of zelfs betekenisdragers in optima forma: letters, die dus ook in een wisselende orde, ja volgorde kunnen geraken. Zo wordt art met een simpele handbeweging tot rat - in de val, in een val van messing draadgaas, allicht. Eames heeft eenmanstentoonstellingen gehad in New York, Athene, Genève en Amsterdam. Vernissage donderdag 26 april vanaf 8 uur · tentoonstelling geopend tot en met 30 mei van 1 tot 6 uur · zondag en maandag gesloten · Galerie d'Theeboom Singel 210 ingang Driekoningenstraat Amsterdam telefoon 248828 privé 237299

Invitation to an exhibition at the Galerie d'Theeboom (Amsterdam). October 1977.

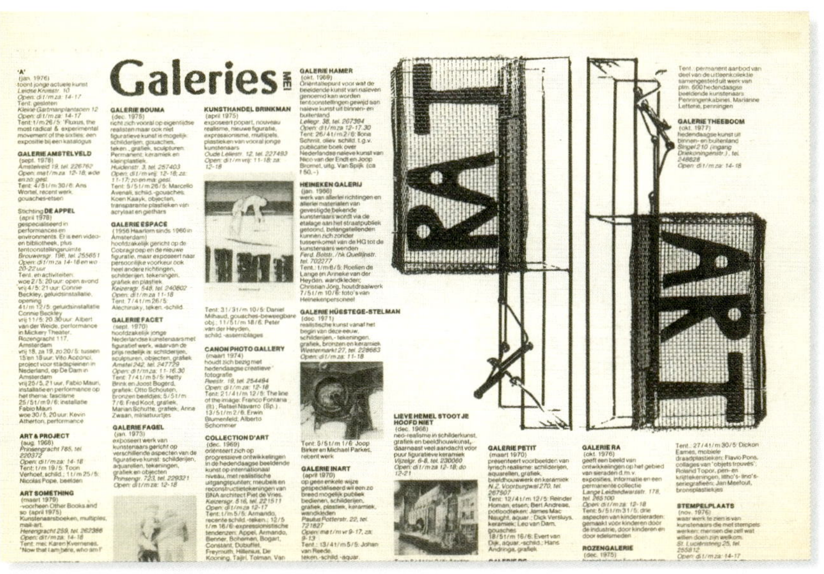

The "Crankshaft Series" was acclaimed by the Dutch press.

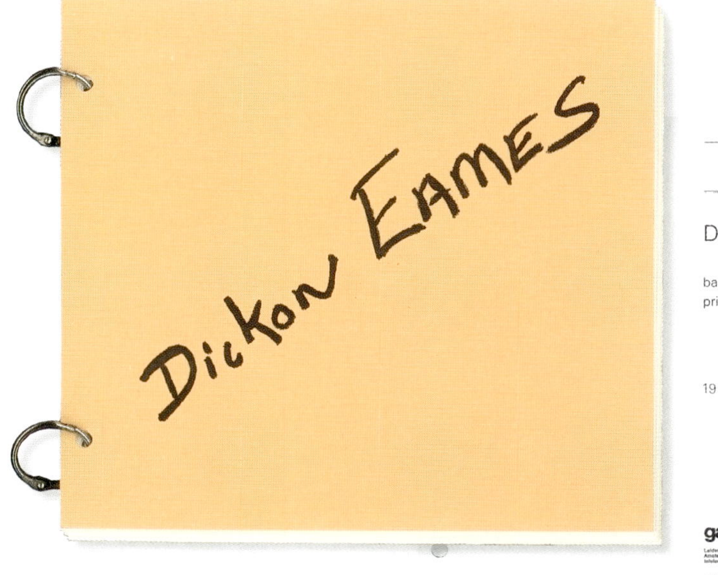

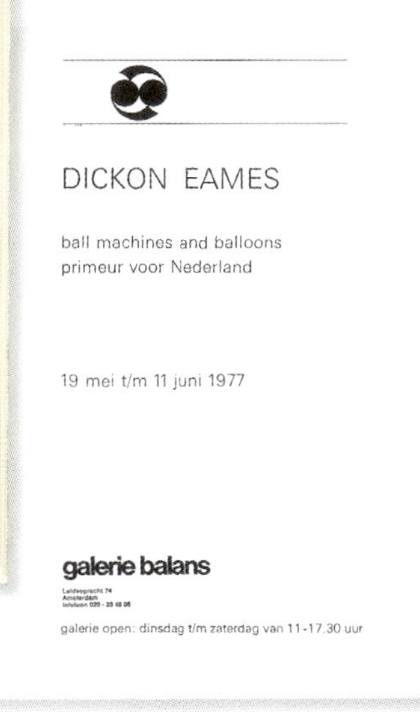

Catalogue of the exhibition "Ball Machines & Balloons". Galerie Balans, Amsterdam. June 1977.

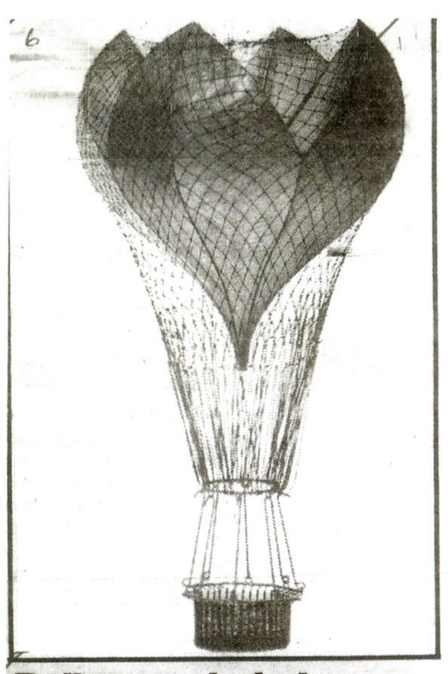

Ballonnen in balans

D'r wordt wat afgevlogen en gefantaseerd over vliegen. Het Amsterdams Ballongezelschap, het Stedelijk Museum en ook nog Galerie Balans laten van zich horen.

Deze Galerie op de Leidsegracht nummer 74, heeft nog tot en met 11 juni de ,,primeur voor Nederland'', zoals ze het aankondigden; de ,,ball machines and balloons'' van Dickon Eames onder dak.

Een alleraardigste tentoonstelling die je een geheel andere kijk op het ,,zachte luchtvaartgebeuren'' doet krijgen. Dickon Eames is een Amerikaan. Maar zoals dat wel vaker het geval is, heeft hij Frankrijk als zijn tweede vaderland gekozen. Op een boerderij in Normandië fabriceert hij zijn ballonnen — die eigenlijk geen ballonnen zijn — maar nog het meeste weg hebben van de allereerste ontwerpen van vliegmachines zo rond het begin van de vorige eeuw toen de luchtvaart nog in de kinderschoenen stond.

"De Echo"
June 8, 1977 (?)

An article published in "De Echo" in June 1977.

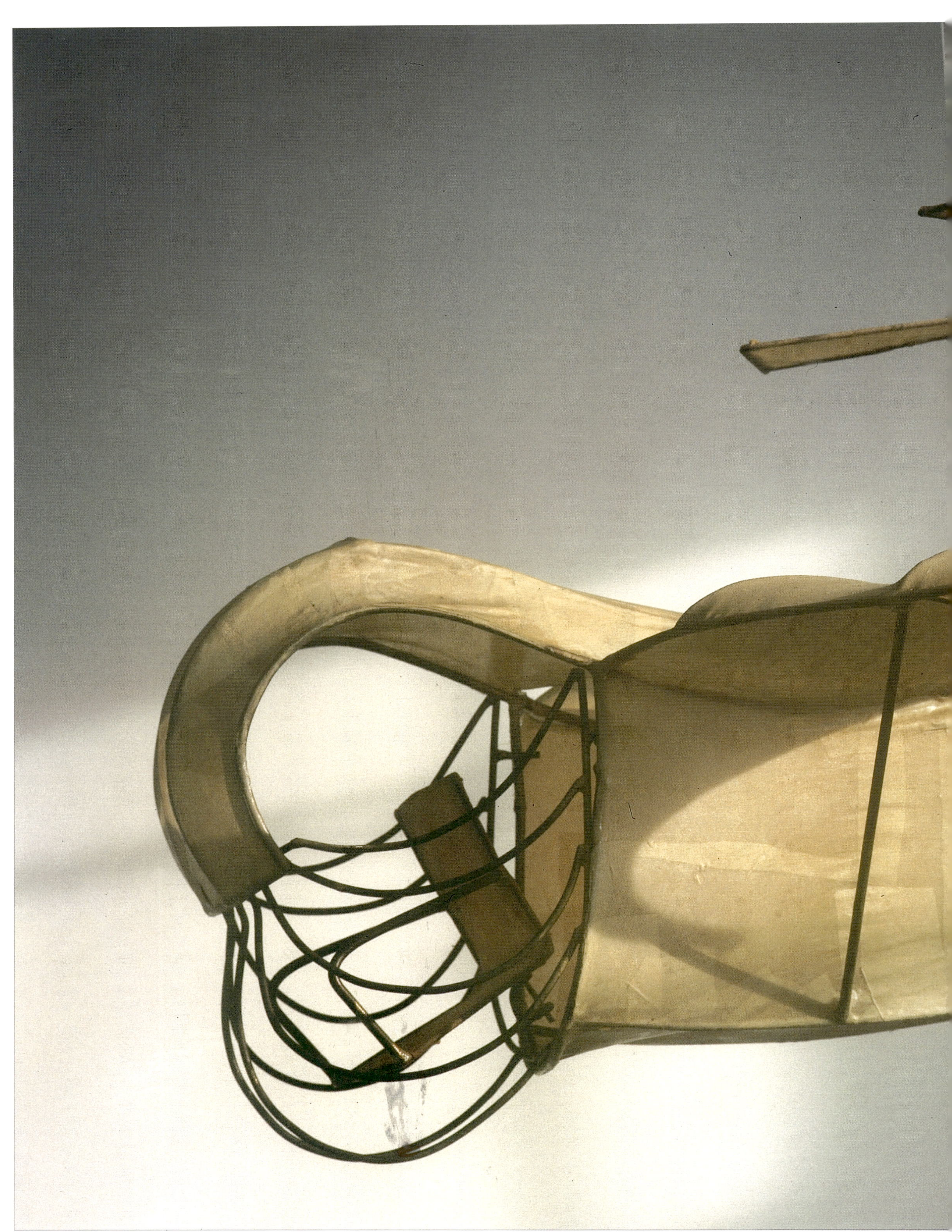

A *"Flying Machine", exhibited in Amsterdam (Galerie d'Theeboom) in 1977.*

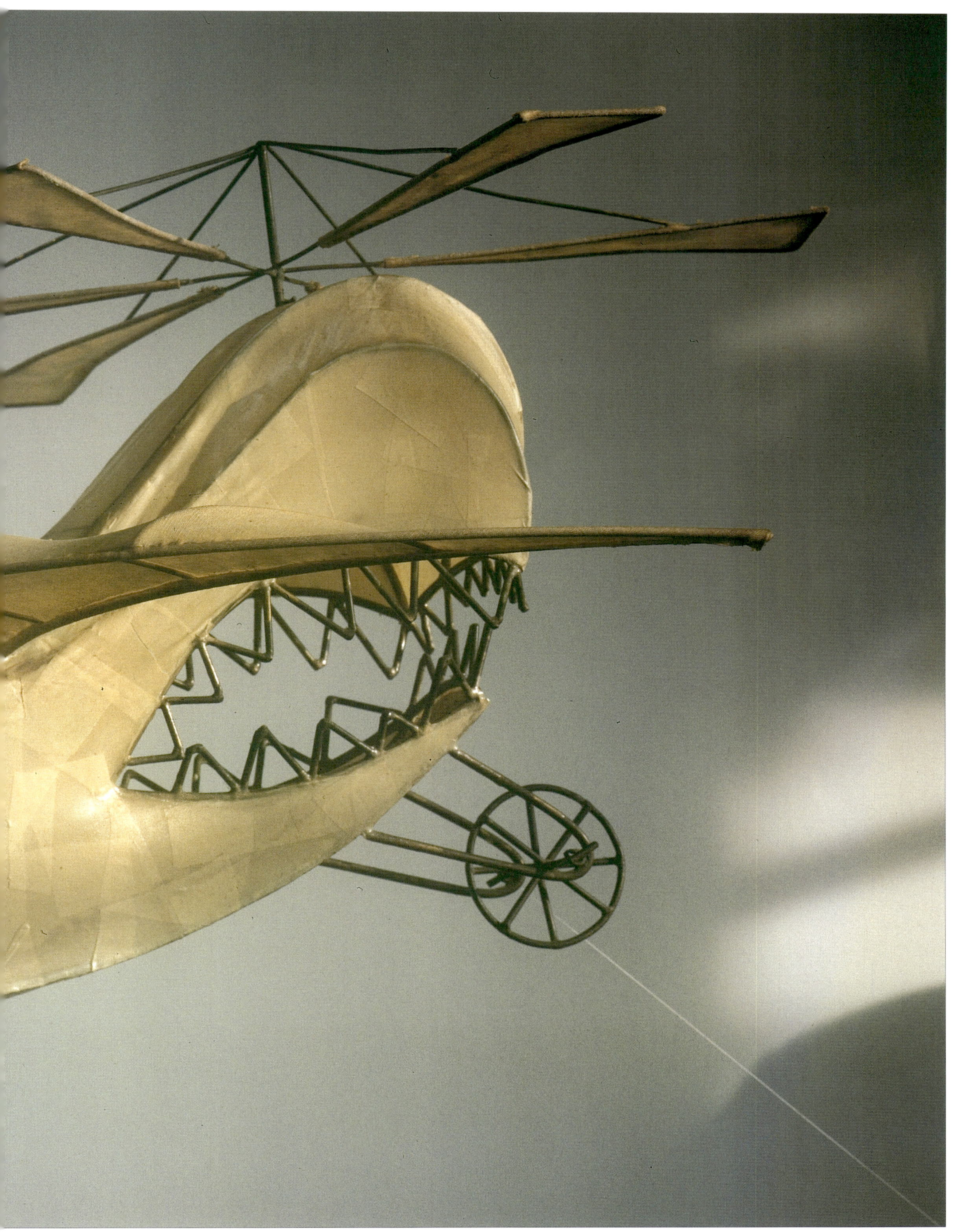

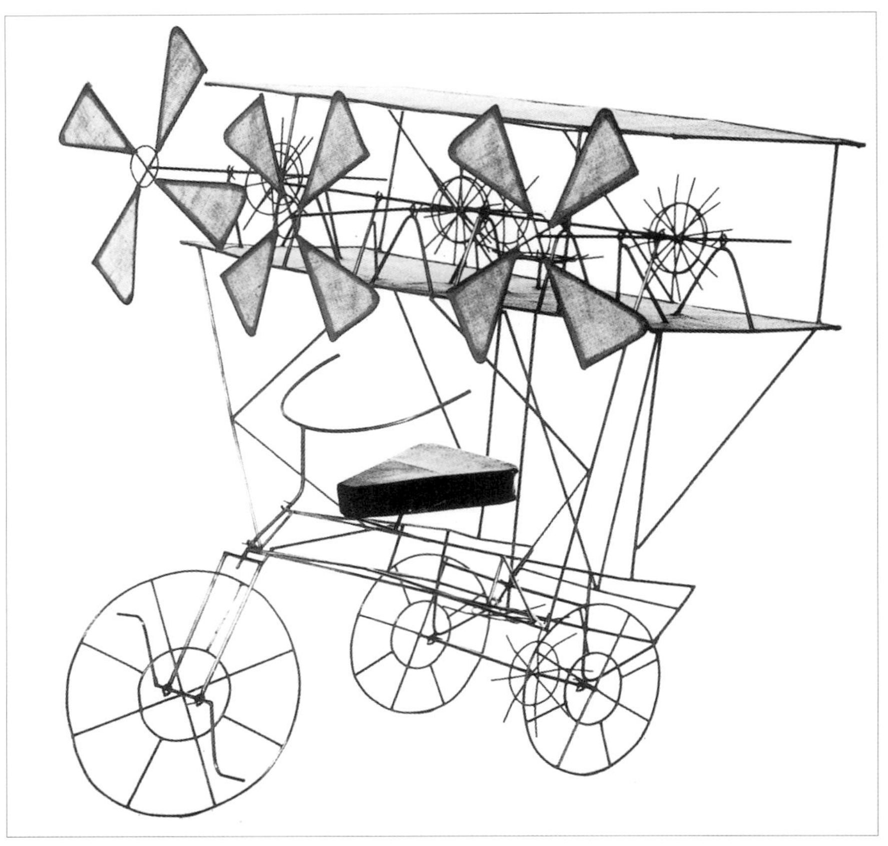

"Flying Bike"

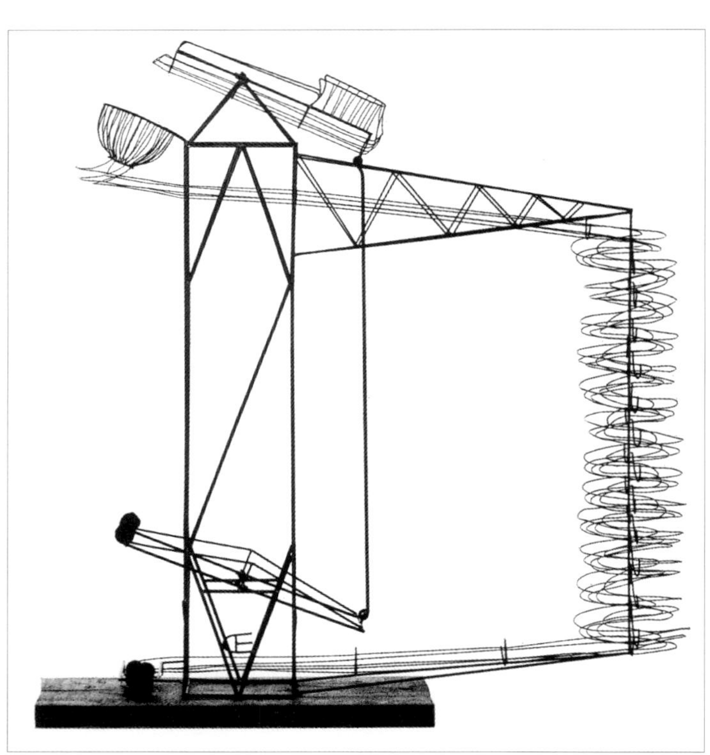

"Something's happening outside the Tower"

"Wall Marbles"

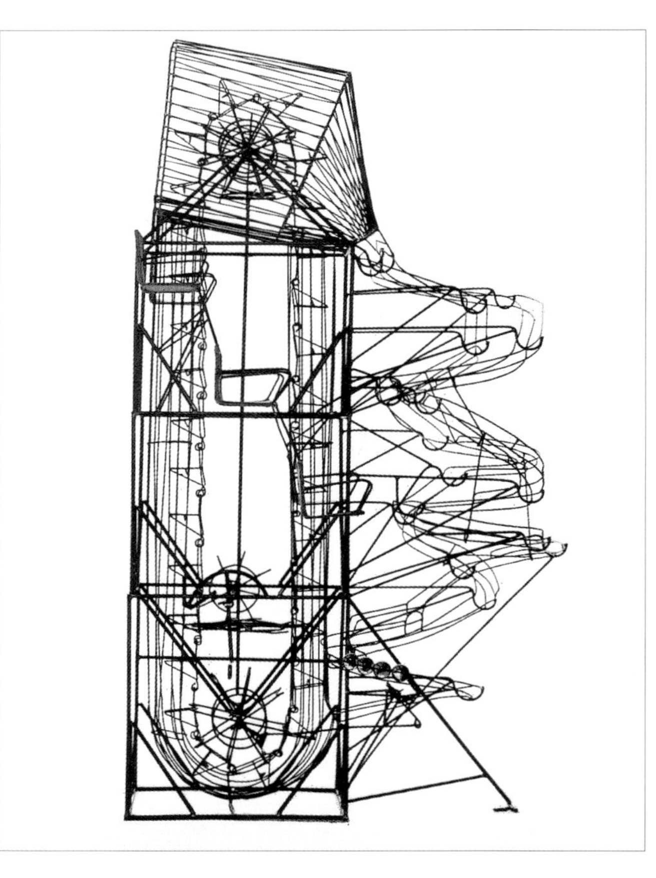

"Marble Machine with Seats"

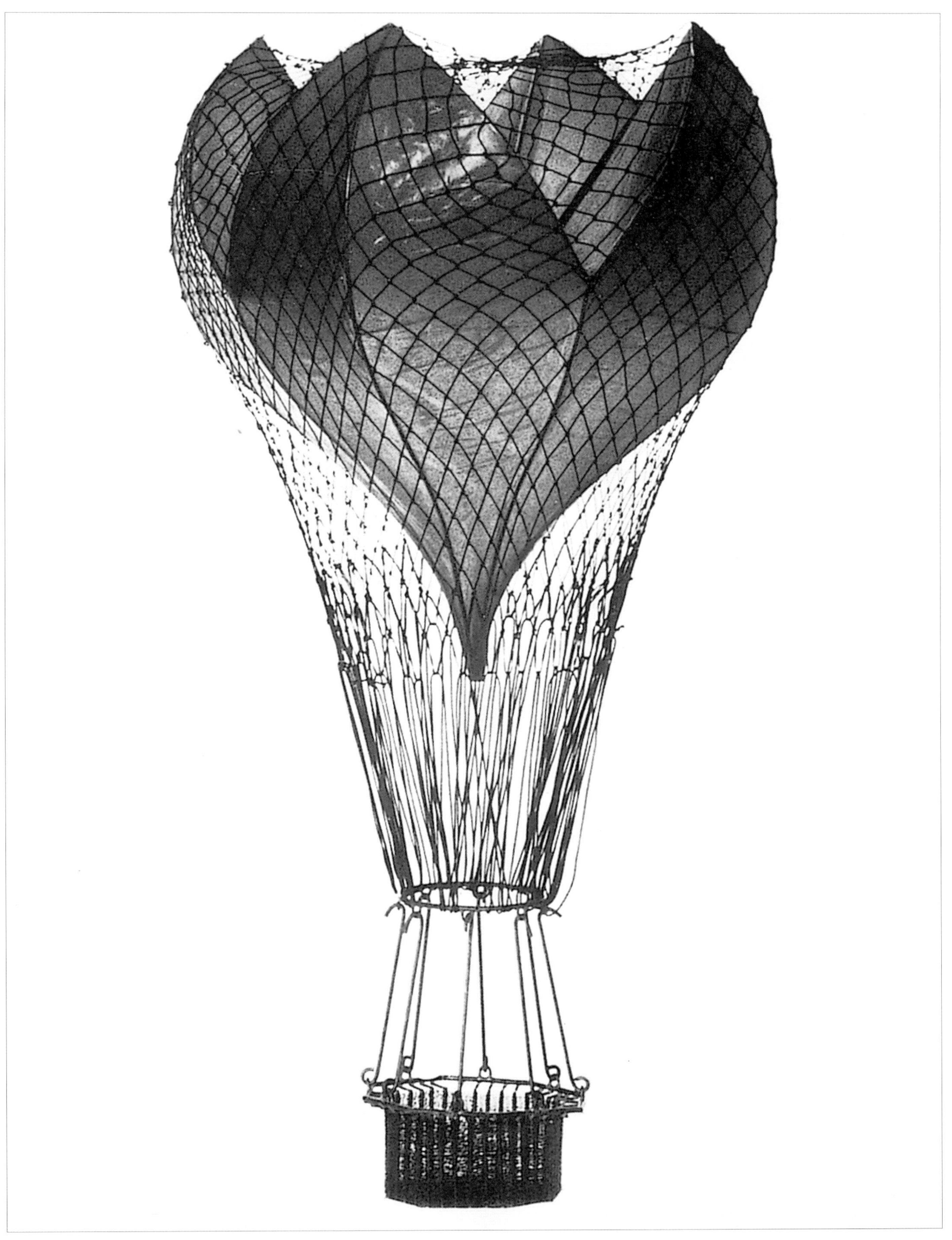

"Top Split Balloon"

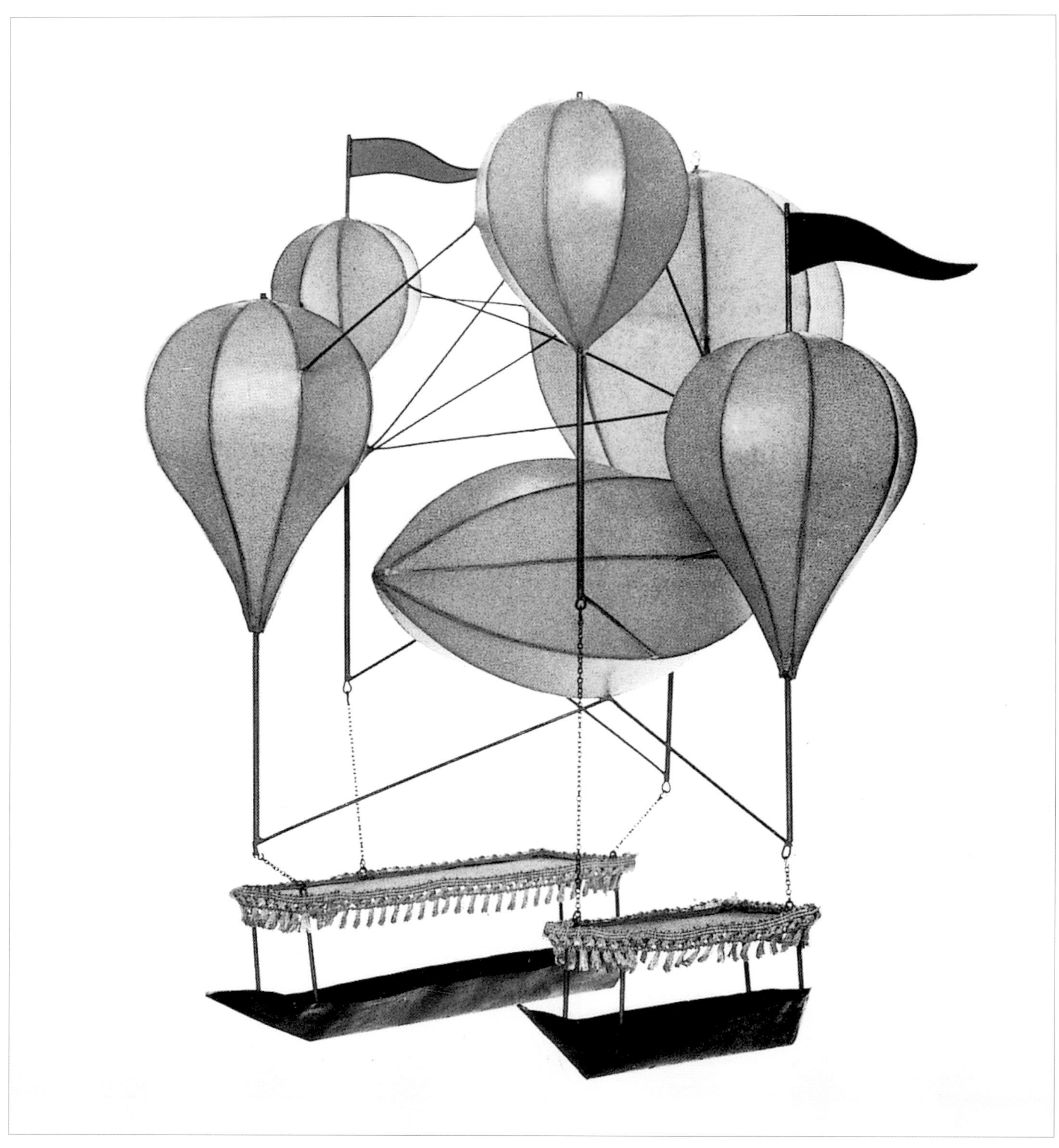

"Carnival"

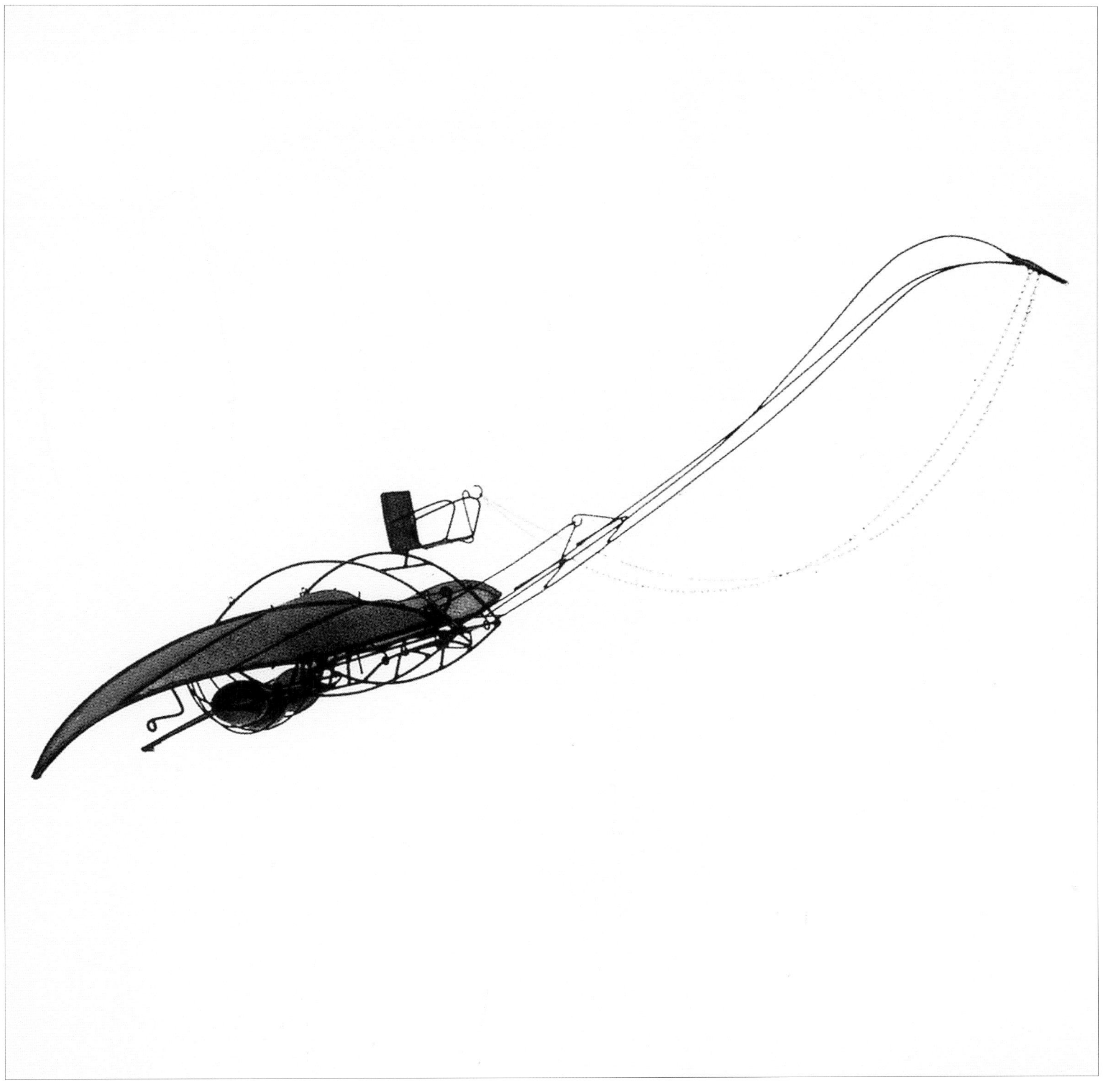

"White Bird with Eggs"

These two sculptures, together with the pieces shown on the previous double page, were part of the series exhibited at the Galerie Balans (Amsterdam) in 1977.

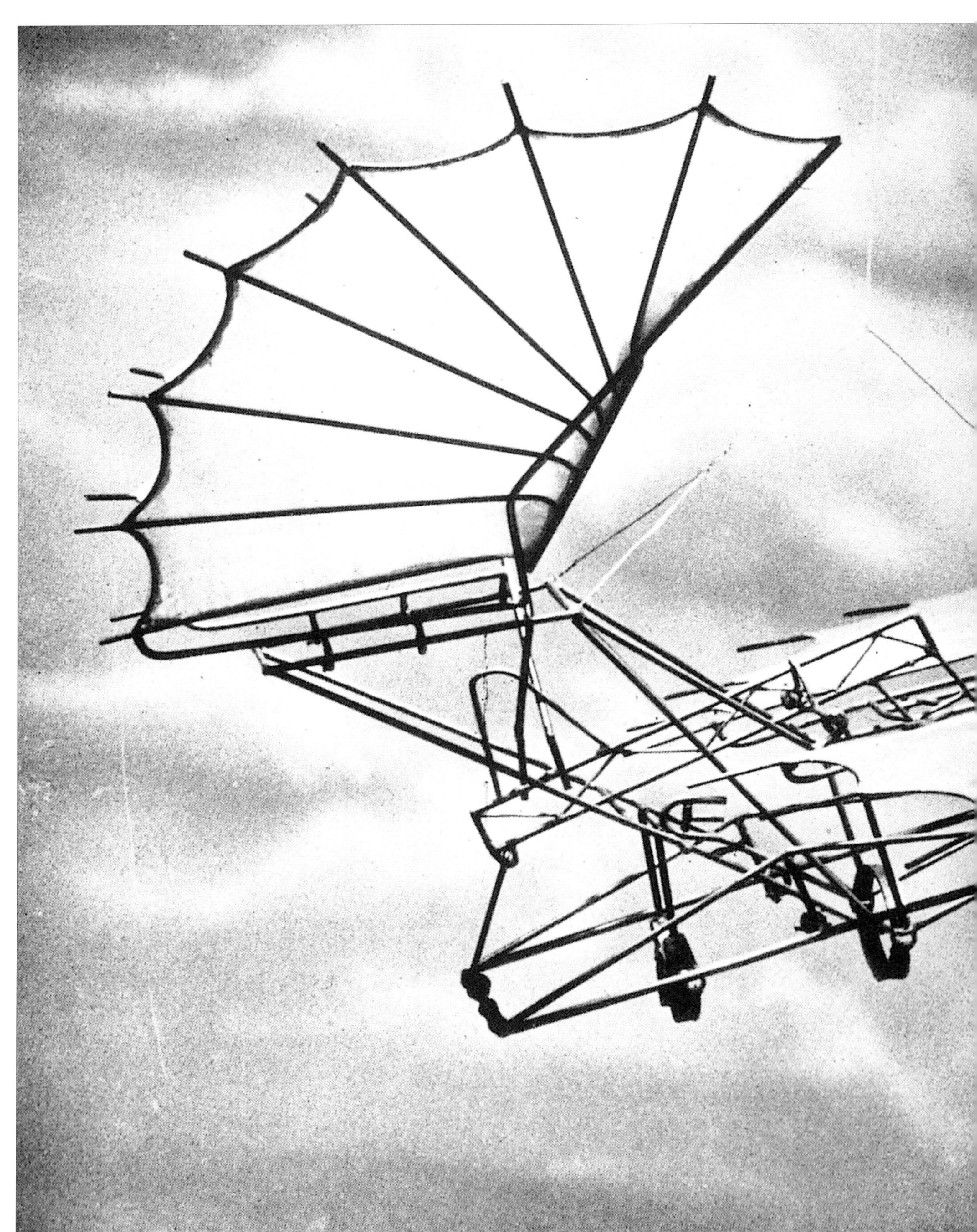

"Flying Machine for a Little Man". Sculpture exhibited in Recklinghausen, 1977.

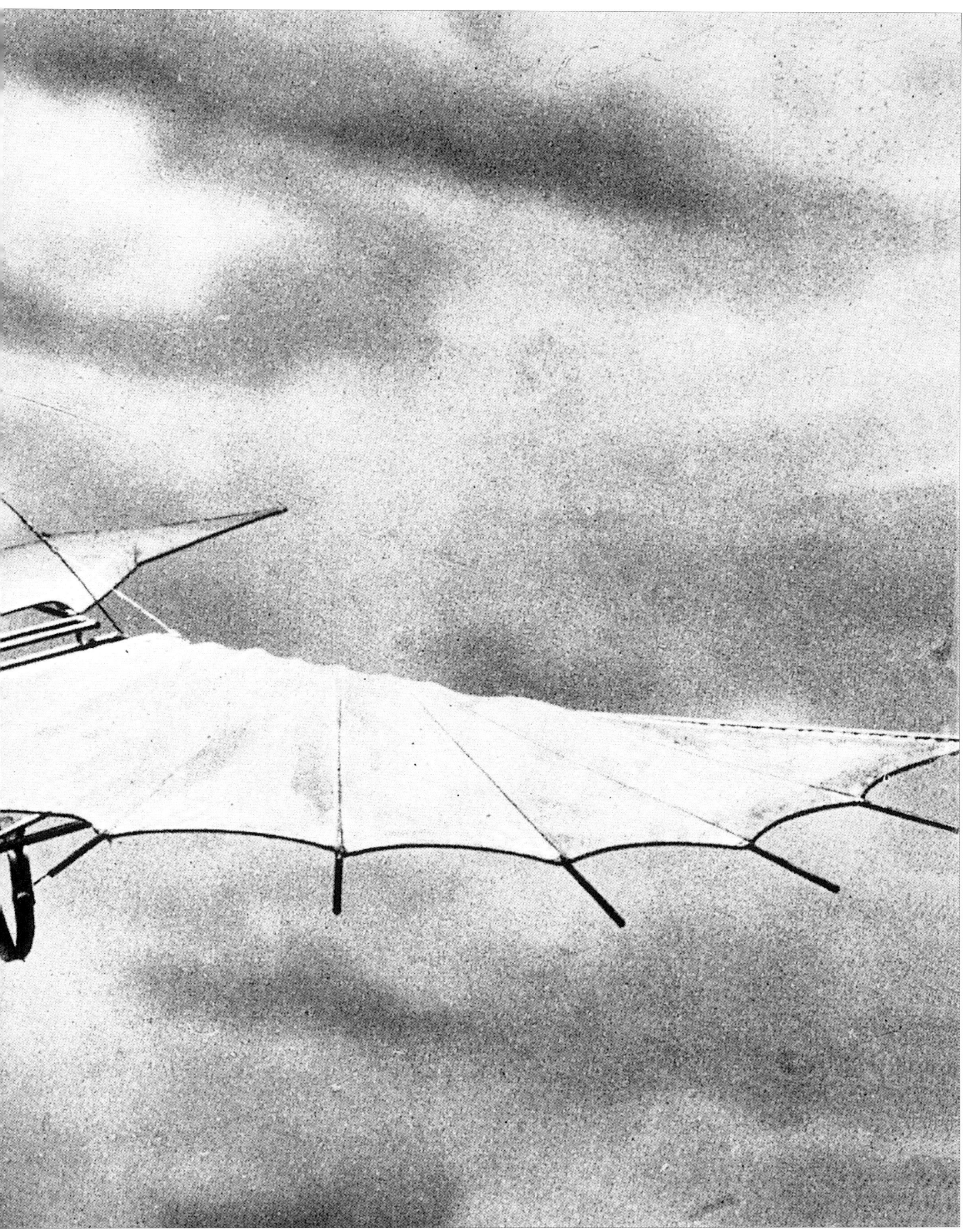

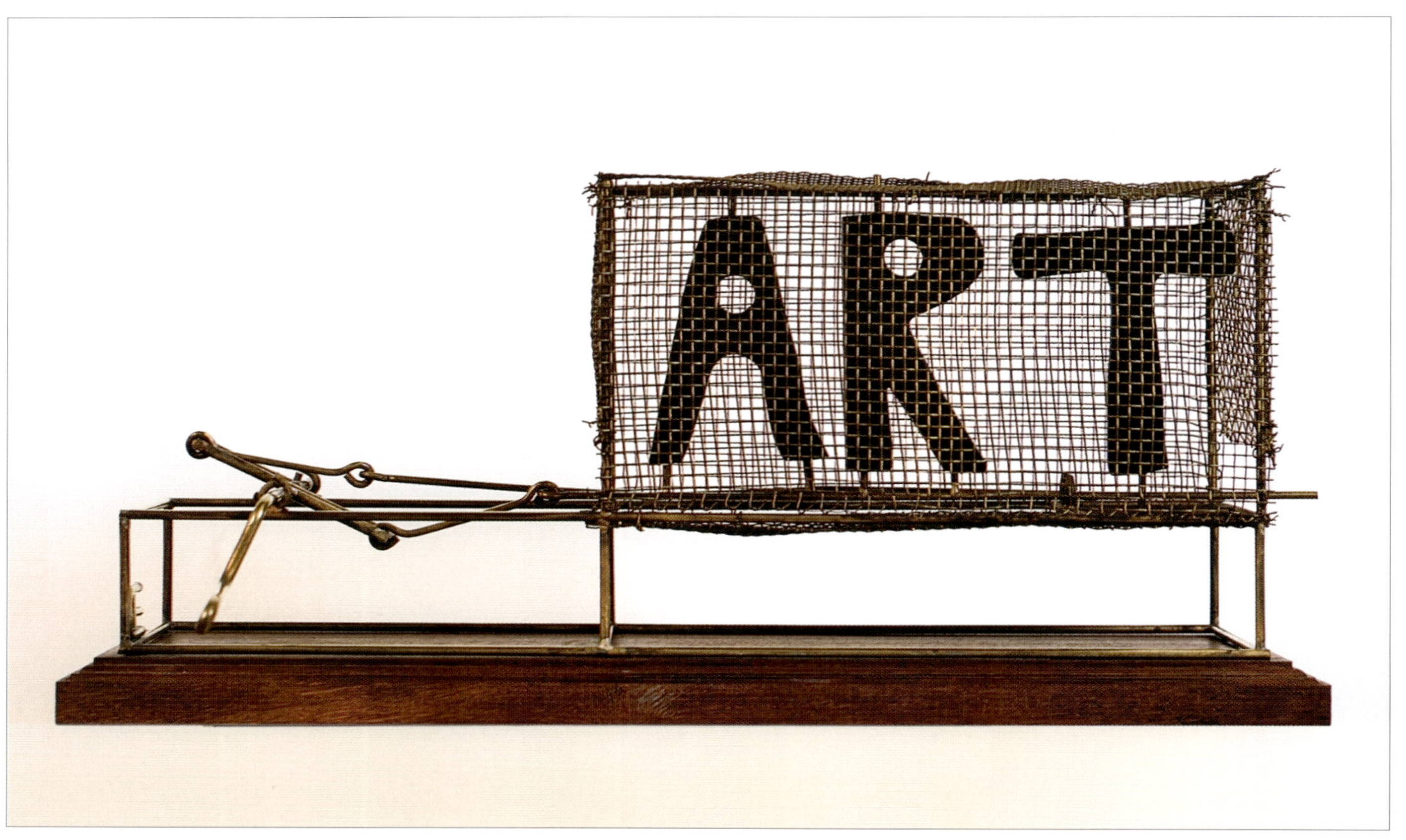
ART

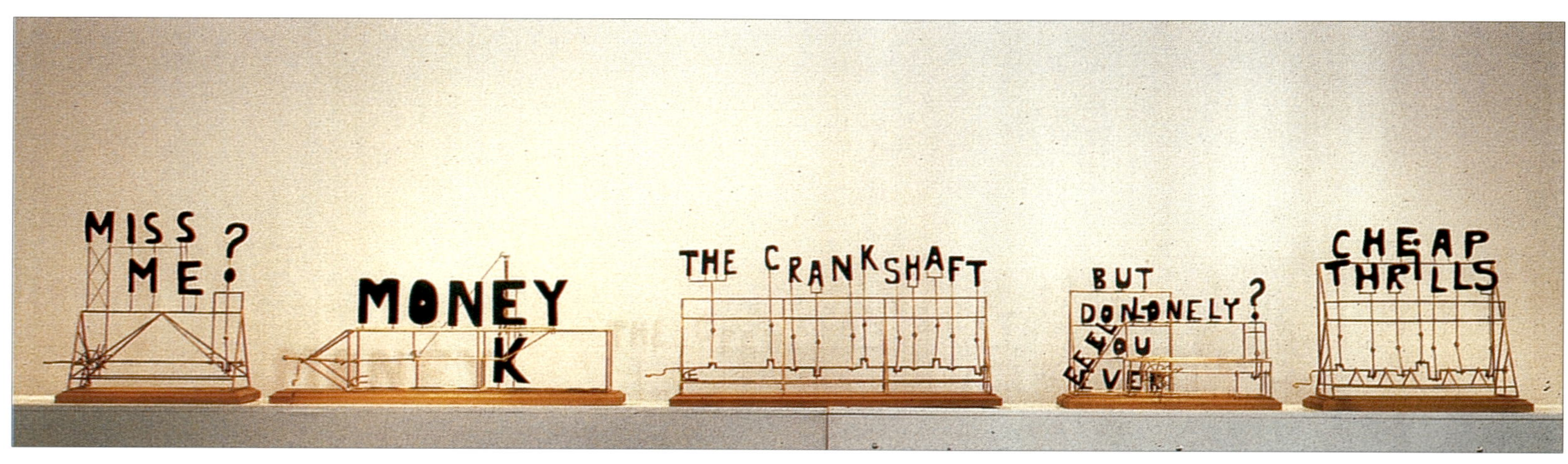
MISS
ME ?
MONEY
K
THE CRANKSHAFT
BUT
DO YOU EVER
FEEL LONELY ?
CHEAP
THRILLS

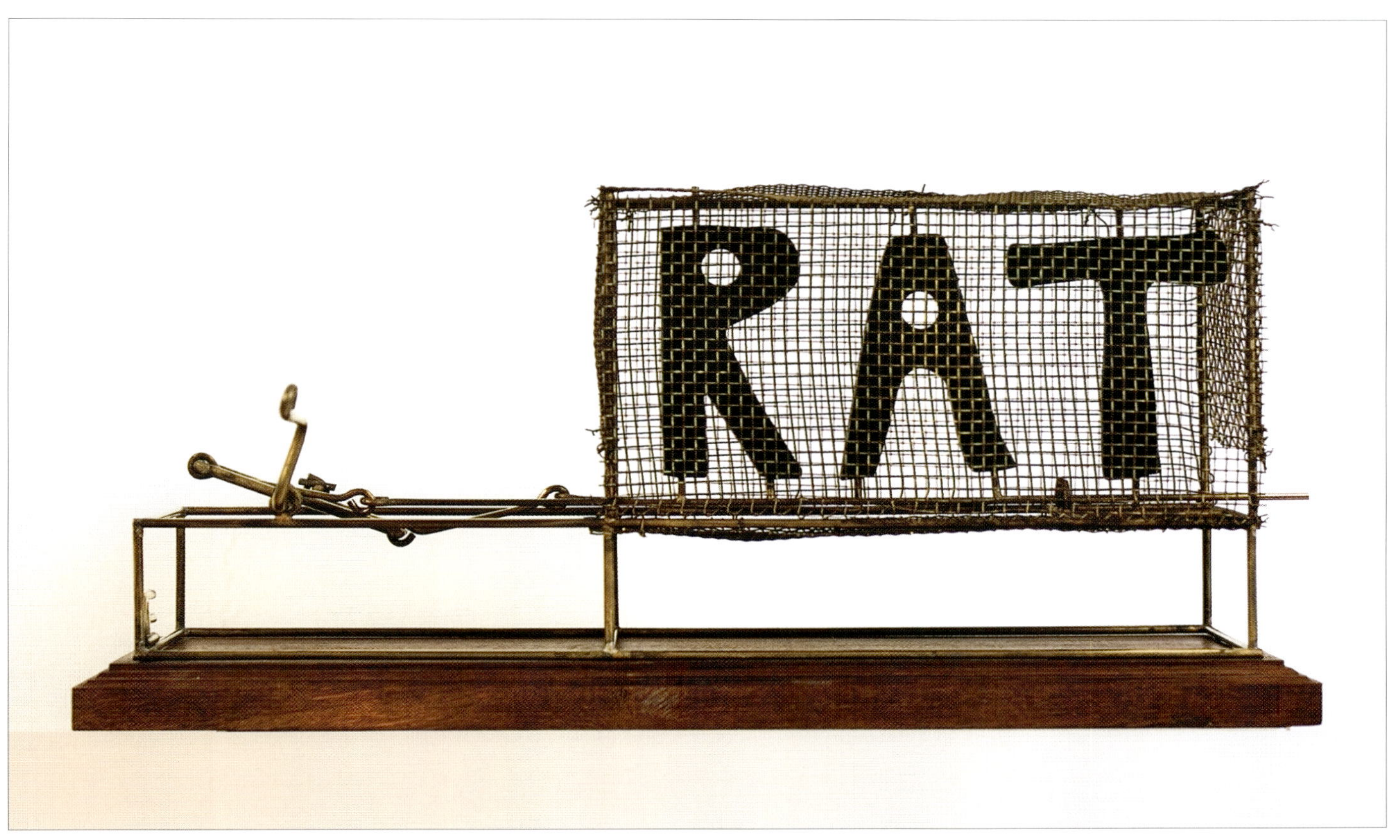

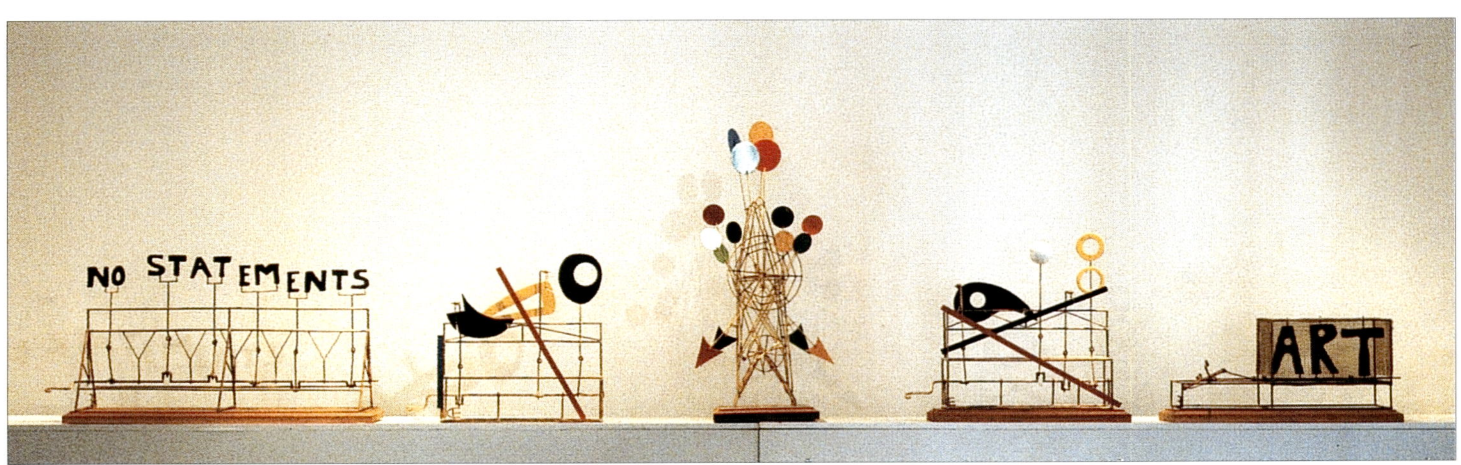

On this double page, and the following double page:
The "Crankshaft Series", exhibited in Amsterdam (Galerie d'Theeboom) in 1977.

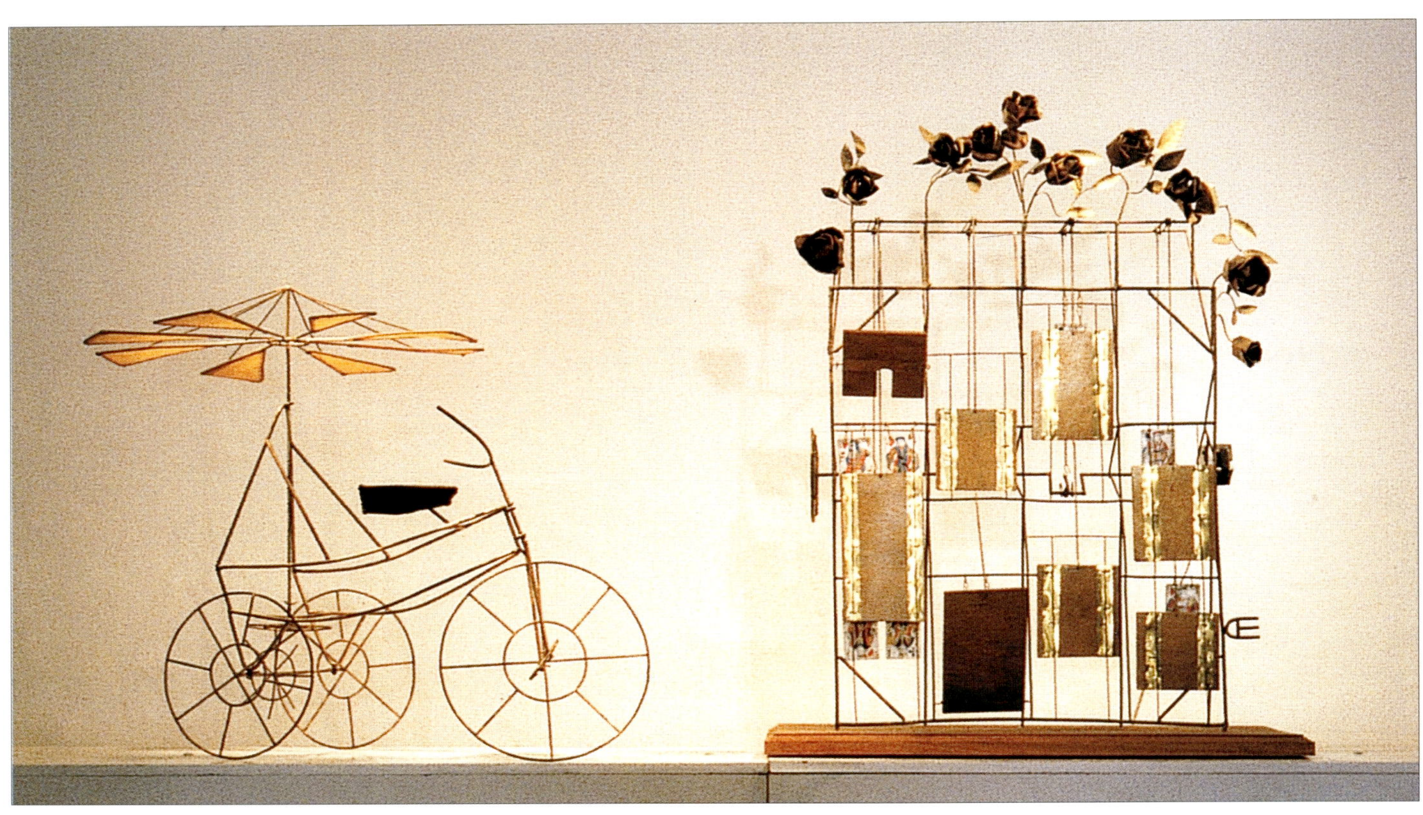

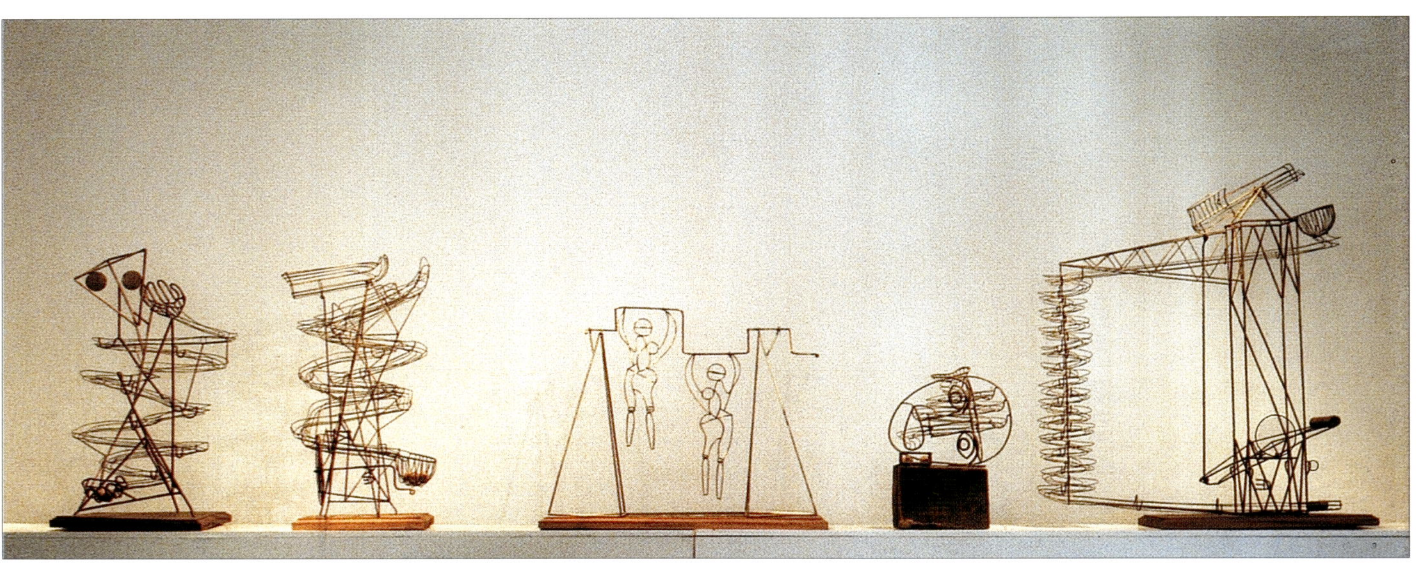

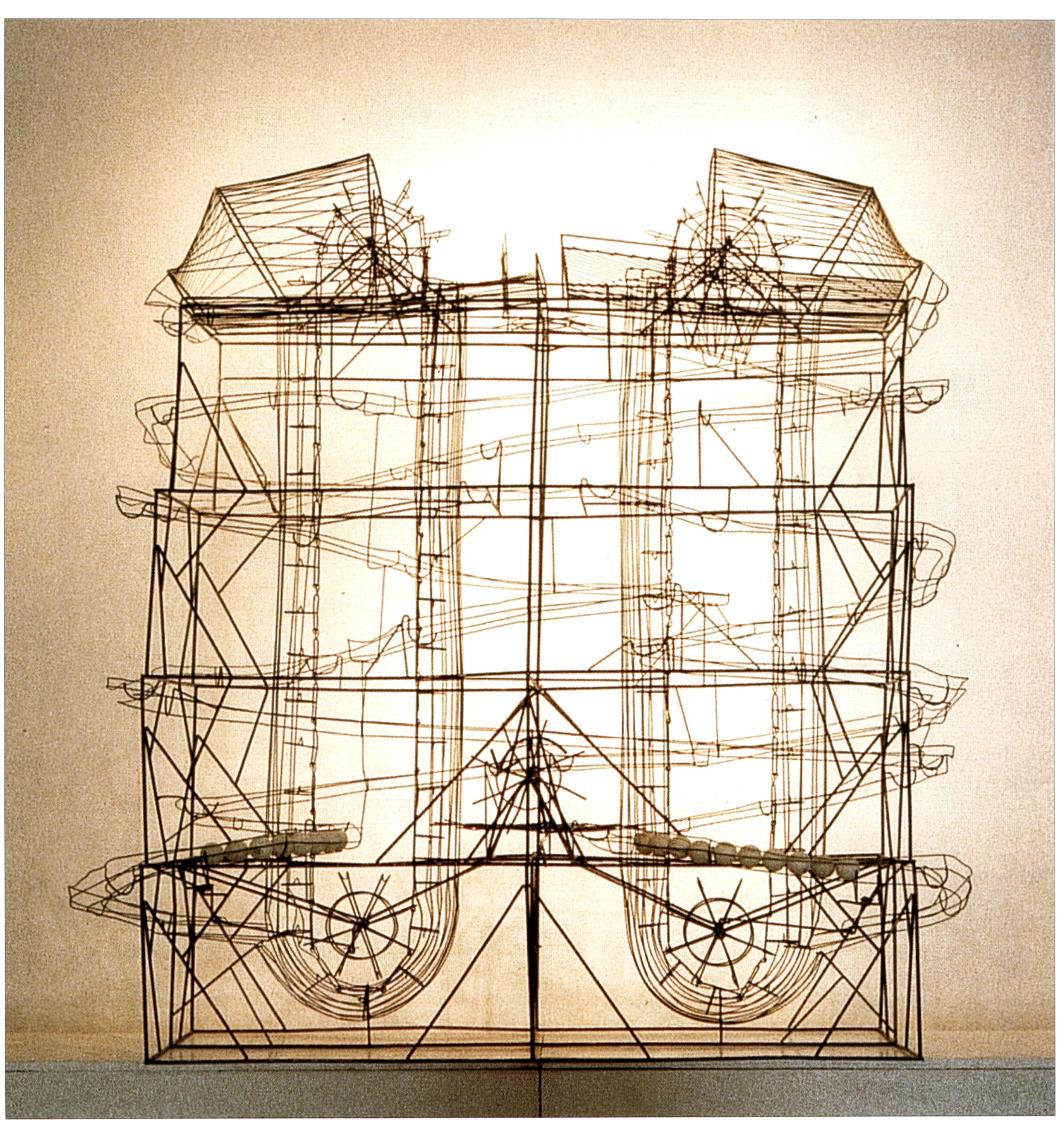

"Big Cork Ball Machine"

The lithograph that Dickon gave Peter Woodd as a wedding gift. 1980.

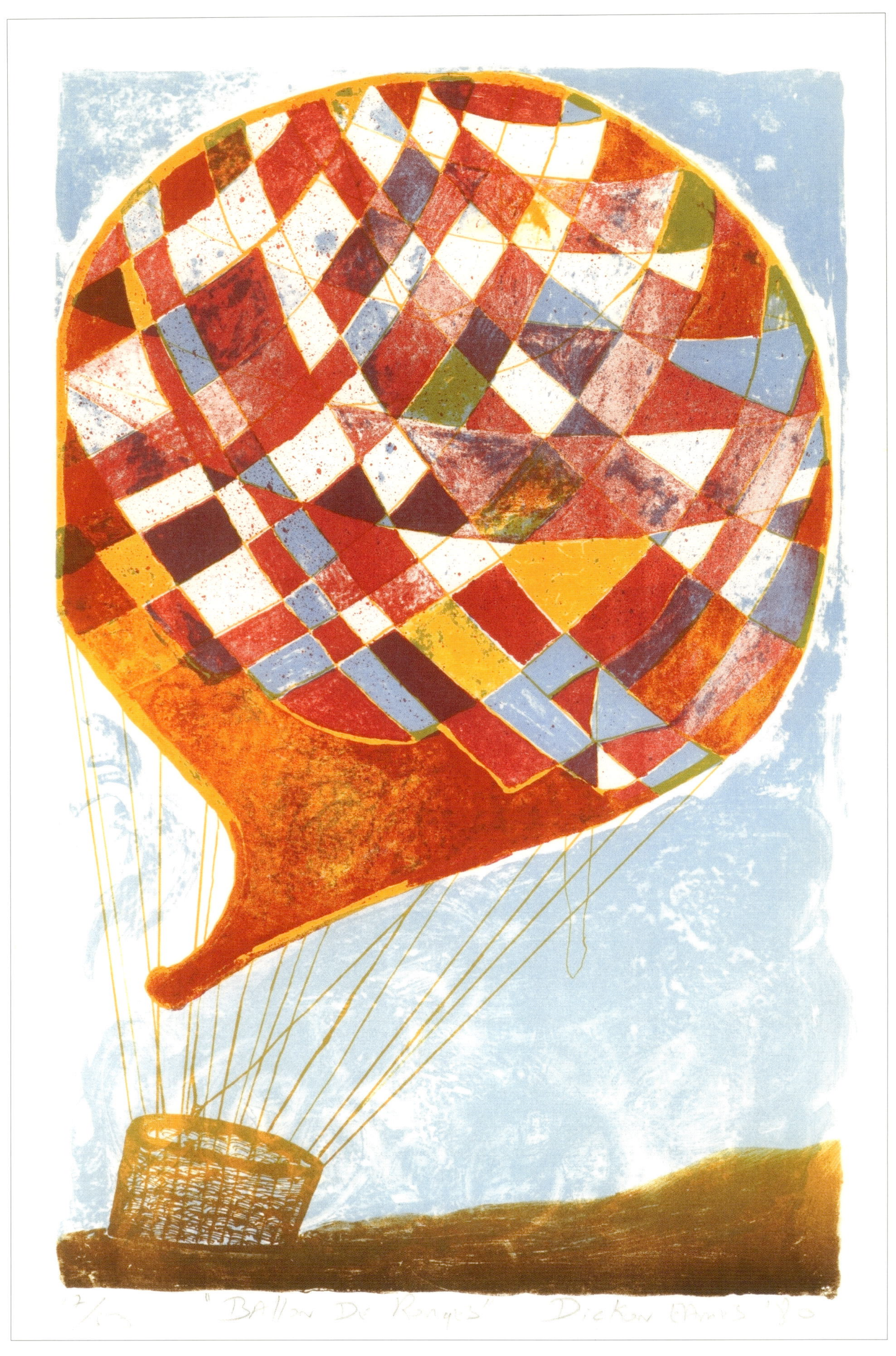

The lithograph that Dickon gave Peter Woodd as a wedding gift. 1980.

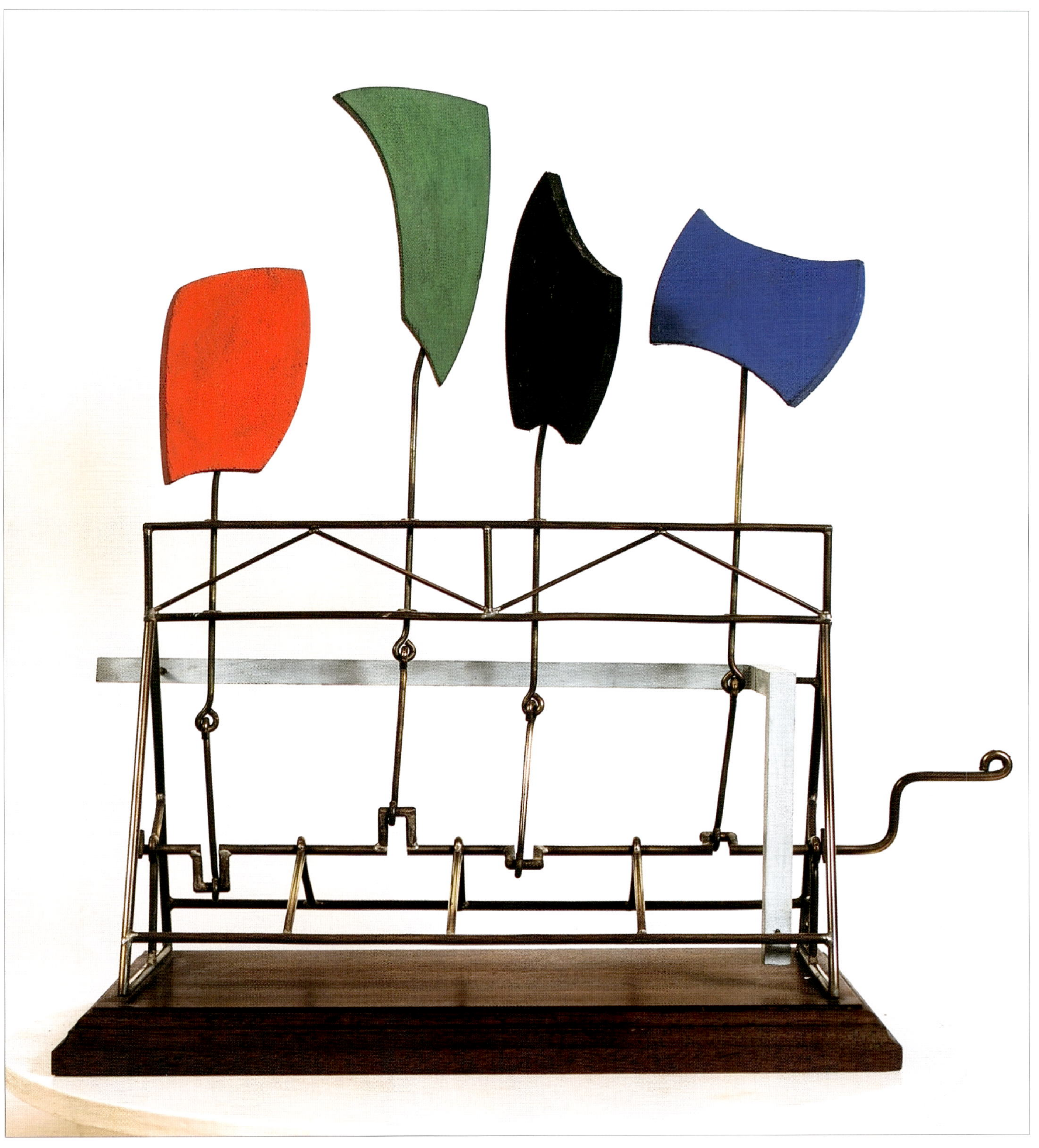

The colored "Crankshaft Series".

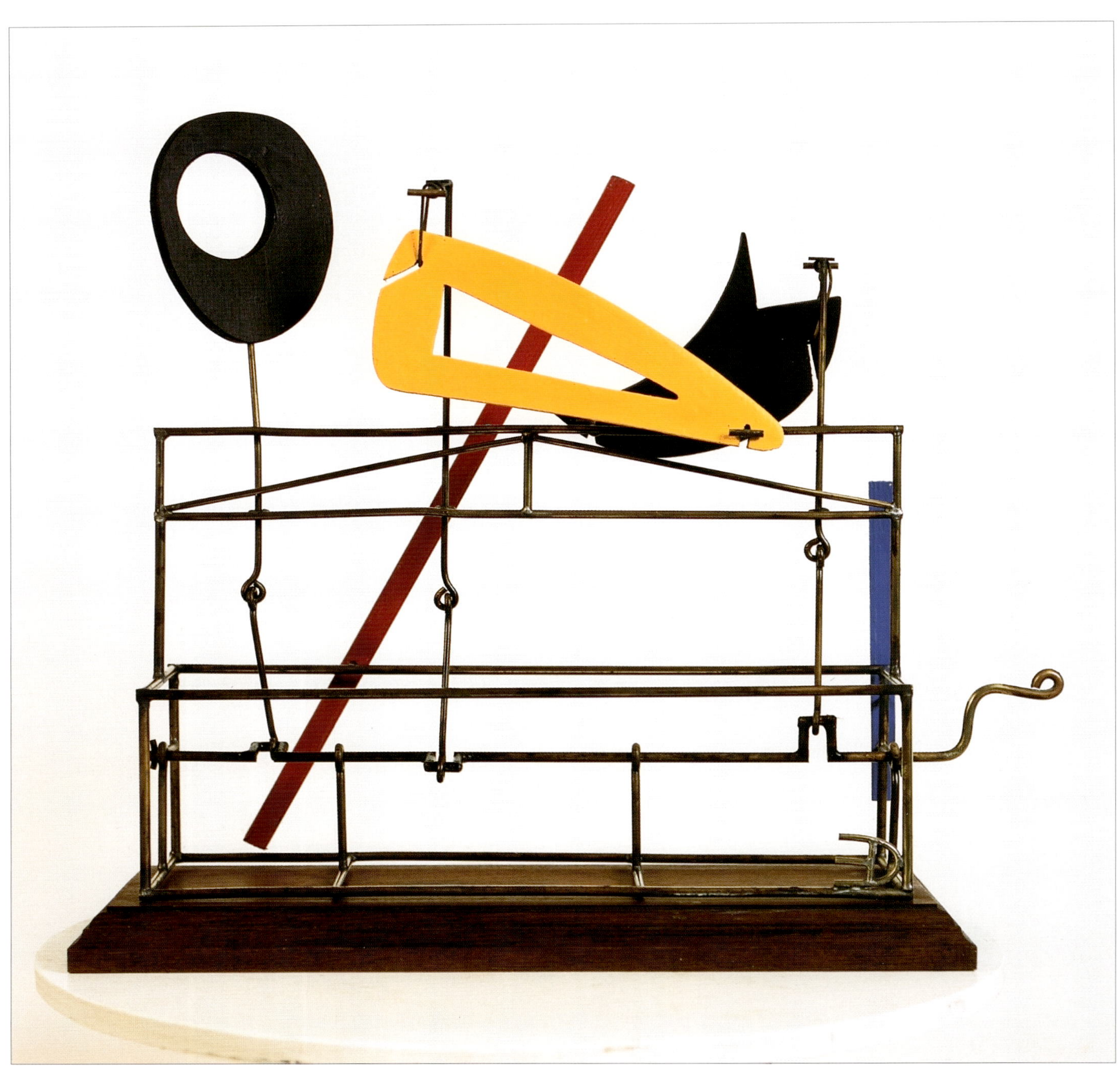

The colored "Crankshaft Series".

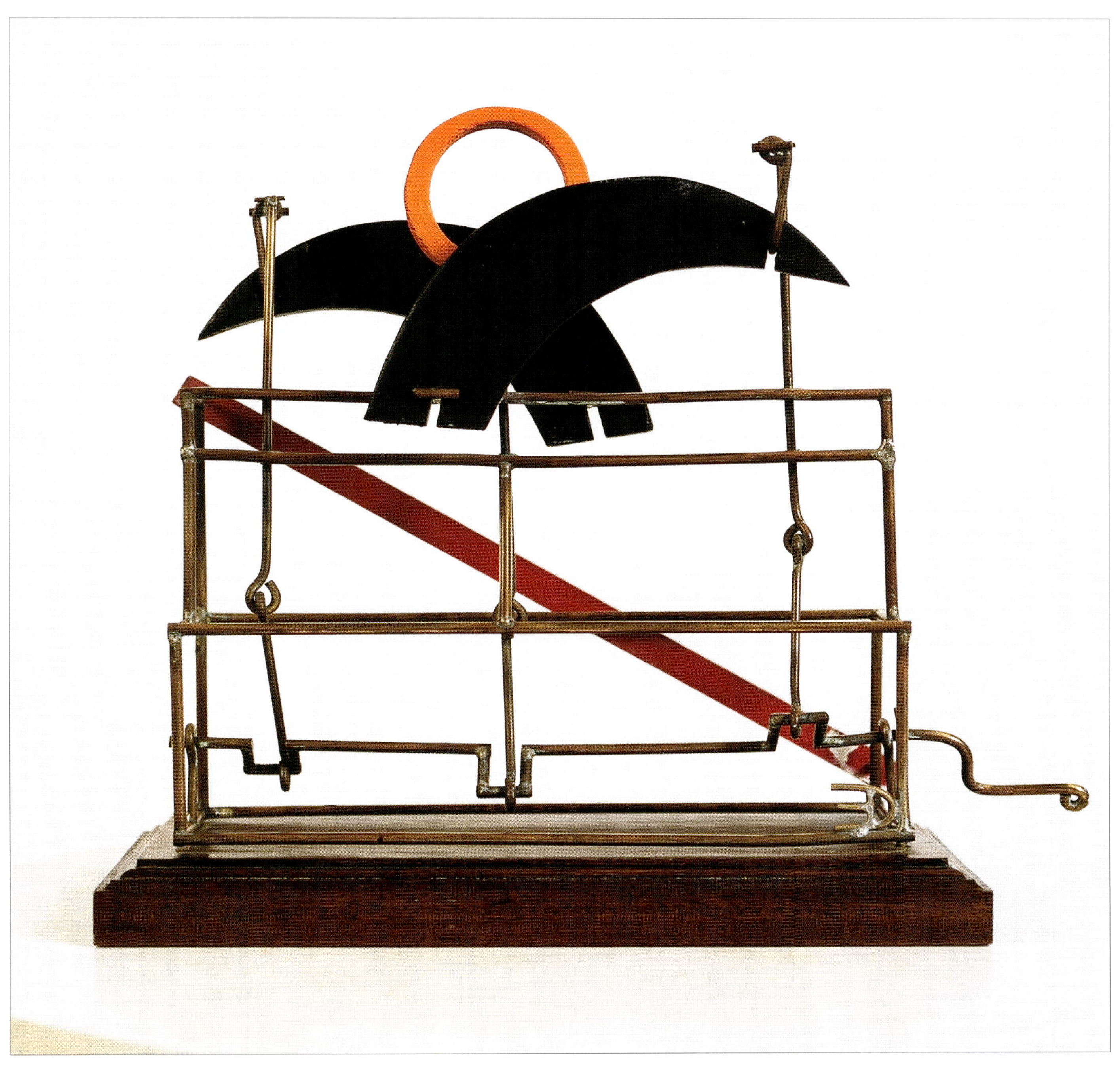

The colored "Crankshaft Series".

Dickon's hologram period can be traced back to my mother. One of her friends was living in Paris with an Englishman called Peter Woodd. Peter and my father hit it off, and before long were looking for ways of using their talents on a joint project. The opportunity soon presented itself. Peter Woodd was extremely interested in the new holograms being produced by pop artists of the period. He returned to London, and in collaboration with John Wolff, manager of the rock group The Who, he created the Holoco company, and later opened his own gallery, Light Fantastic. Dickon threw himself into the project, delighted to explore a new, experimental outlet where his knowledge of physics and geometry could be brought spectacularly into play.

Peter introduced Dickon to Holoco's art director, Anton Furst. The two artists found themselves on the same wavelength, and their prolific partnership got off to a flying start. Together they explored and deconstructed concepts, transgressed the traditional codes, tested the borderline between reality and the reality of illusion, as exemplified in a brilliantly designed coffee table, or in the classic figure called the Tesseract, a four-dimensional cube. Dickon also used the medium to pay a discreet tribute to one of his masters, Magritte, with the holographic image of a high heel crushing an egg.

After four years of a highly productive partnership, Anton Furst left for Hollywood to work on the films of Stanley Kubrick. For both artists, it was the end of the hologram period.

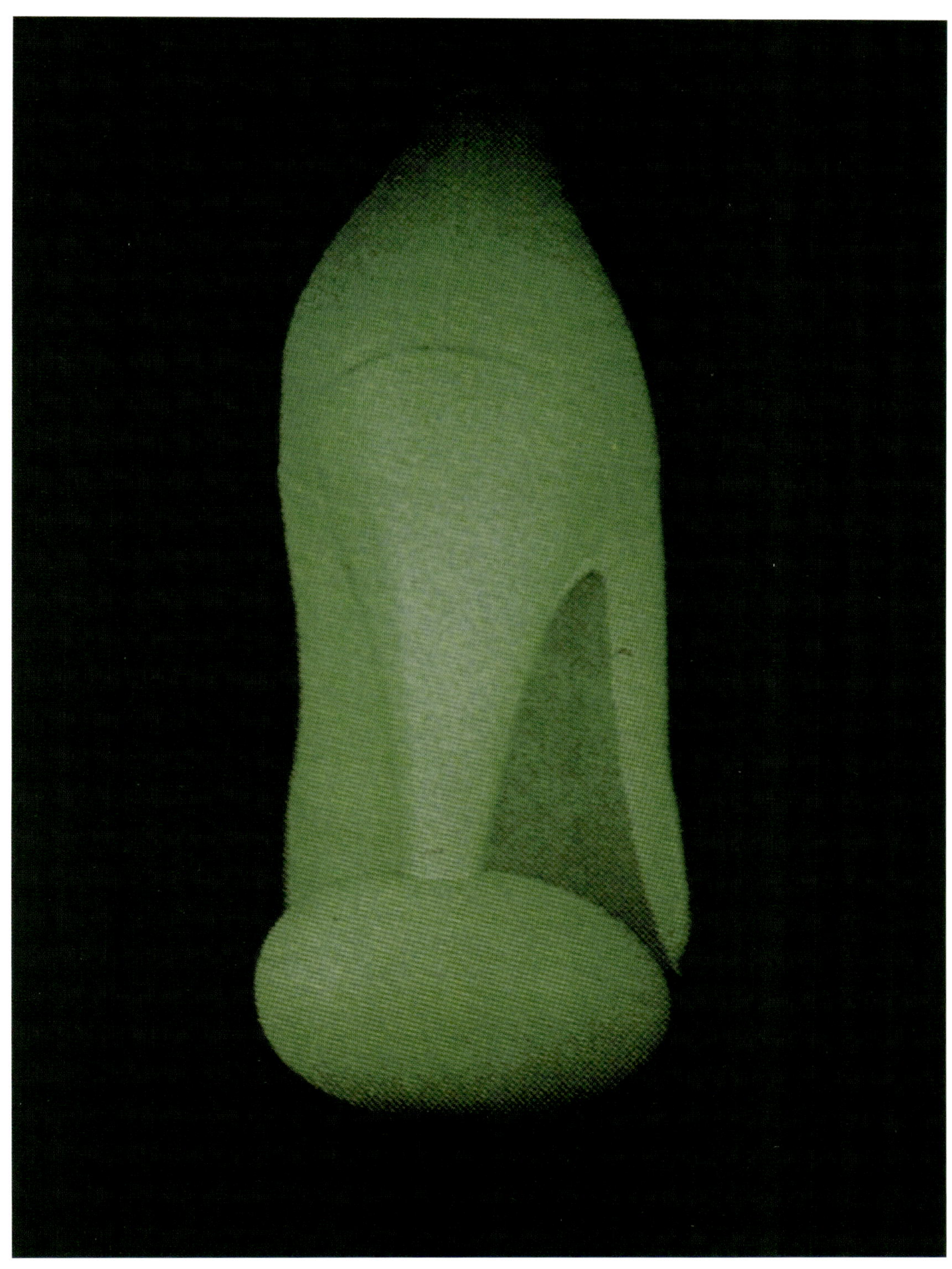

Her shoe: "Oops".

Star of David.

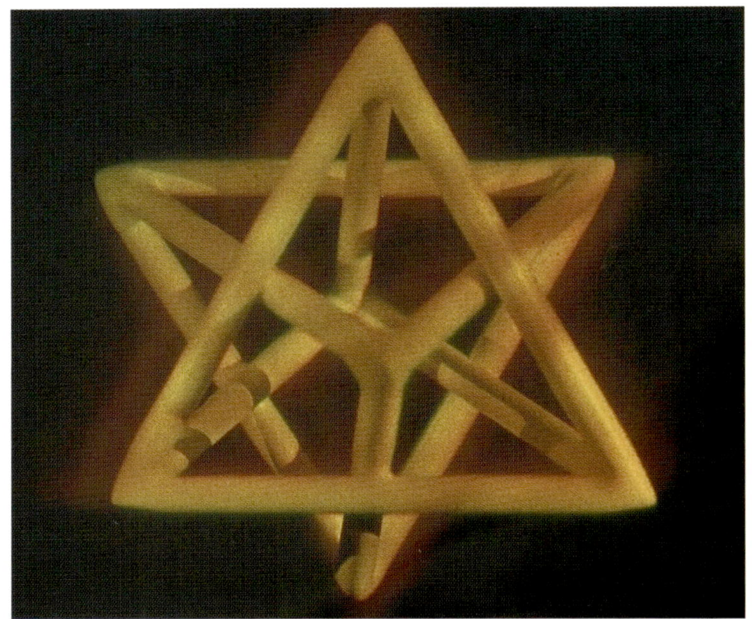

Hard currency.

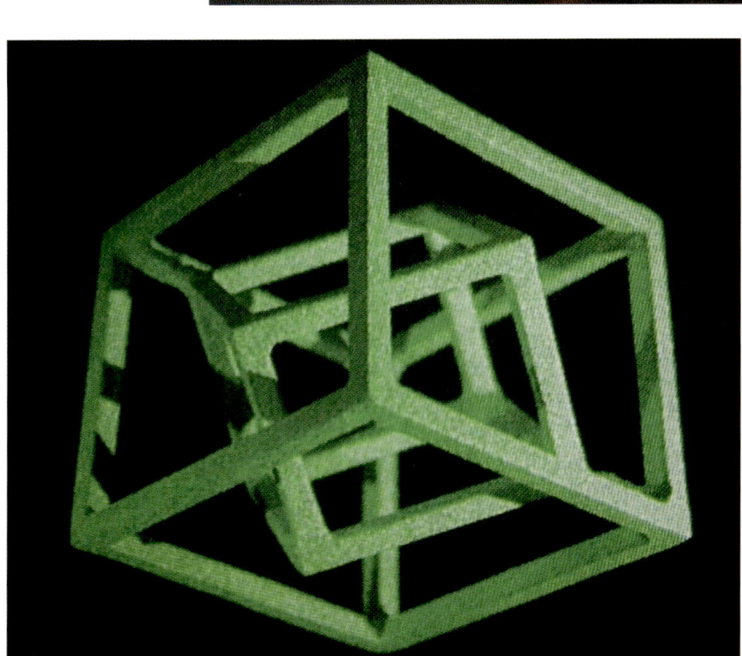

Square in square.

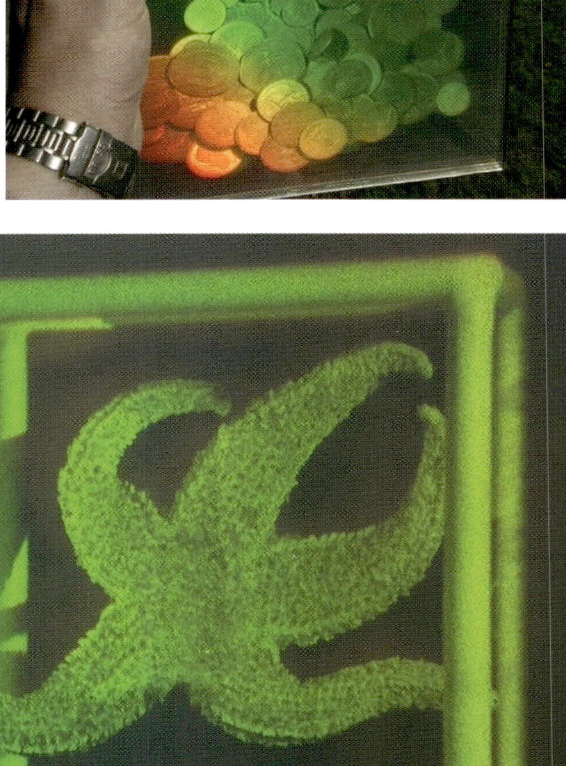

Starfish in square.

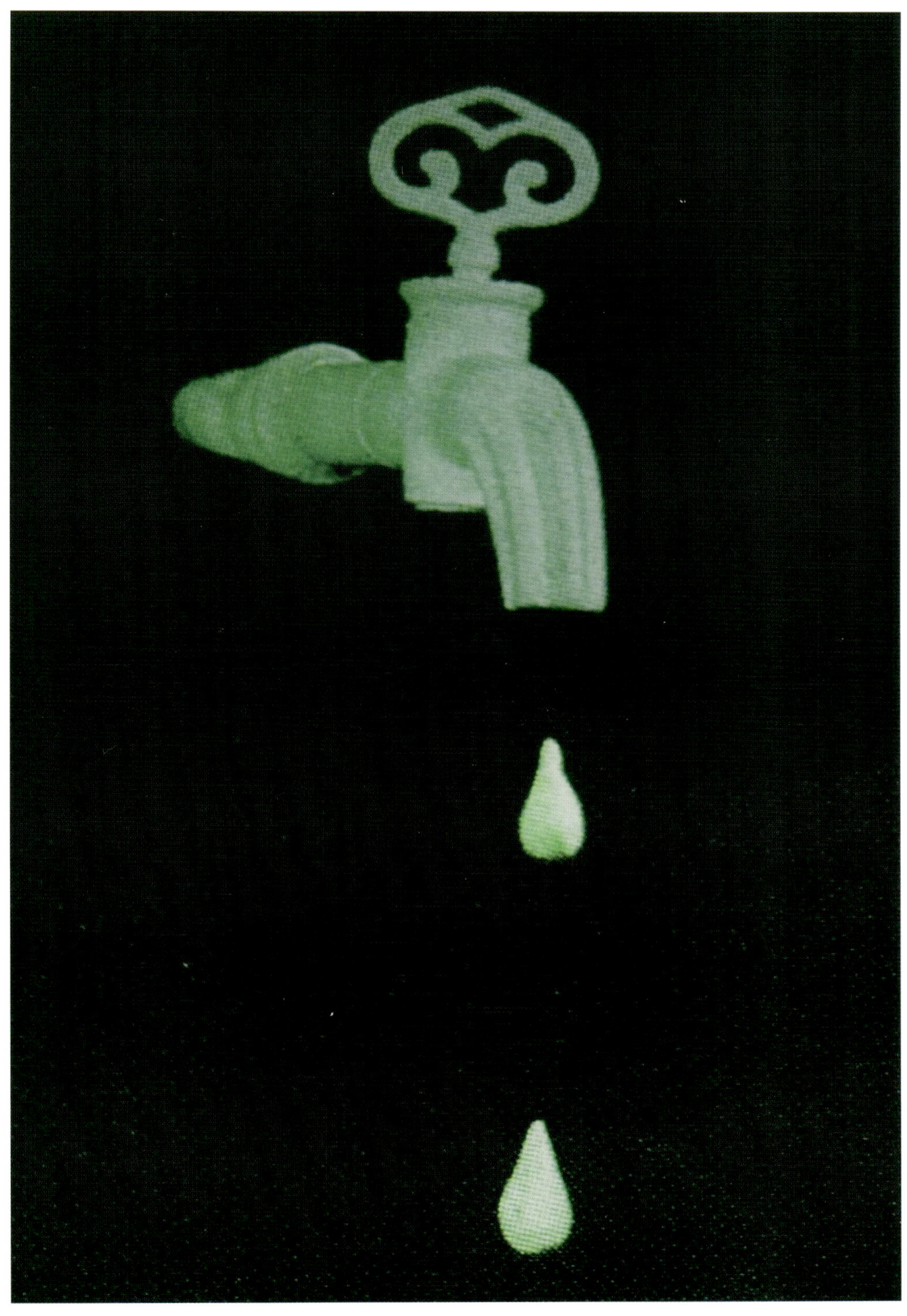

French tap, leaking.

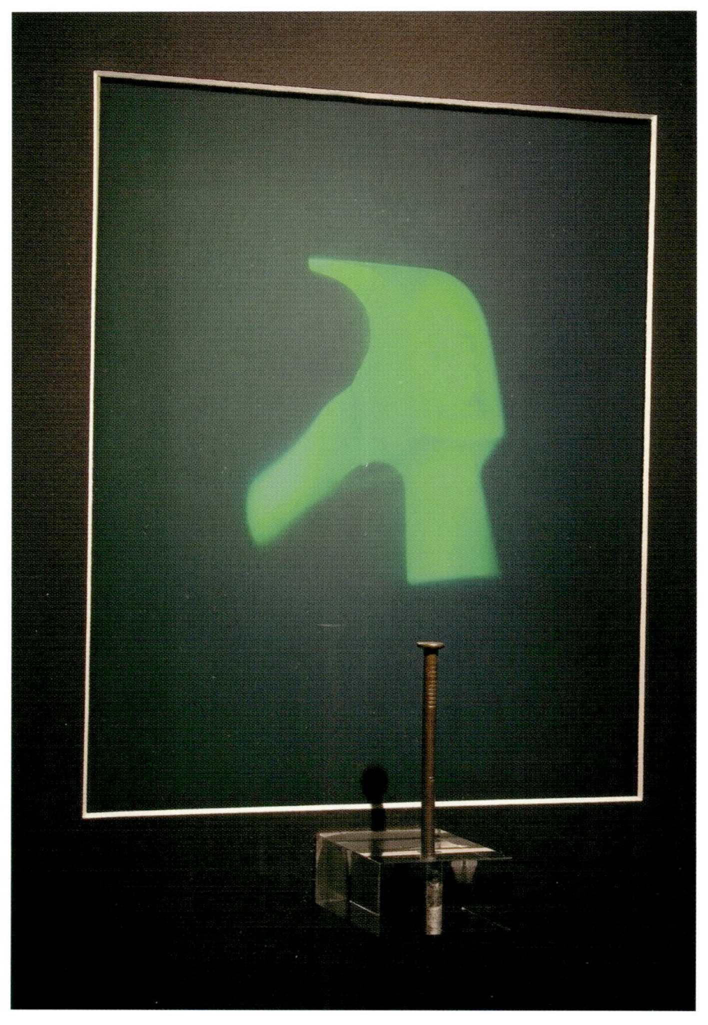

Hammer and nail. *

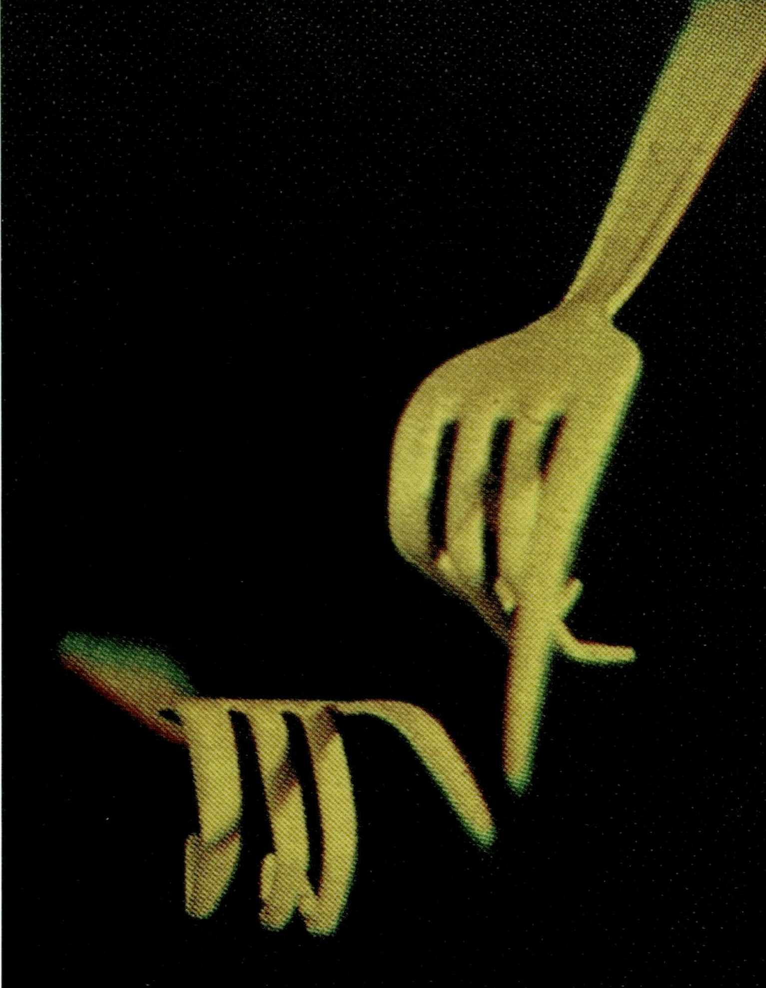

Famous painting.

Sweet hearts.

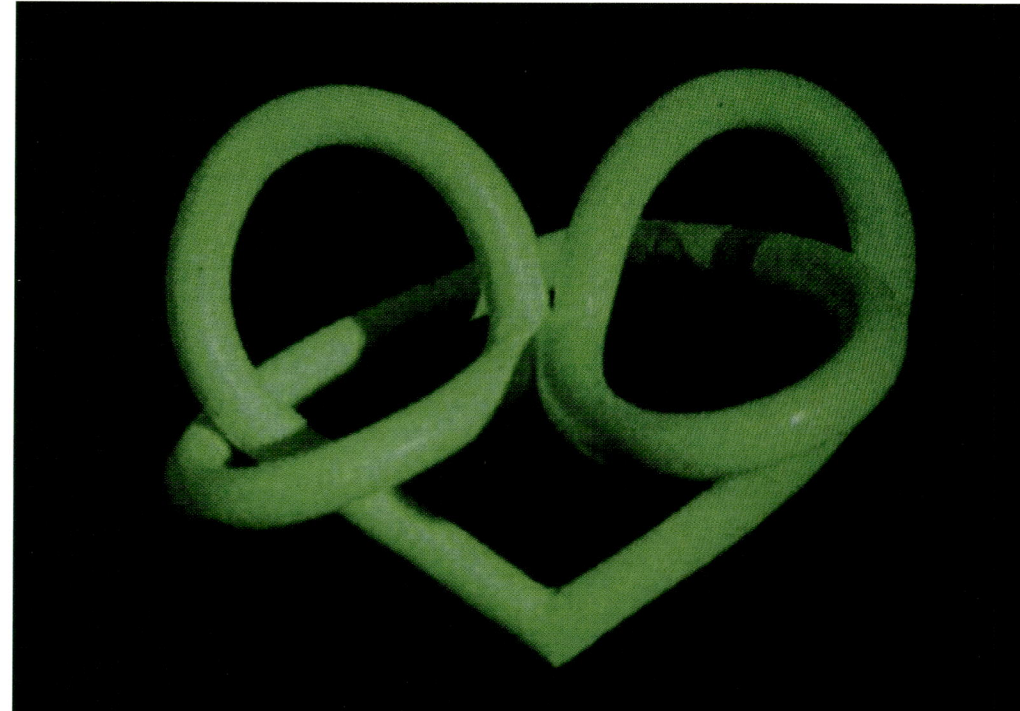

* Photo Olav Skipnes.

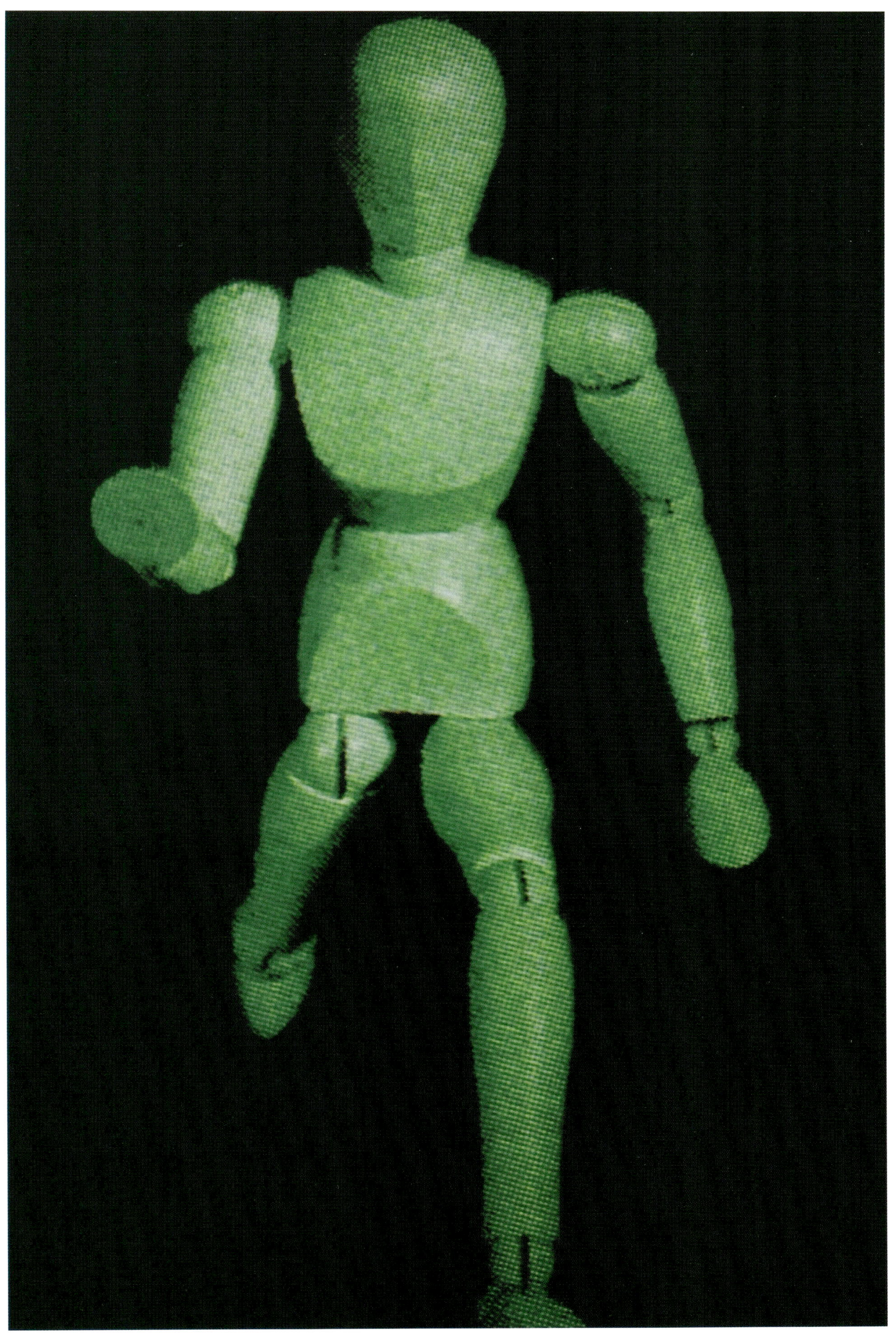

Running man.

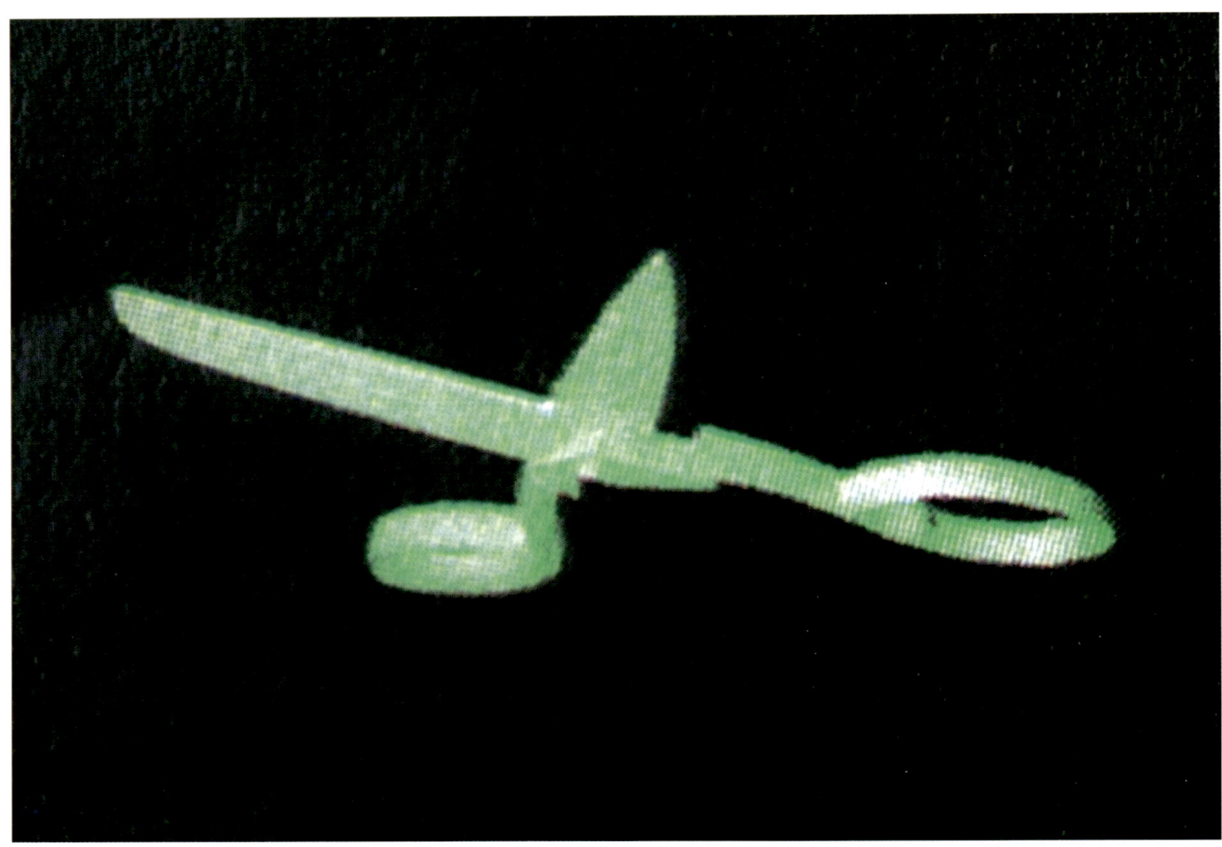

Scissors.

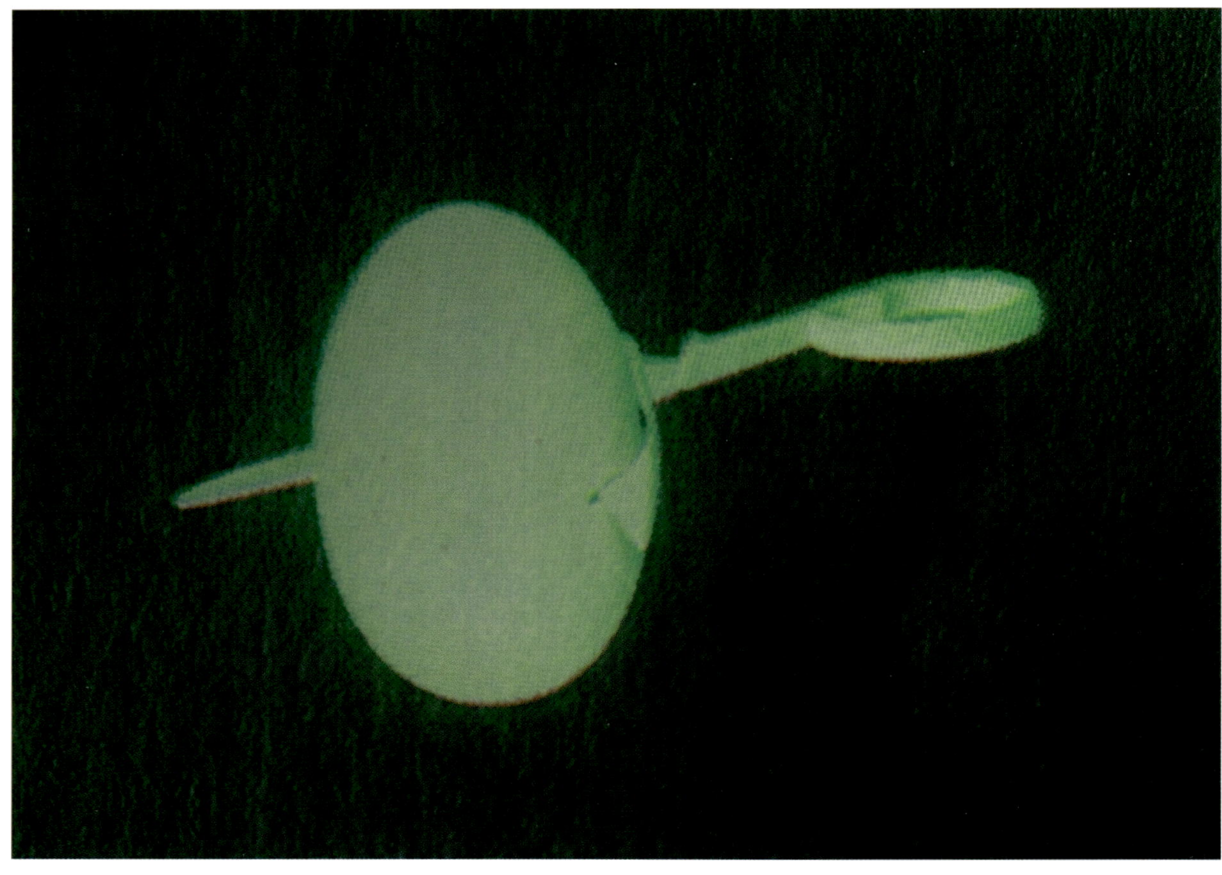

Sliced egg.

But is it Blurred in Front or is it my Light —

Money — good in Transmission —

Sissors & Egg — This TAKE much Better to First But would Like to See it in Reflection (ABRicote)

Lights out — Same as Above Transmission good But Try A Few in Reflection in ABRicote.

Horseshoe — Should Be shot with Plate Virtical instead of Horizontal i.e. 10 virtical 8 horizontal

Running MAN — Could Be shot in All Coulores. — Maybe Even try Transmission?

Hearts — Green Hearts Are A no go. Any other Coulor.

Horshoe — Same As Above — ABRicote Remember we have A master of Just A shoe.

Forks — in ABRicote Are A Big Success

Chair — Seems ok in the soft Green Coulor of my Proof.

Pipe — would Do well in ABRicote

Dripping tap — I Don't Like The Drips, Too Corny, sorry Pat. But we have A master of Just the Tap.

Dickon's notes to technical director Patrick Flynn, indicating the changes to be made to the holograms in progress.

The year of 1986 saw the start of another phase in the life of Dickon Eames: a period of major exhibitions in a Parisian gallery in the rue Guénégaud, on the Left Bank, close to the Institut de France and the Ecole des Beaux Arts.

Once again, it was a prolific, rich period. Themes sprang to life in the propitious harmony of the house, the studio and the surrounding countryside.

Dickon Eames was now an artist of some standing. Celebrities and critics attended his openings. His works struck a resonant chord and were selling well. Dickon enjoyed the pleasant upheaval and excitement of these Paris shows, happy to be the center of attention and also happy to head back to his studio in Normandy.

In ten years, he had eight major solo exhibitions on as many themes. The first, "Les Tuyeaux" (Pipes), was a tremendous success. Almost all the pieces were bought up immediately. 1987, 1988, 1989 ... each show presented a new angle on Dickon's work. After the "Série Grise" came "The Aviary", a polychrome collection of pieces in stainless steel, including a large palm tree. The bird theme was back again, this time with new force and mastery. Although I like them all, this series has a special place in my affections. Here I see the continuity of my father's vision in its most accomplished form, a celebration of technique and substance, a mature and joyful reinterpretation of his earlier "Flying Machines".

Later came the astonishing "Hard & Soft" series, full of virtuosity and humor - a tribute to the Hollywood stars of the Forties - followed by "Les Fontaines", where Dickon's "hydraulic" skills came to the fore: simple, almost transparent mechanisms controlling the flow of water.

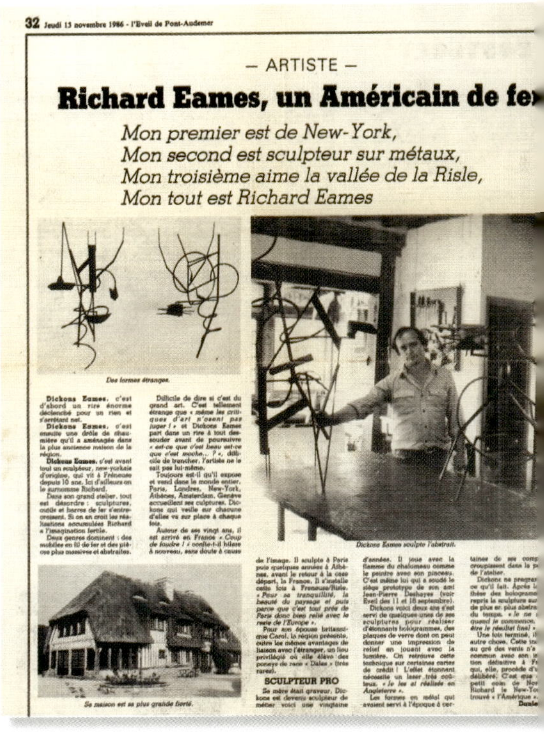

The weekly regional "l'Eveil de Pont-Audemer" shows Dickon working in h studio. 13 November, 1986.

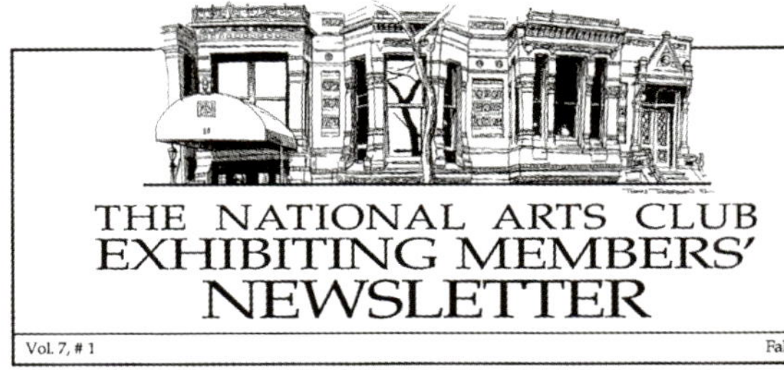

"Les Fontaines" also made news on the other side of the Atlantic as seen in an article published in this reputed fine arts review.

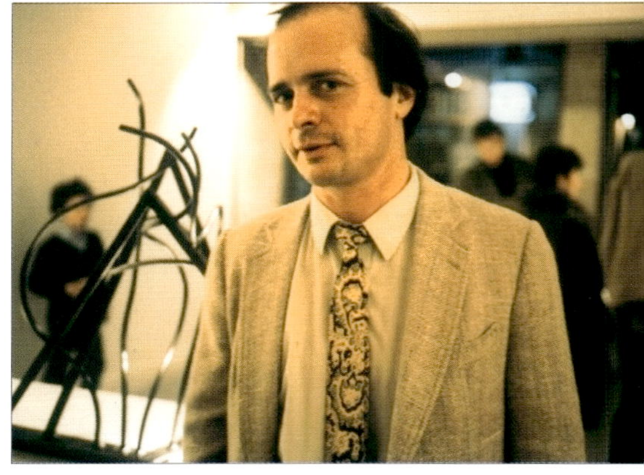

This first show at the Galerie Riedel (Pari is the start of a cycle of major exhibitions devoted to the work of Dickon Eames.

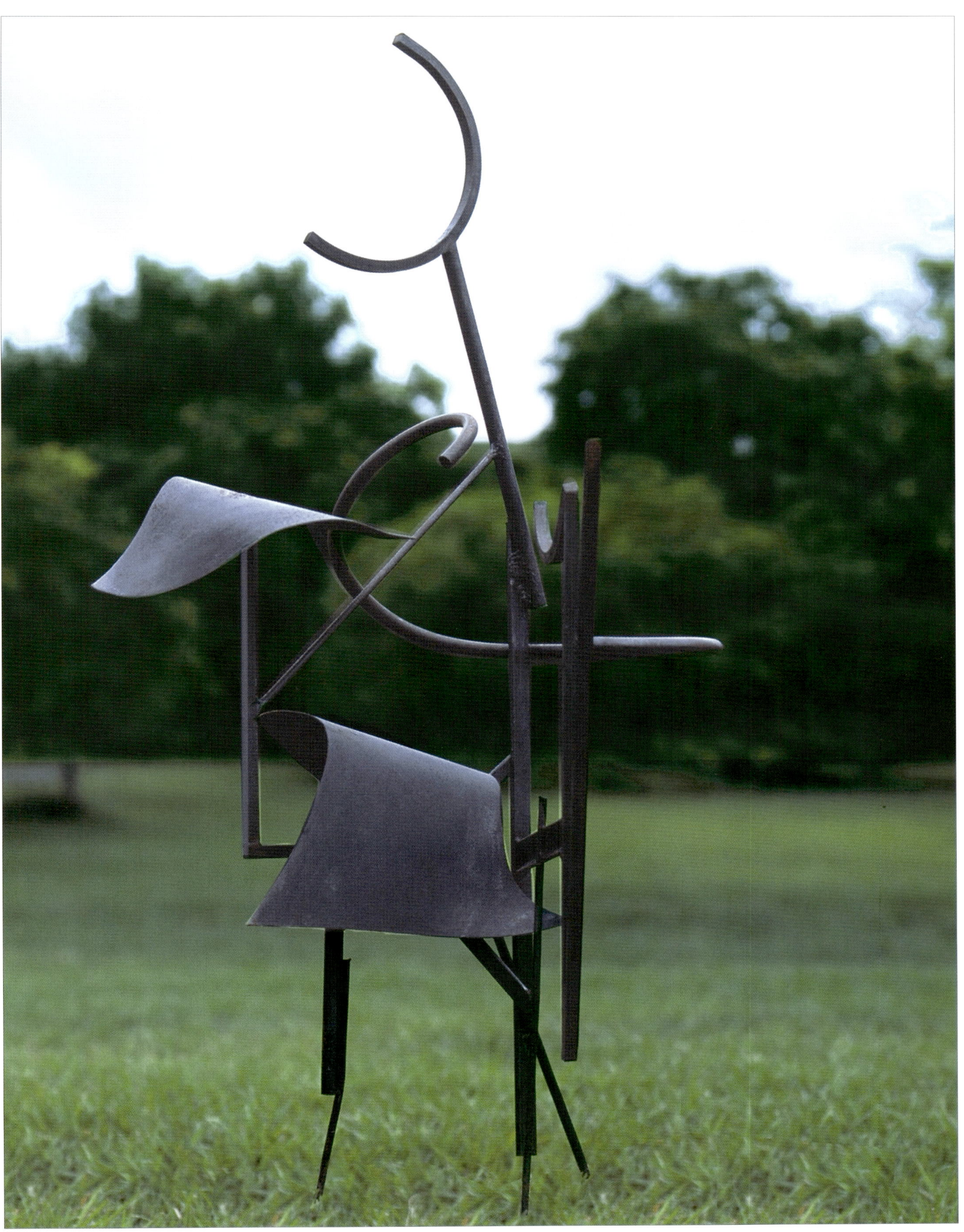

This work is now in Carol's home in Puerto Rico.
It was first shown at the Galerie Riedel in 1987, at the exhibition "Sculptures Récentes".

This extended spate of exhibitions ended with "Les Guerriers Orientaux", or Oriental Warriors, which signaled a new departure in Dickon's work. It was a significant transition: from sculpture to installation. The complexity of installation art appealed to his collector's instinct. He got hold of Chinese newsprint and sought out new materials, like the porcelain insulators used on power lines. One day as he walked through the local market with Carol, he was struck by the pure, sensual contours of a tomato. He made a mold of it and used it for the body of his warriors. He made maquettes, an unusual practice for Dickon. It was an approach very different from his past method of working, going against the current of his past successes. His gallery was sceptical: "Why change, when everything is going so well?"

For Dickon the question was irrelevant. His work was a process of constant research in which change and renewal were essential. He had no interest in "mass producing" his most popular creations. He was the first to be pleased when his work was publicly recognized, but he had to move on.

The Oriental Warriors should have opened up new paths in the art of Dickon Eames. They should have been the springboard for yet more themes, yet more explorations with materials and techniques. Fate decided otherwise. The Oriental Warriors are a testament that is difficult to decipher. Where was Dickon heading when he embarked on this new phase in his art? Sadly, we shall never know.

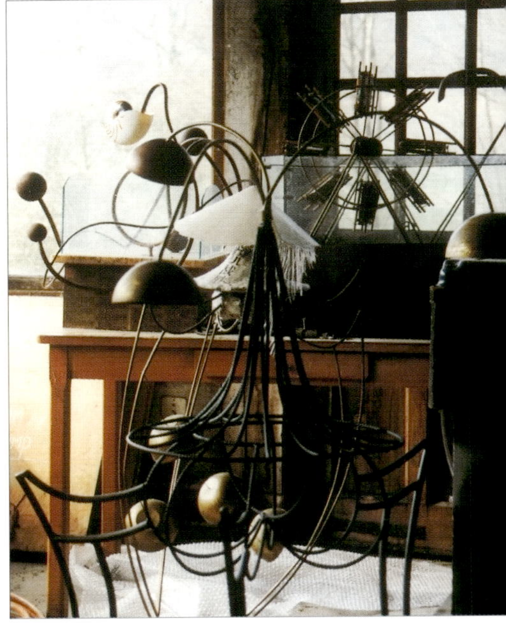

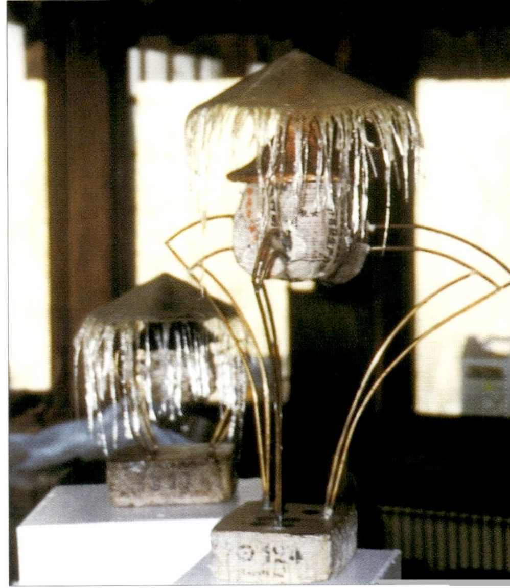

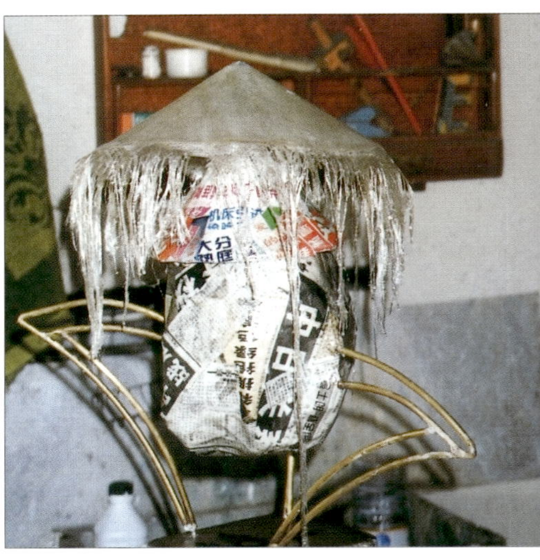

The "Guerriers Orientaux" (Oriental Warriors) coming to life in the studio. Dickon is preparing the last exhibition to be held during his lifetime.

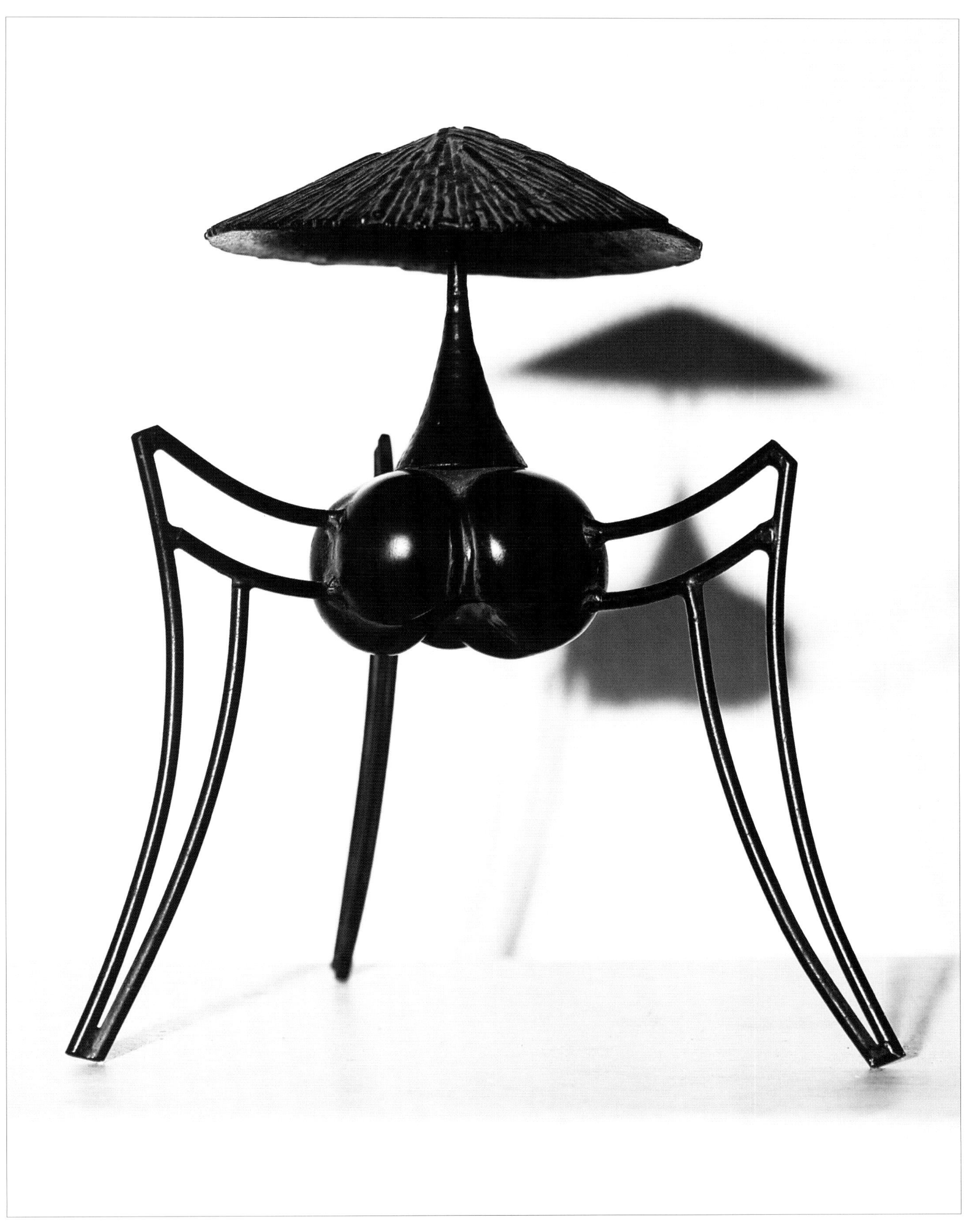

"Guerrier Oriental", whose body was inspired by the contours of a tomato ...

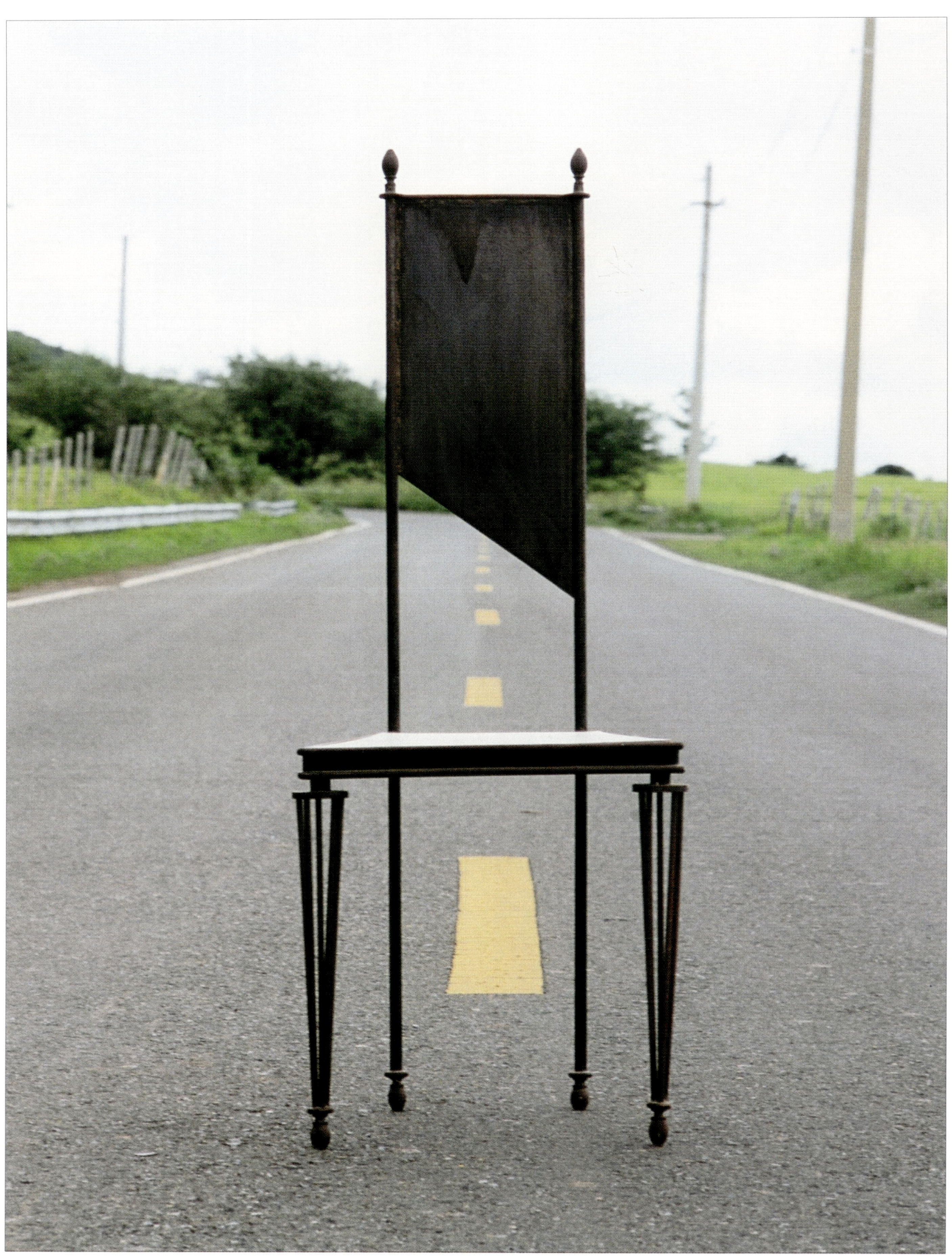

"Louis Chaise". A play on the name of France's hapless king, Louis Seize, and Dickon's own way of celebrating the bicentenary of the French Revolution. Work created in 1989.

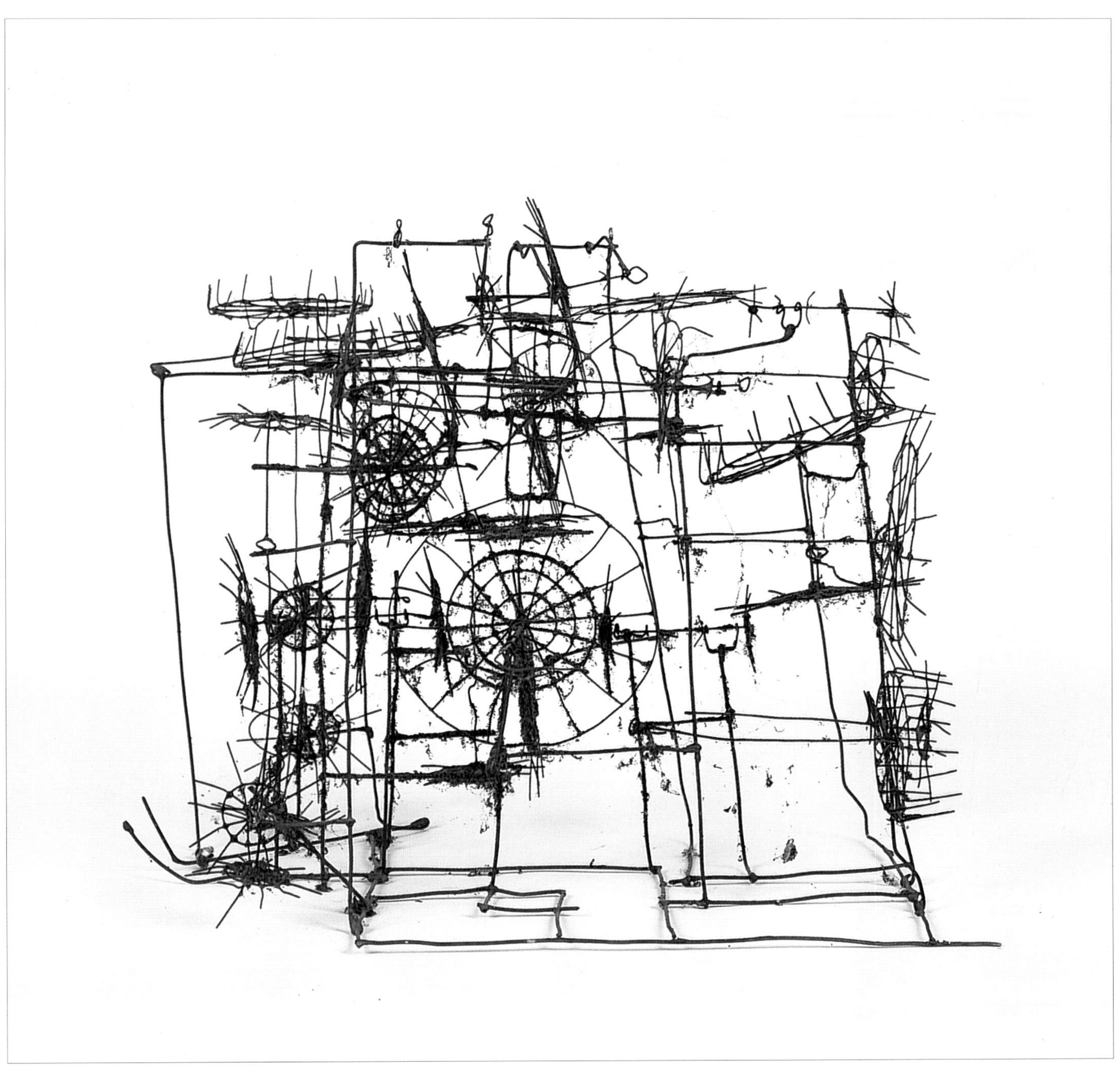

Dust: first machine 1979.

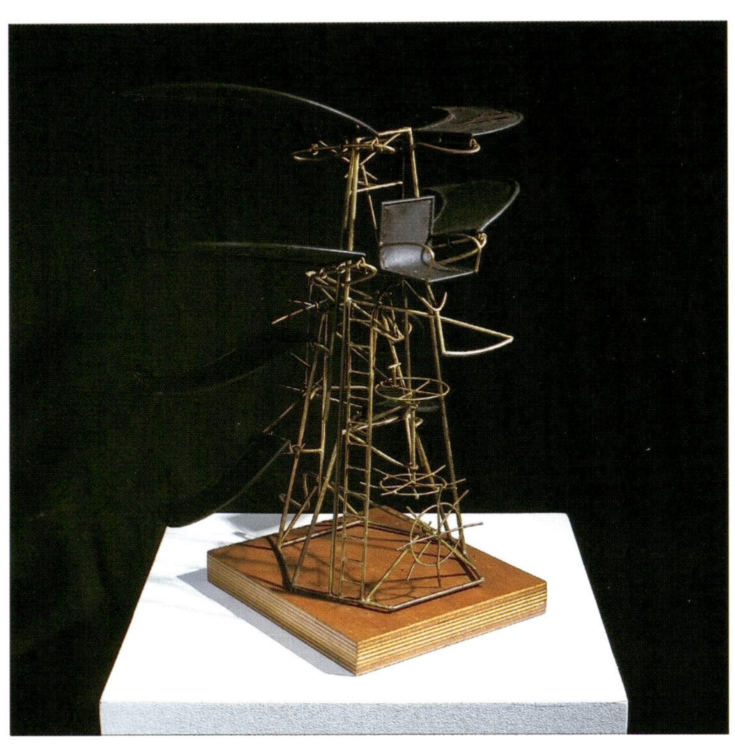

Flying Tower with eight wings.

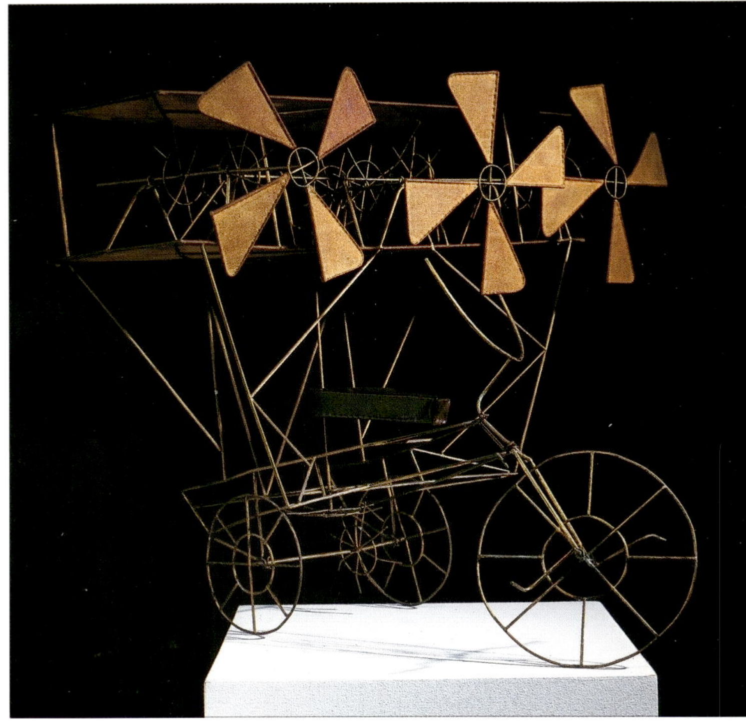

Flying Bicycle I.

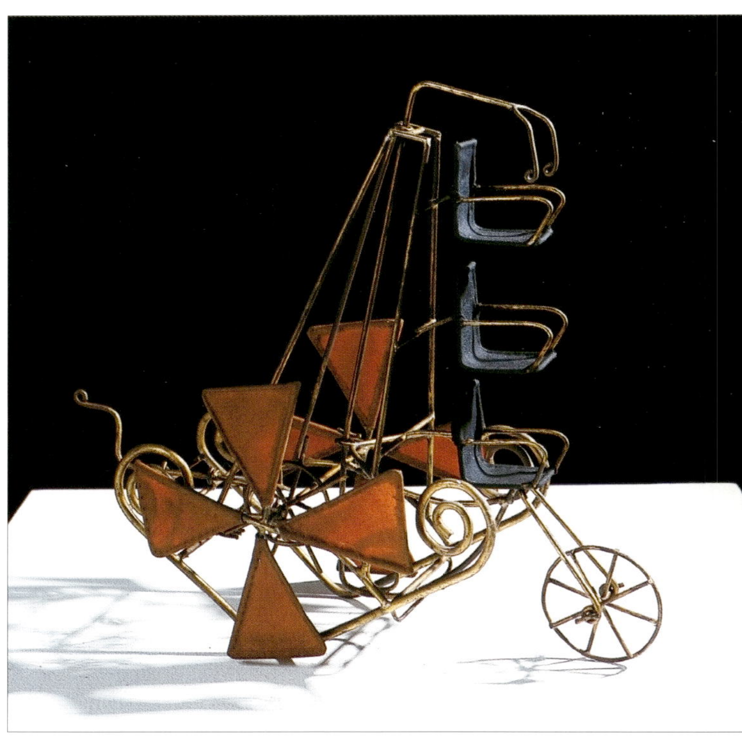

Three seat sleigh.

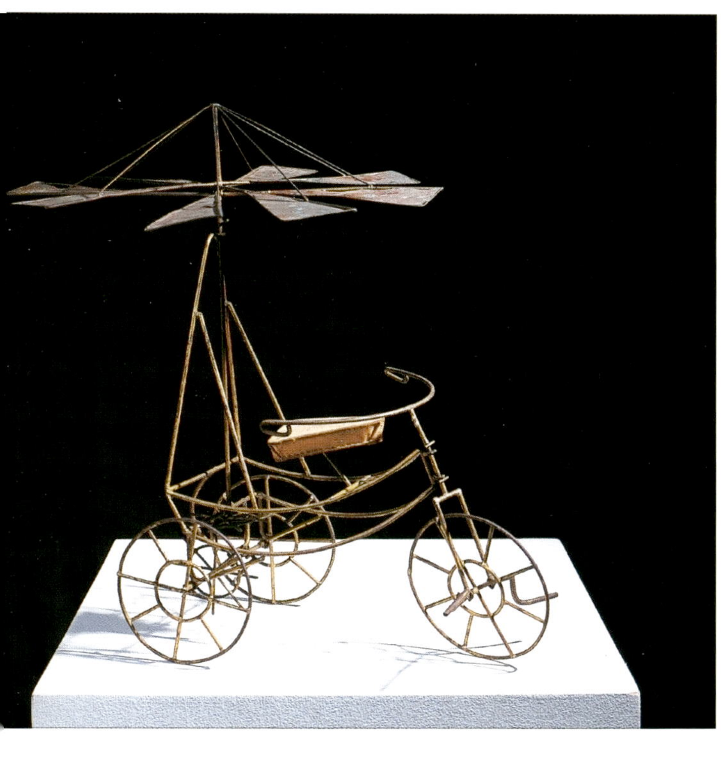

Flying Bicycle III.

FLYING MACHINES

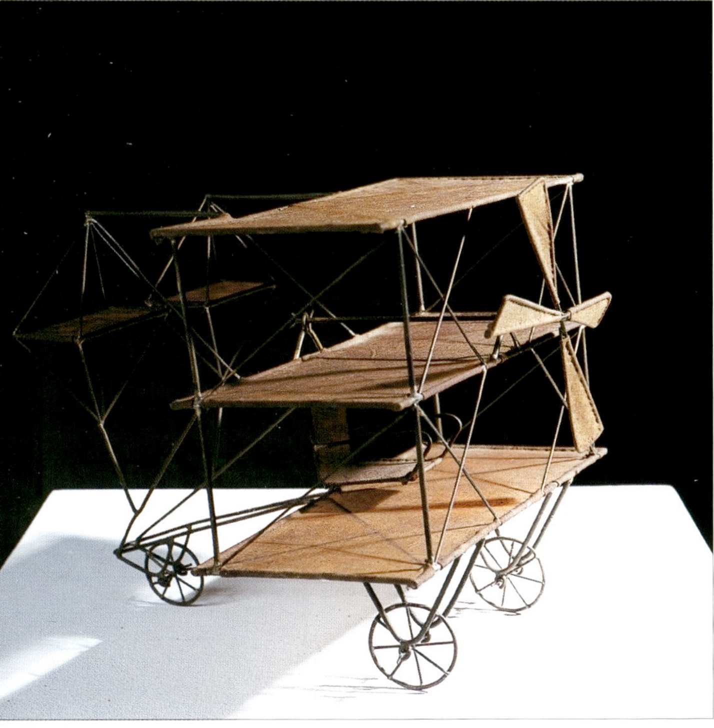

Three wing airplane.

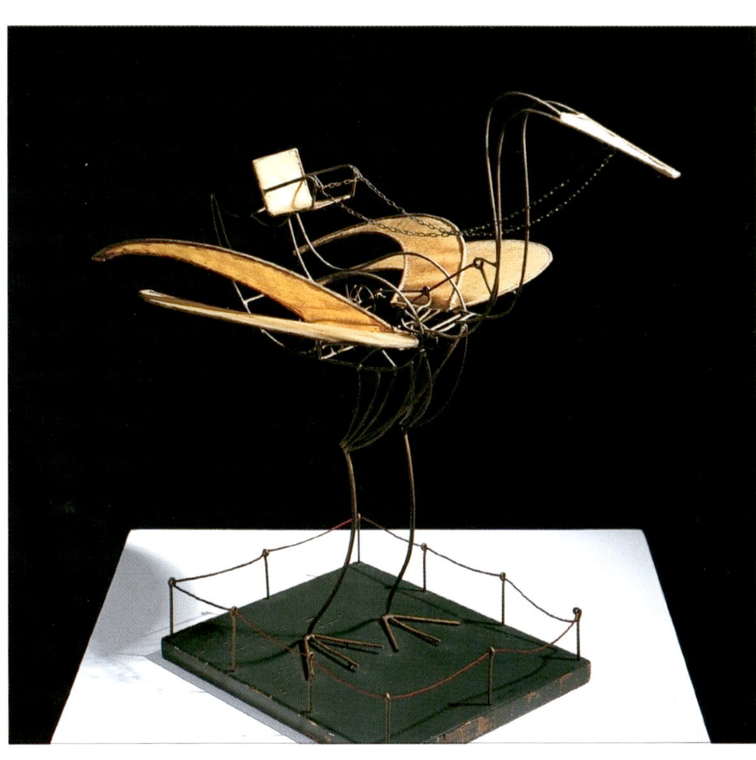

Rare bird.

THE CRANKSHAFTS

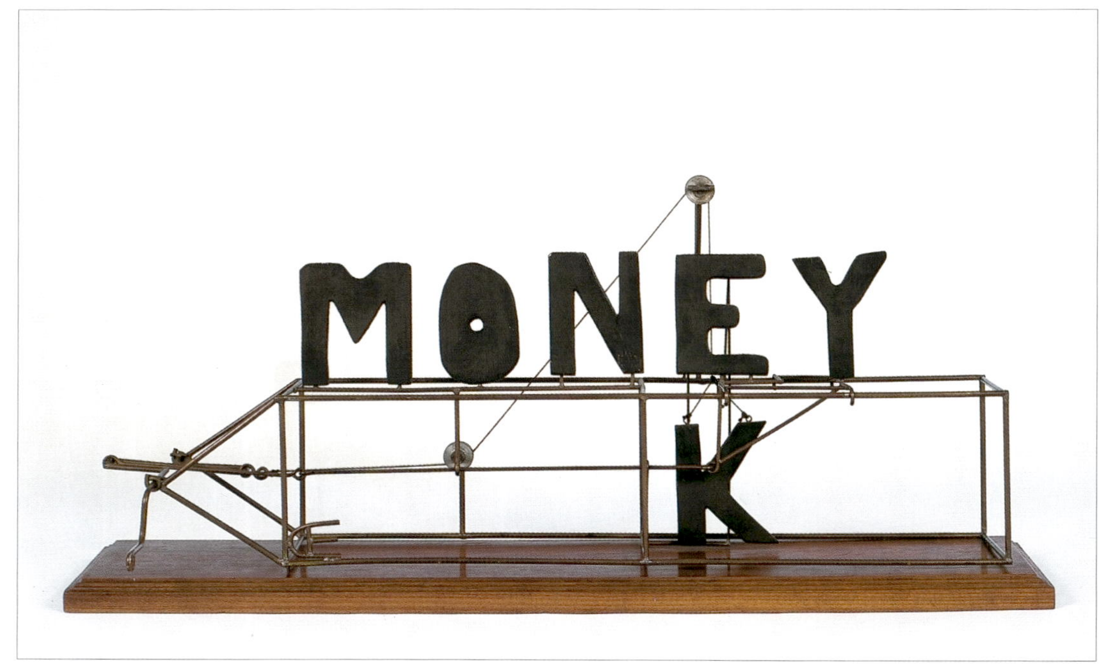

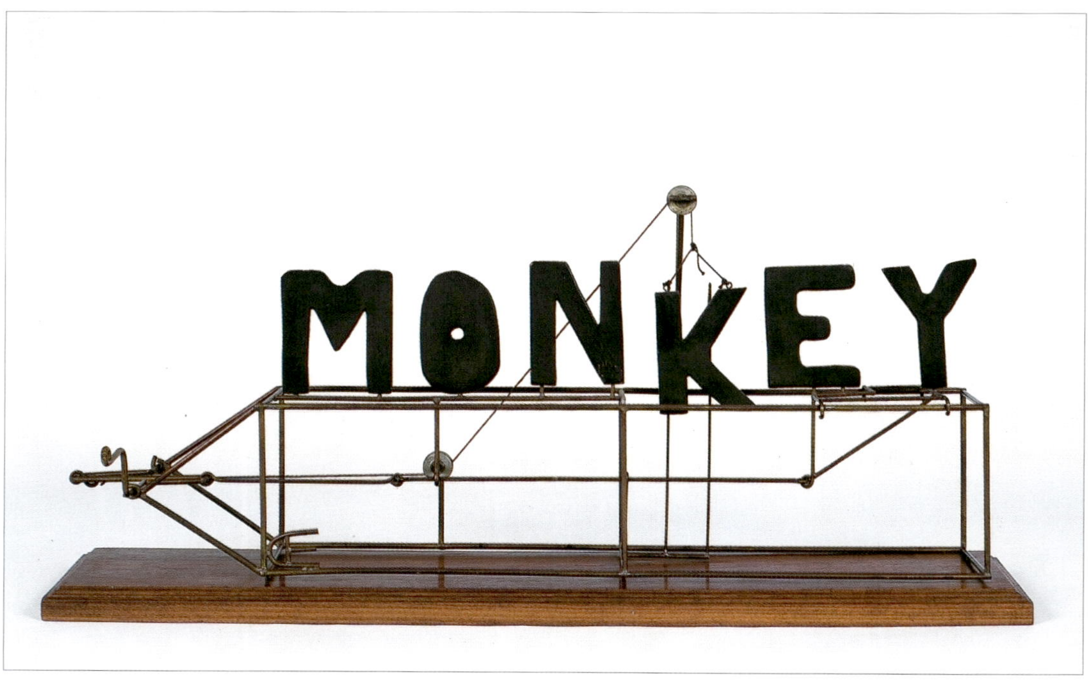

Money / Monkey.

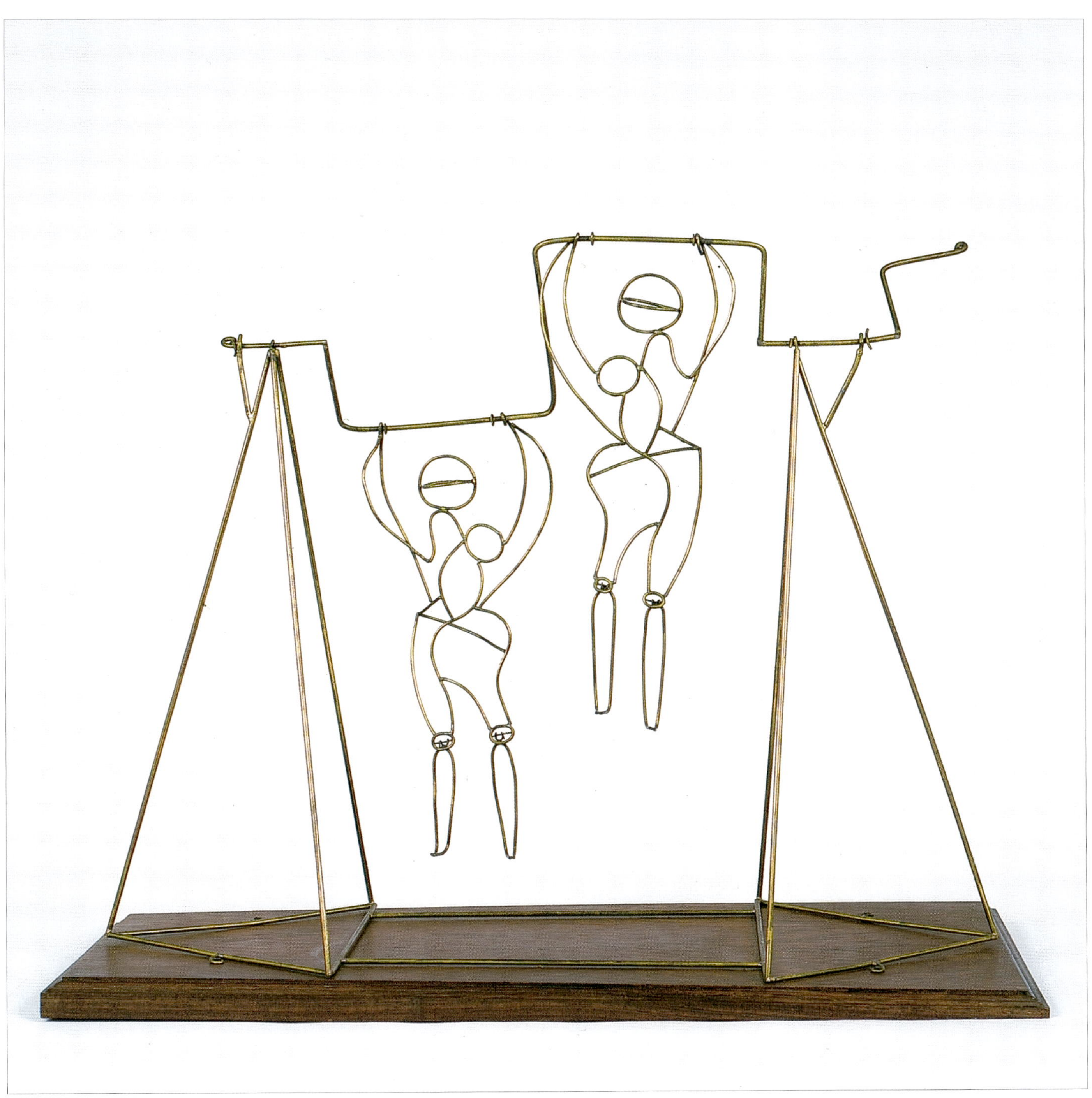

Les Acrobates.

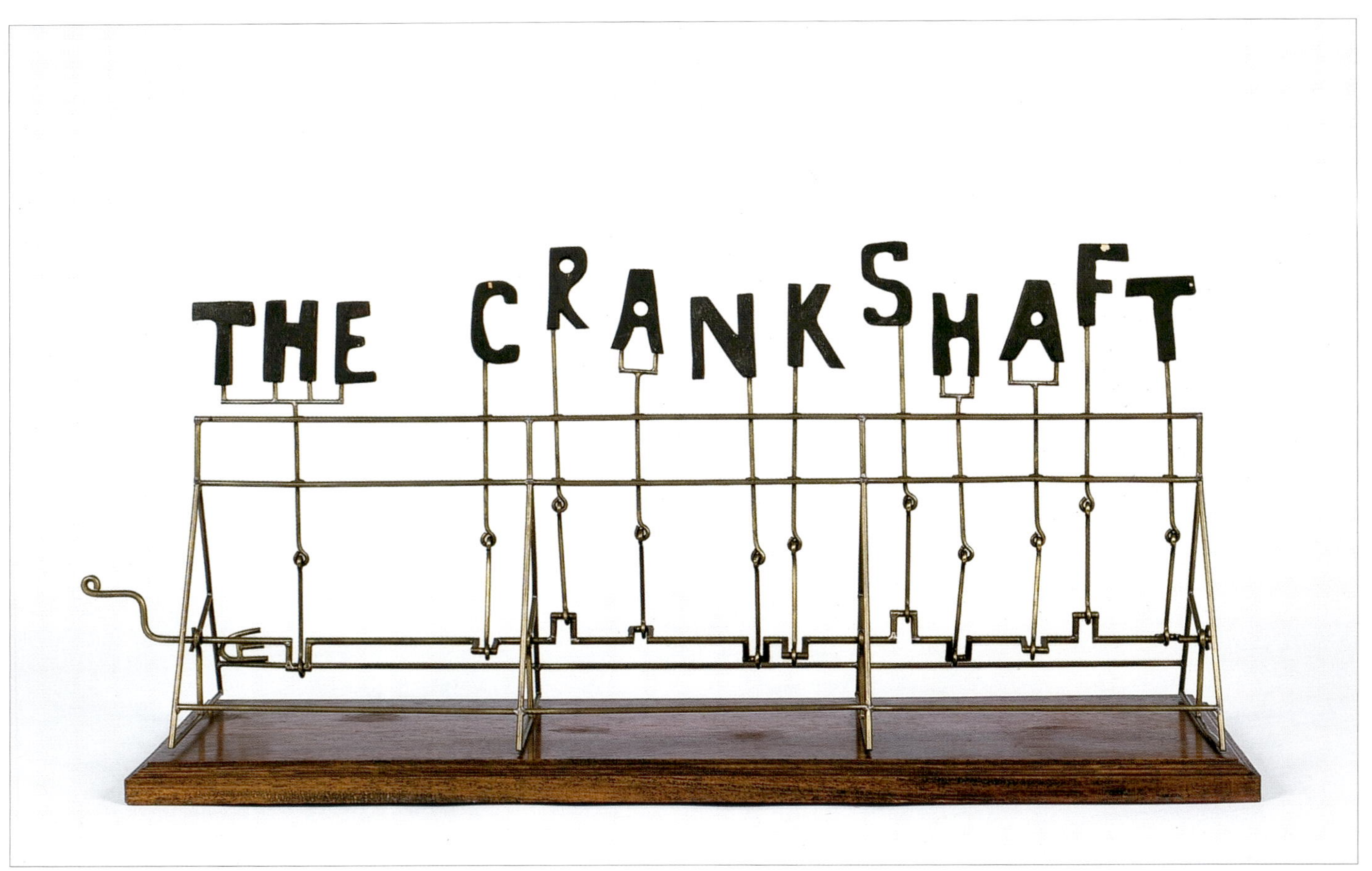

The Crankshaft.

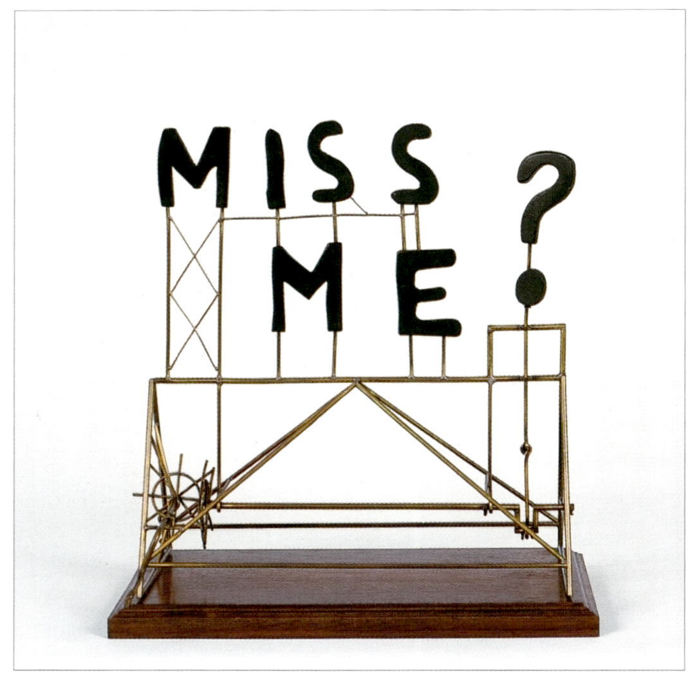

Miss Me.

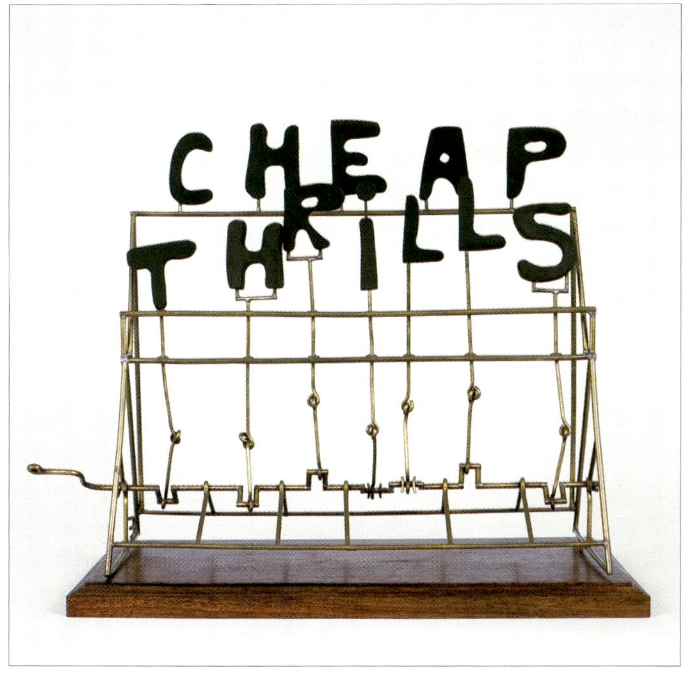

Cheap Thrills.

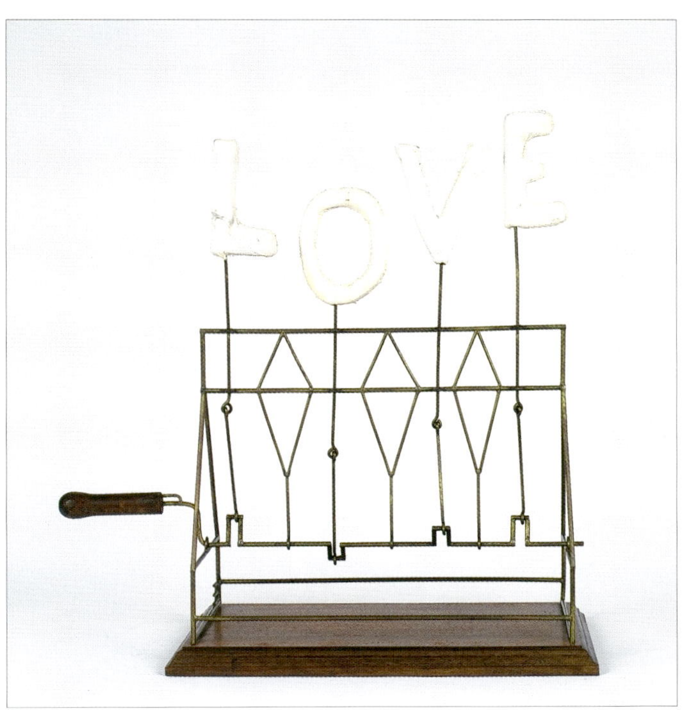

Love.

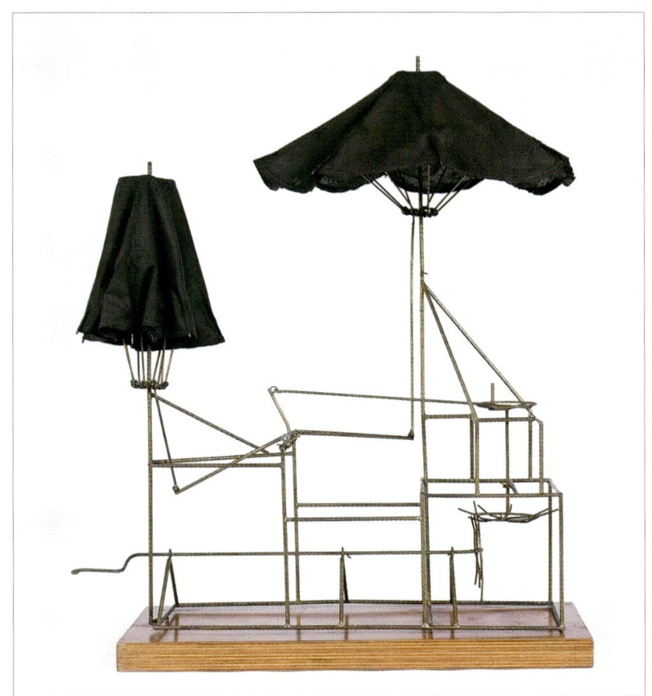

Umbrellas.

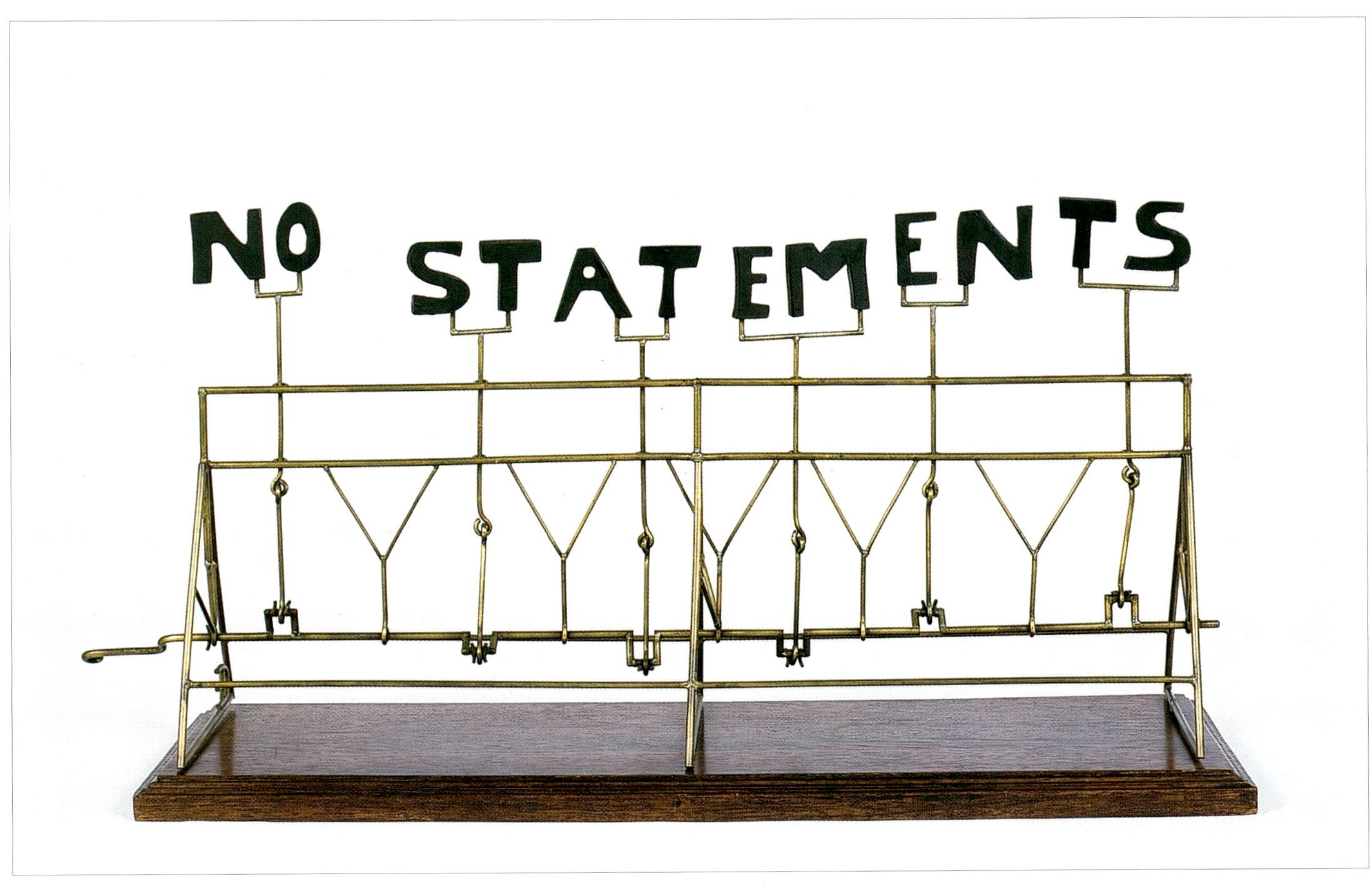

No statements.

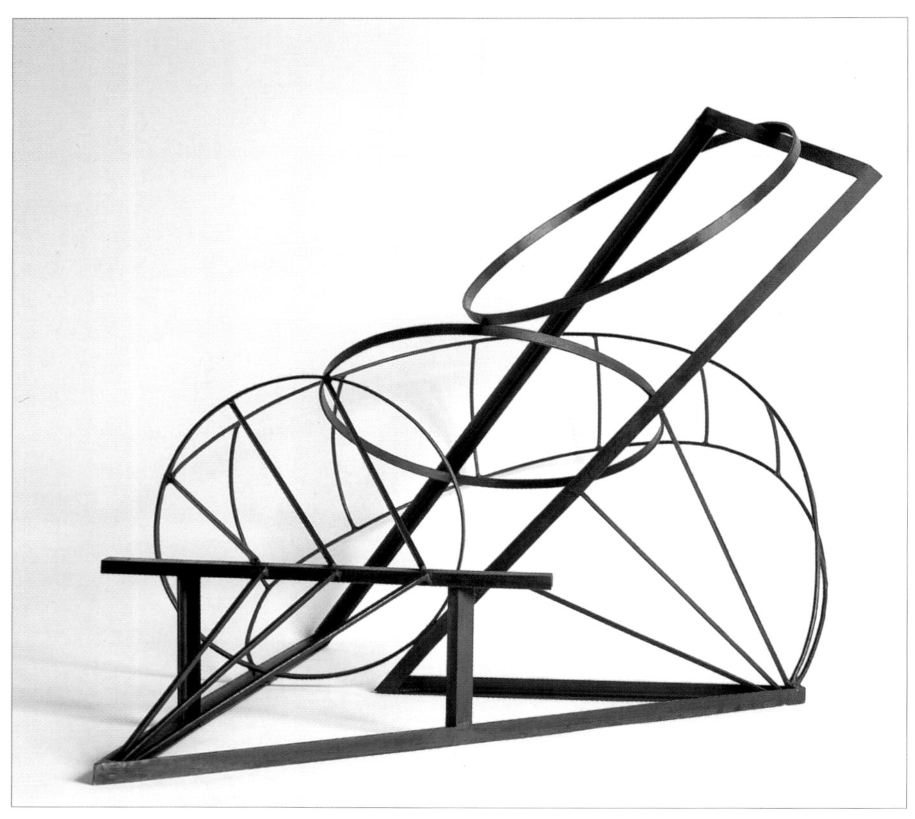

Ladder II.

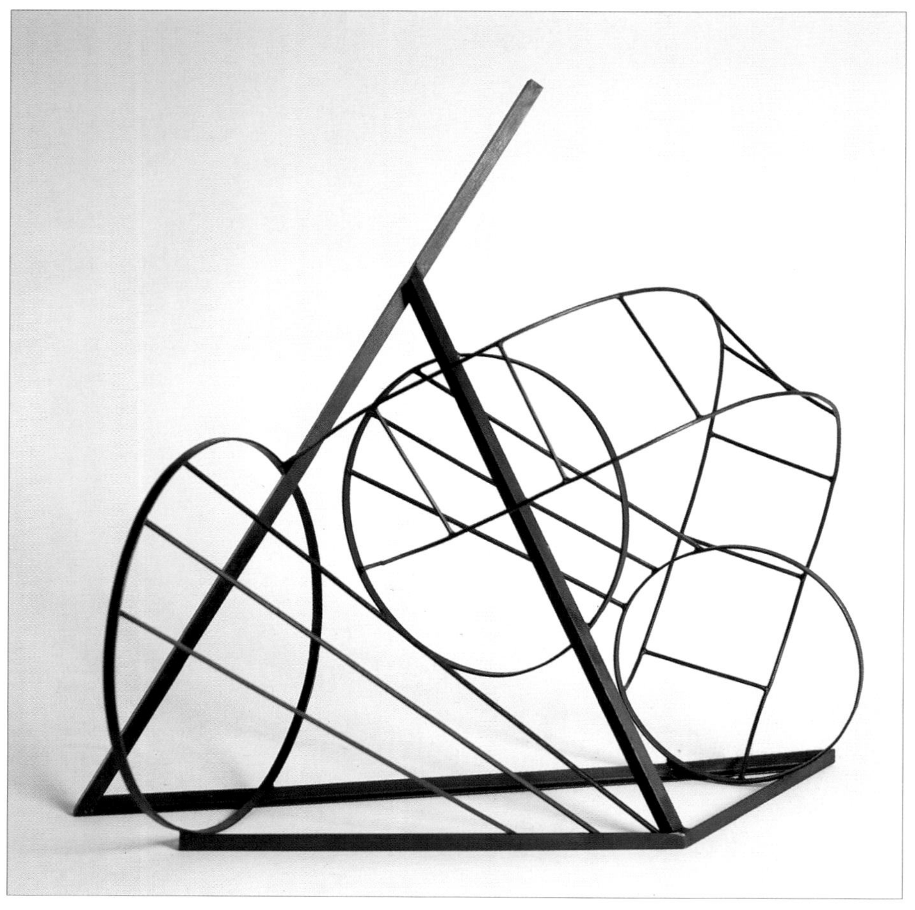

Ladder I.

STEEL

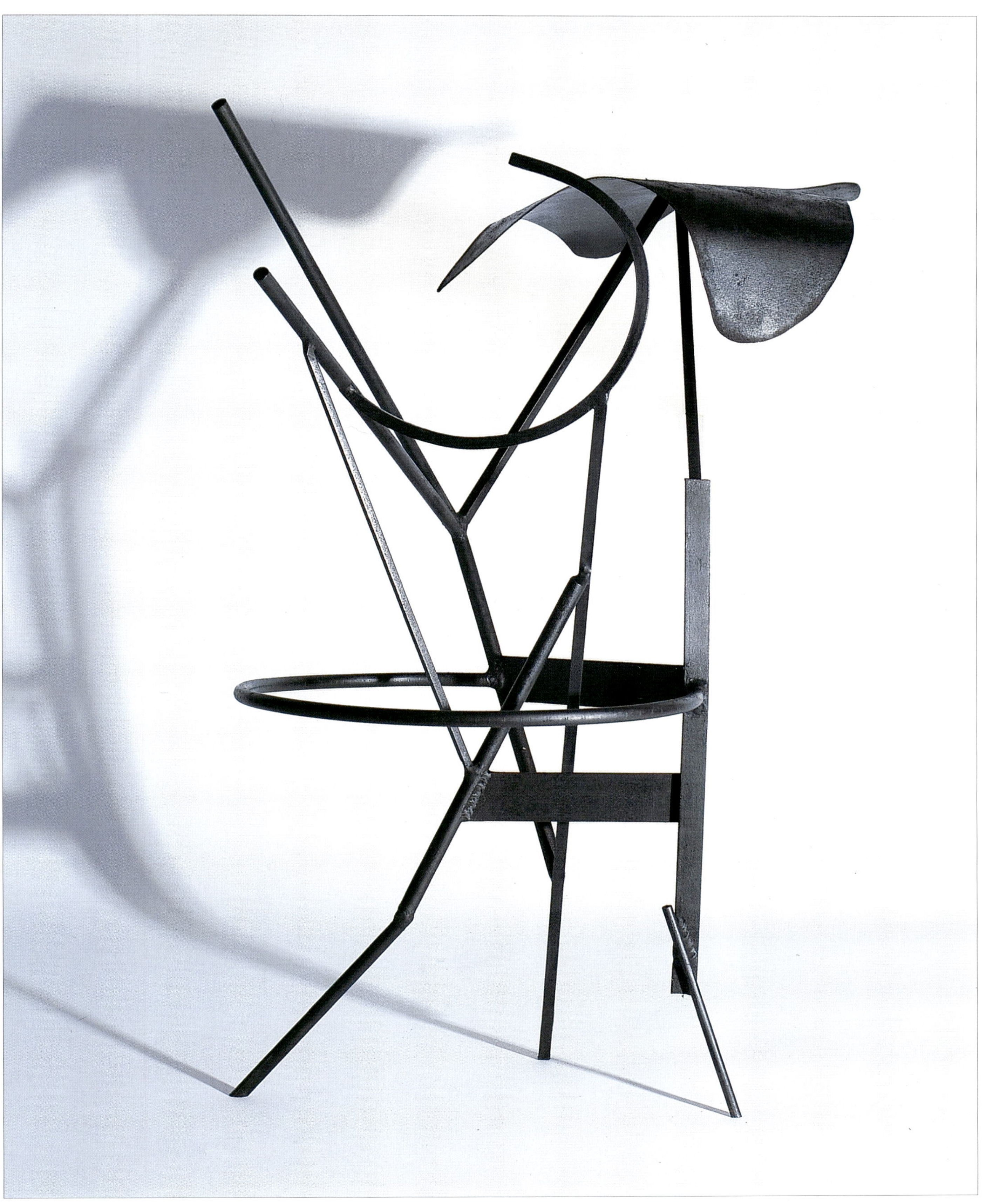

Abstract with hat.

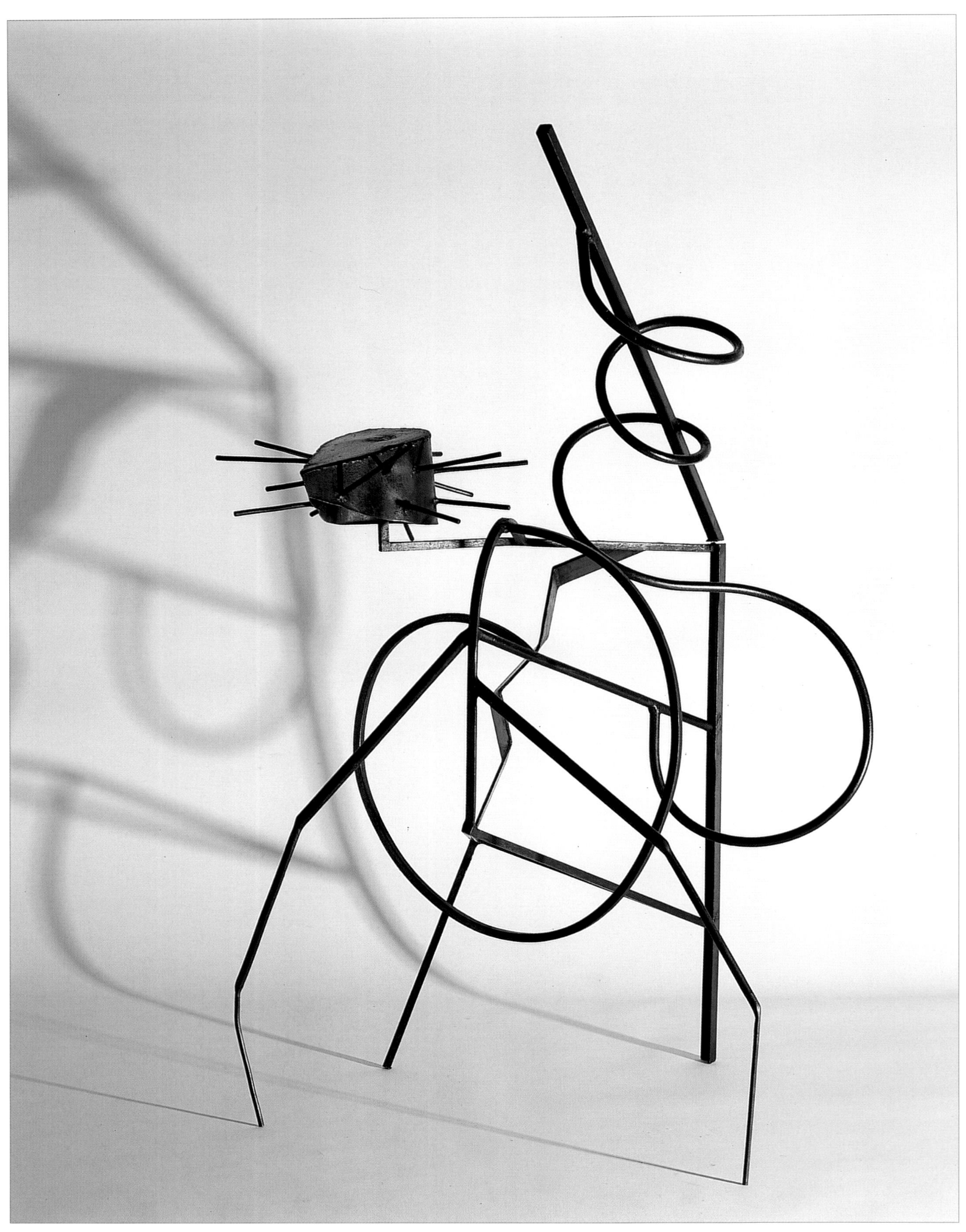

Monsieur.

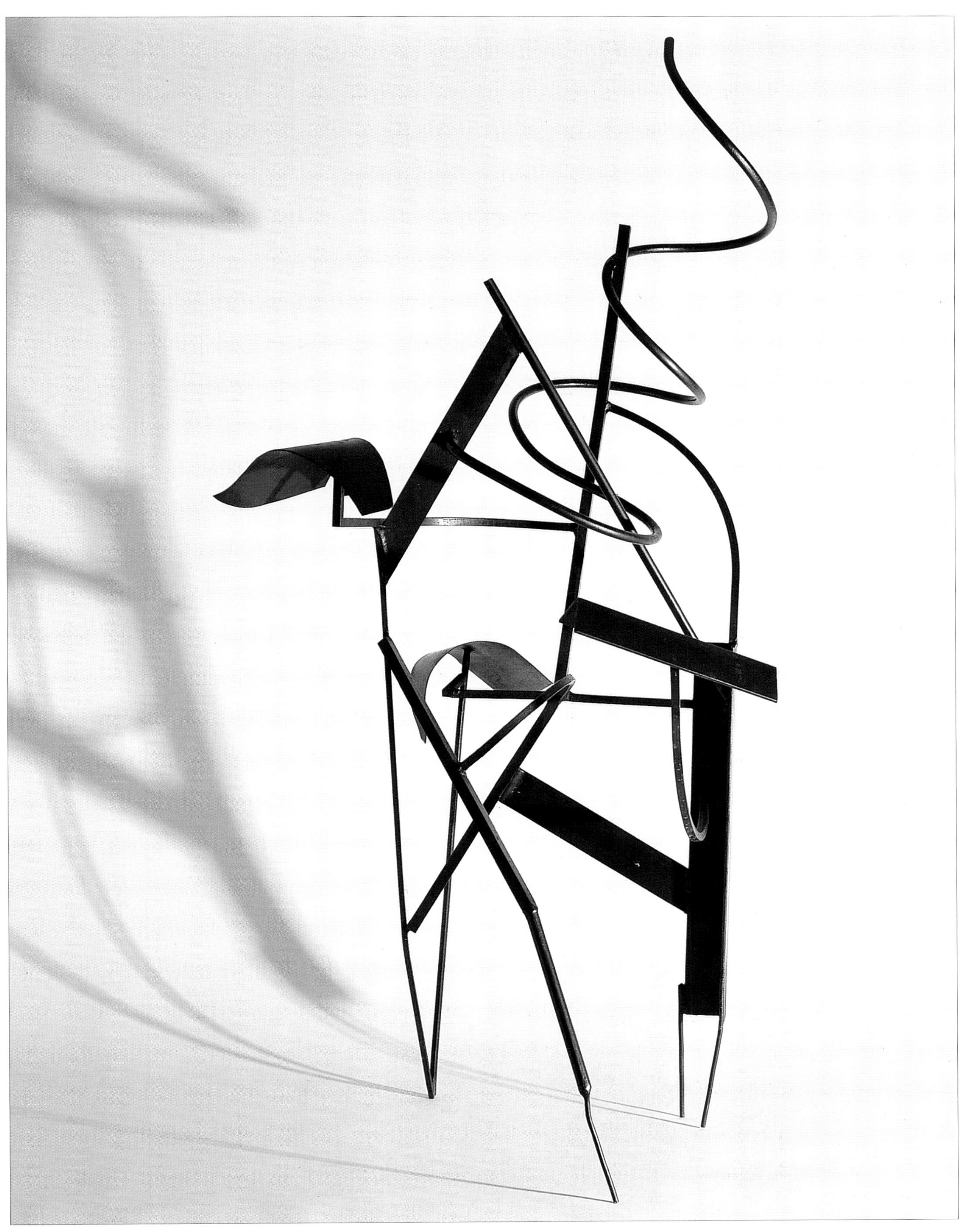

Madame.

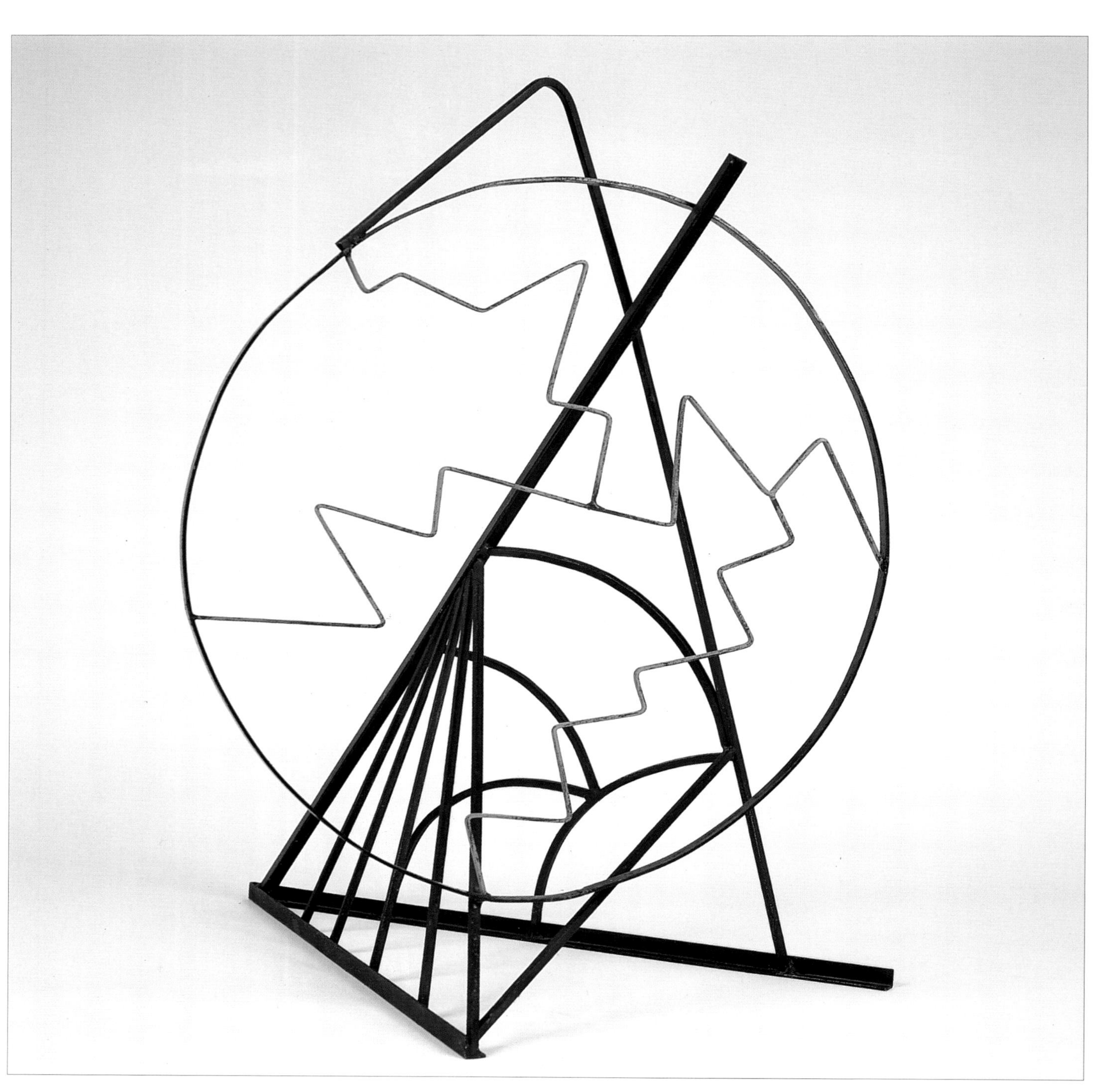

Untitled.

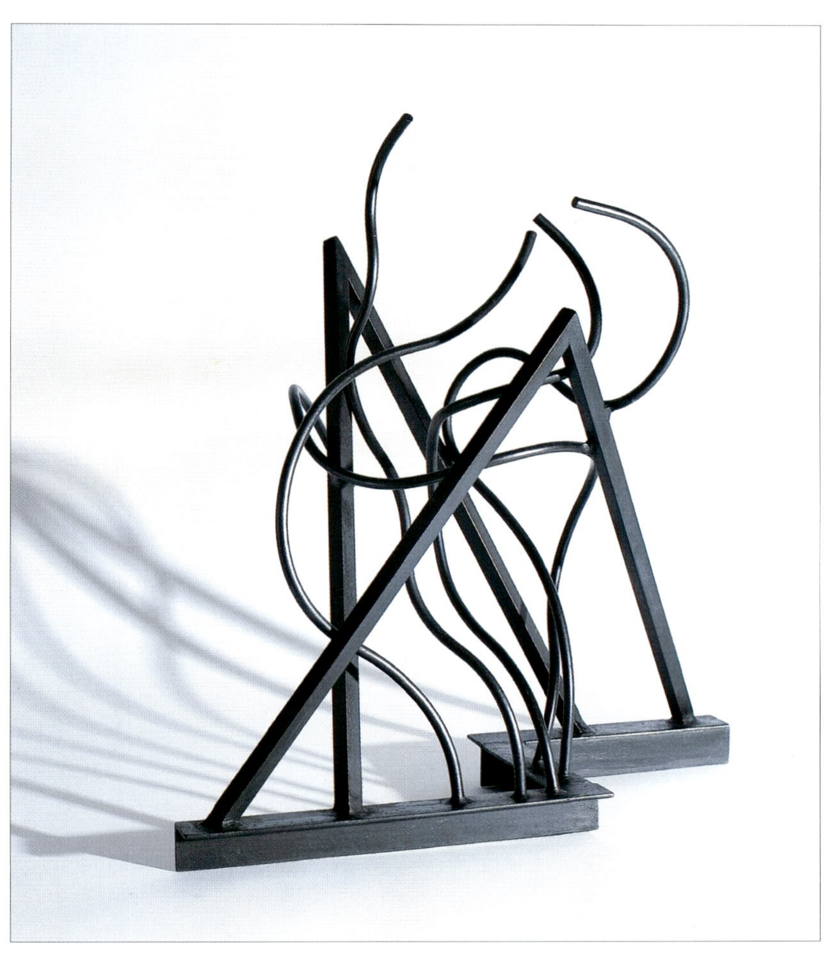

Uni medium.

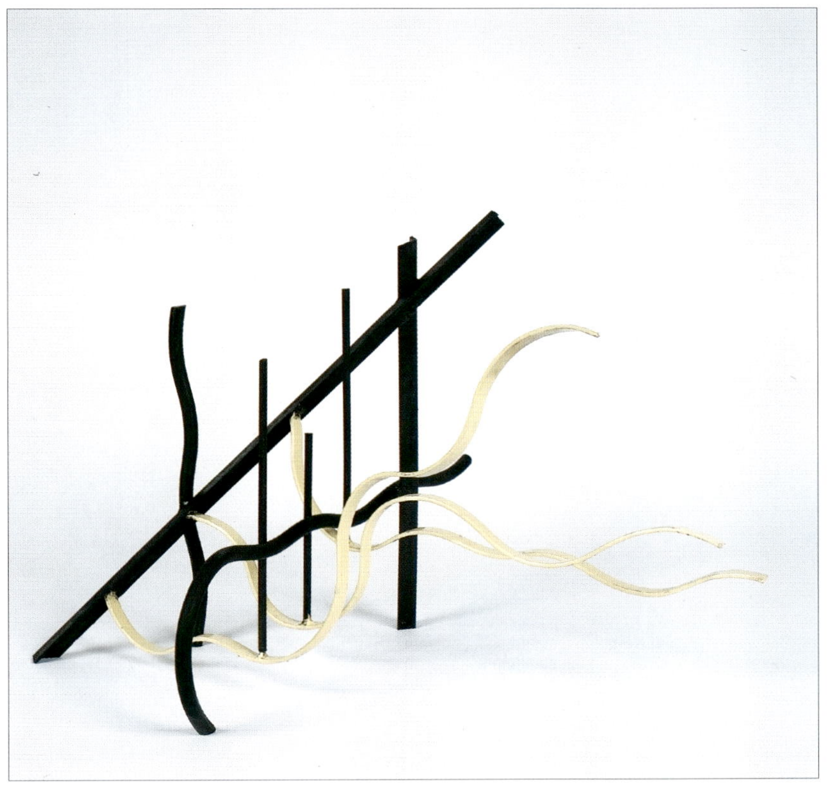

Bye Bye.

TUYAUX

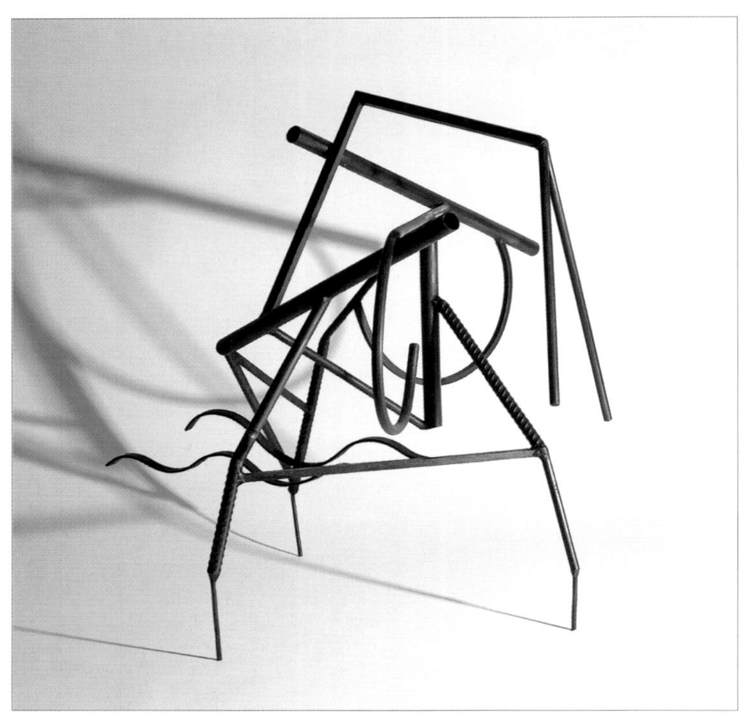

Tuyau Bye Bye.

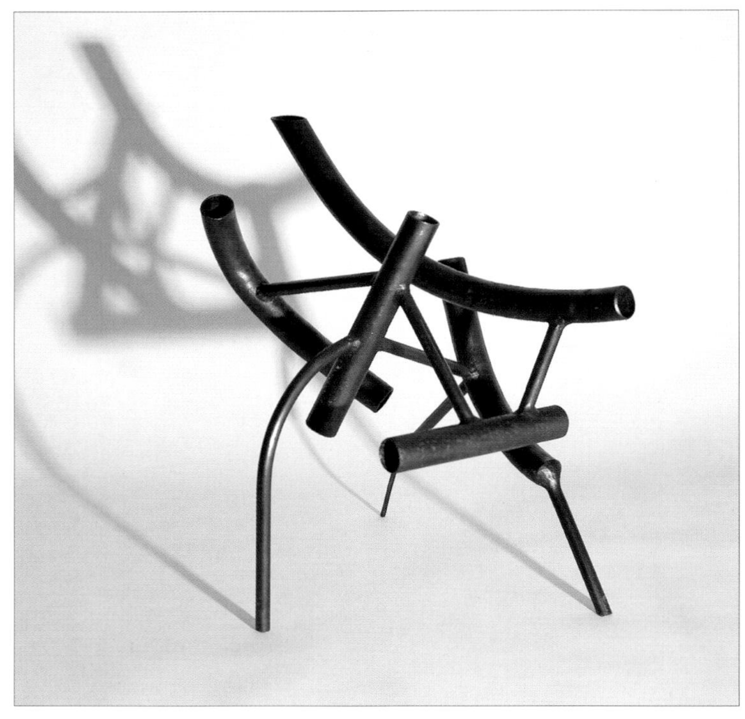

Tuyau IV.

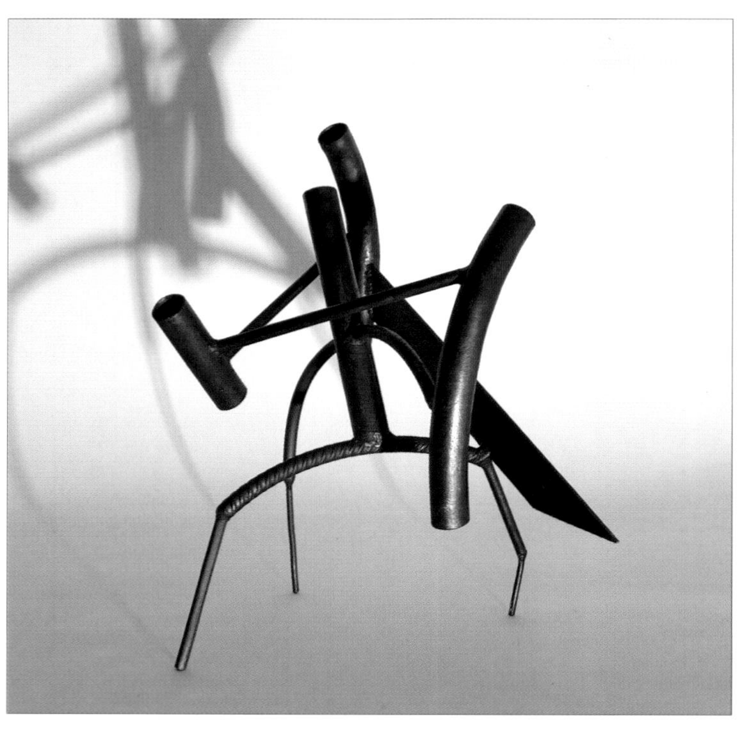

Tuyau III.

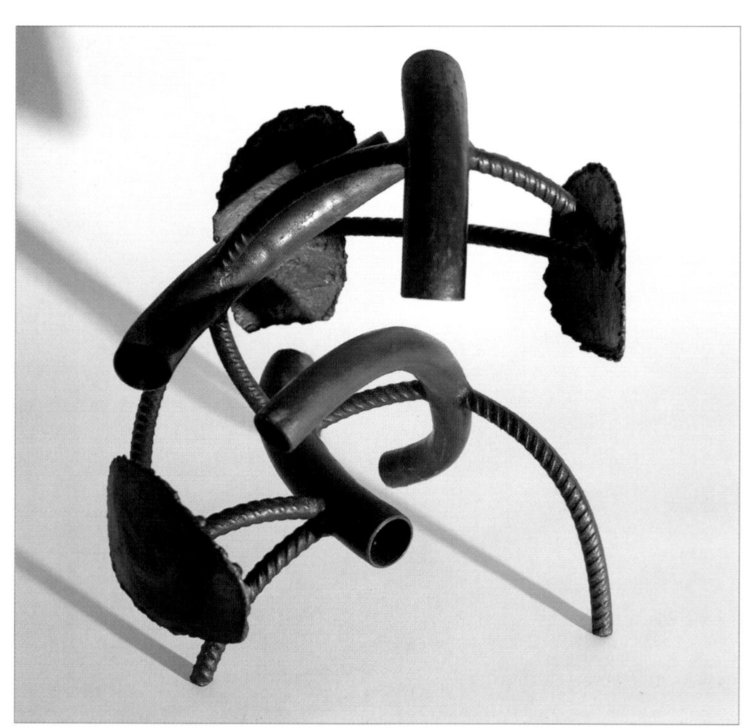

Tuyau X.

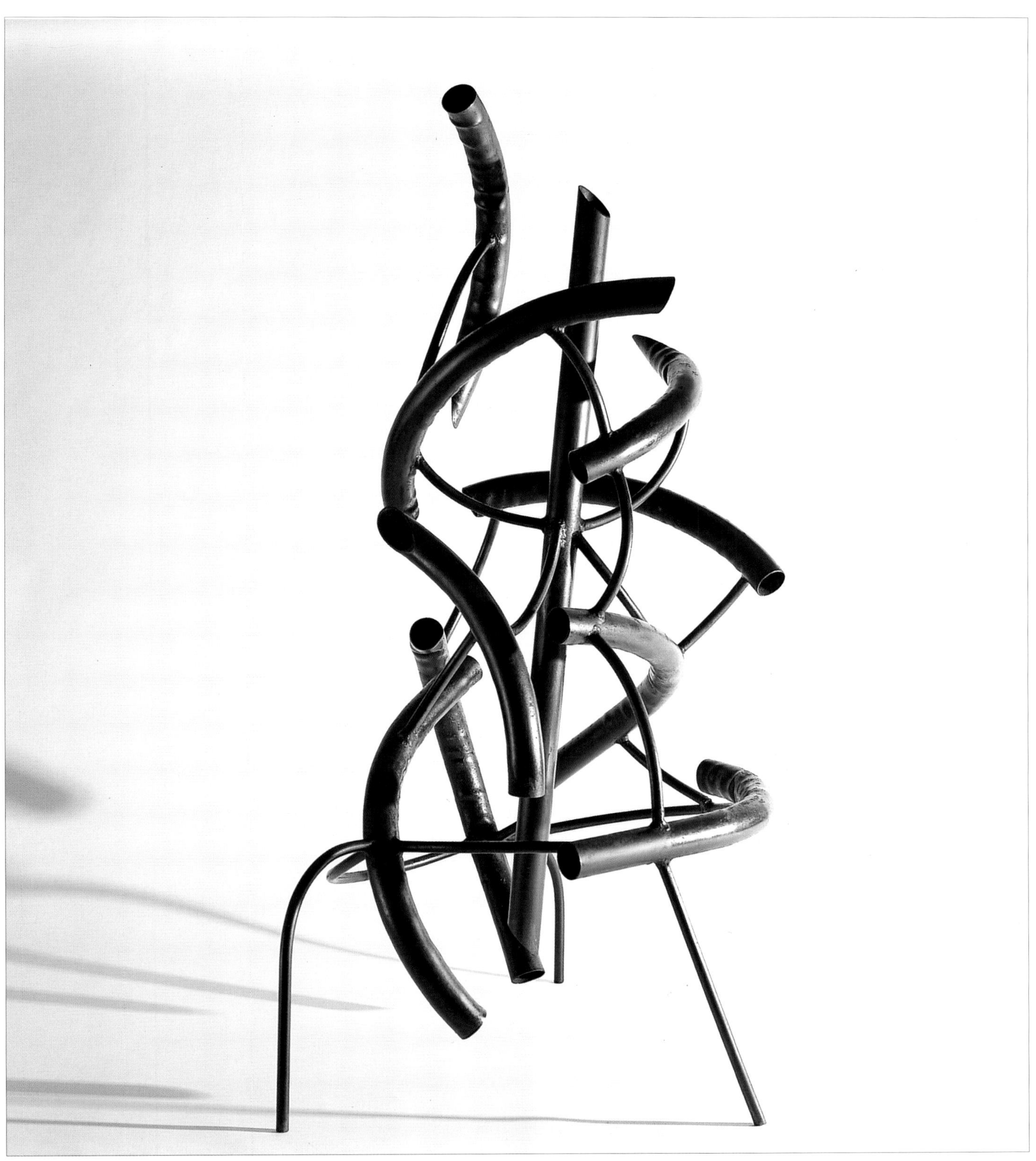

Tuyau XIII.

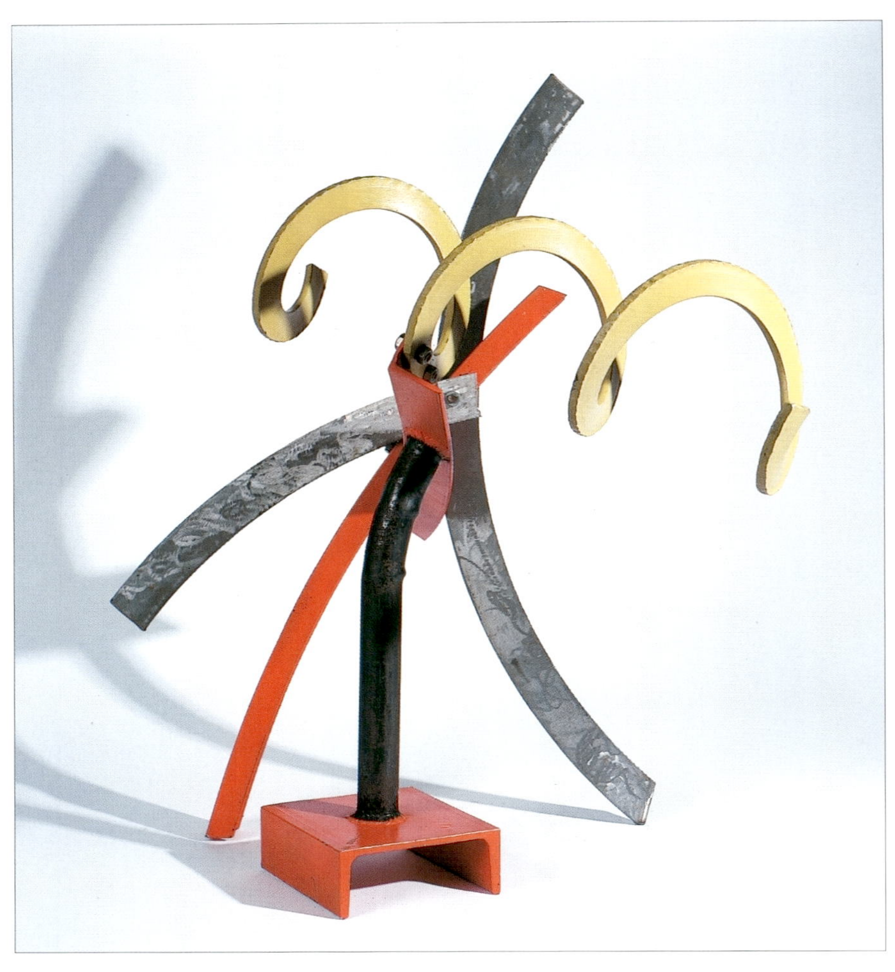

Light Hearted.

RECENT SCULPTURES

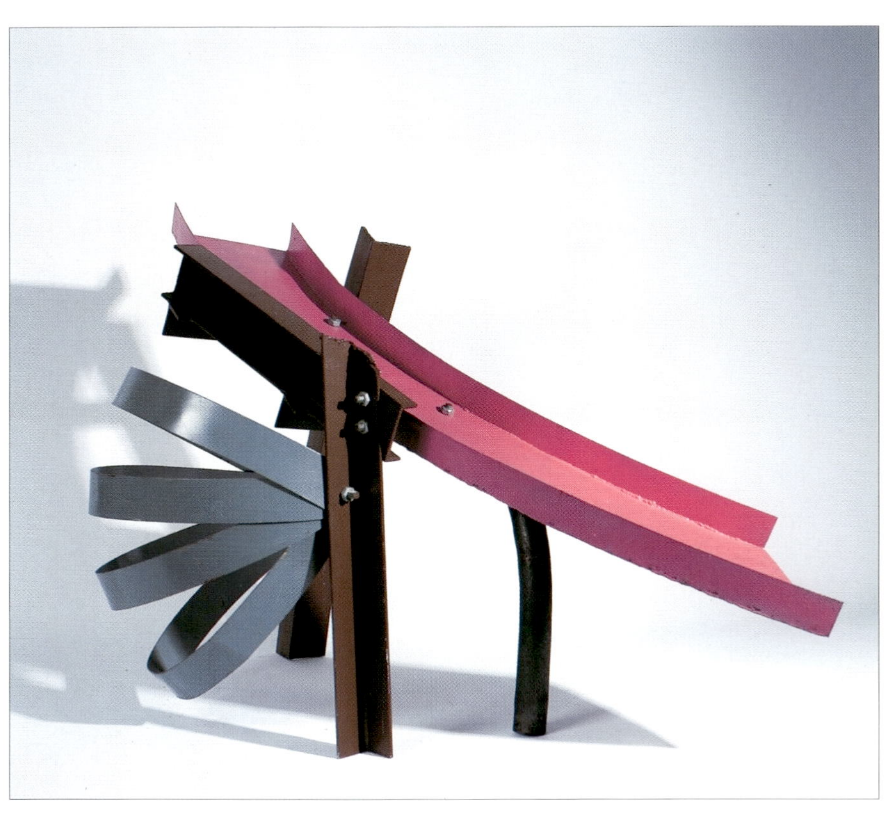

Pink Slide.

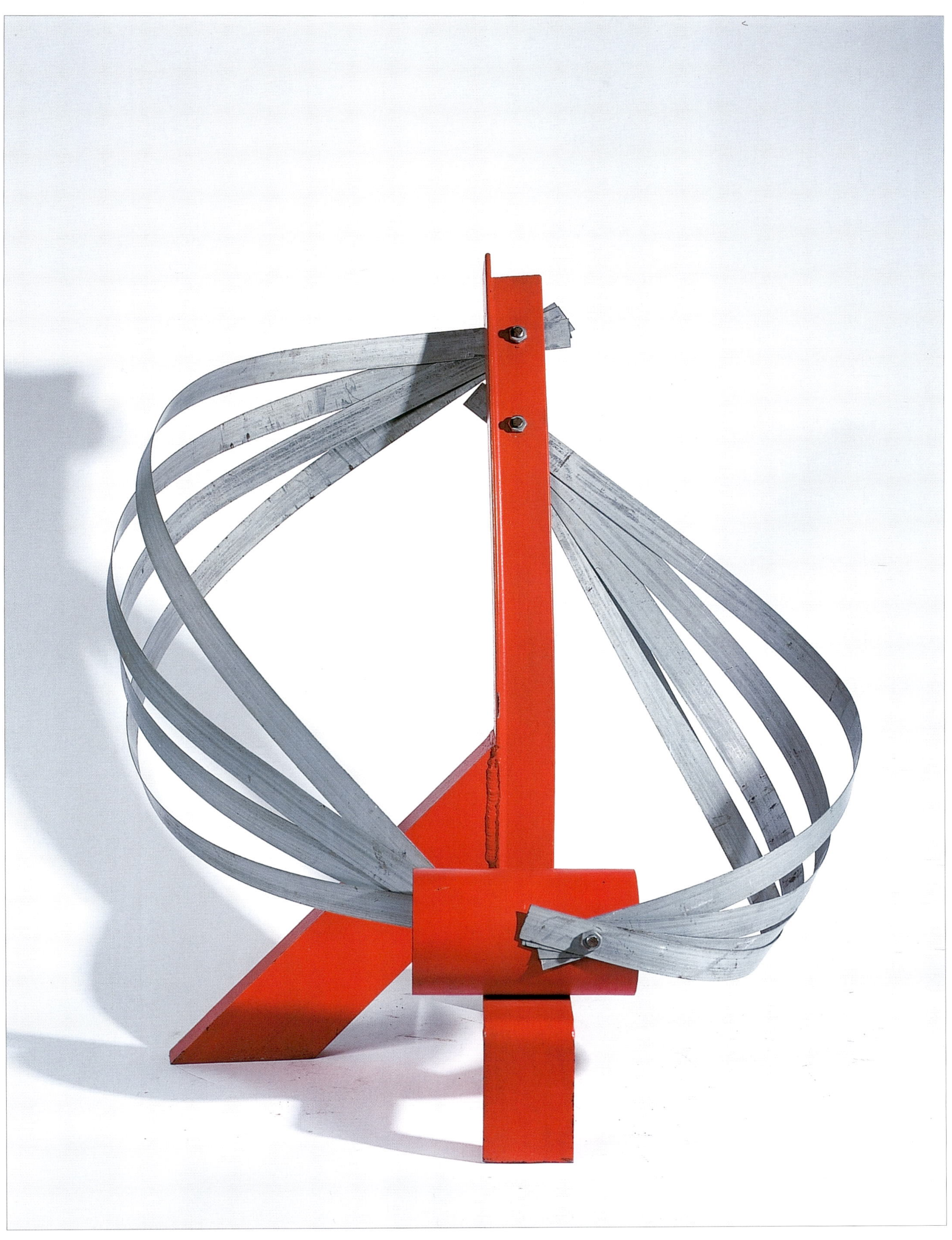

Scarlet.

COULEURS

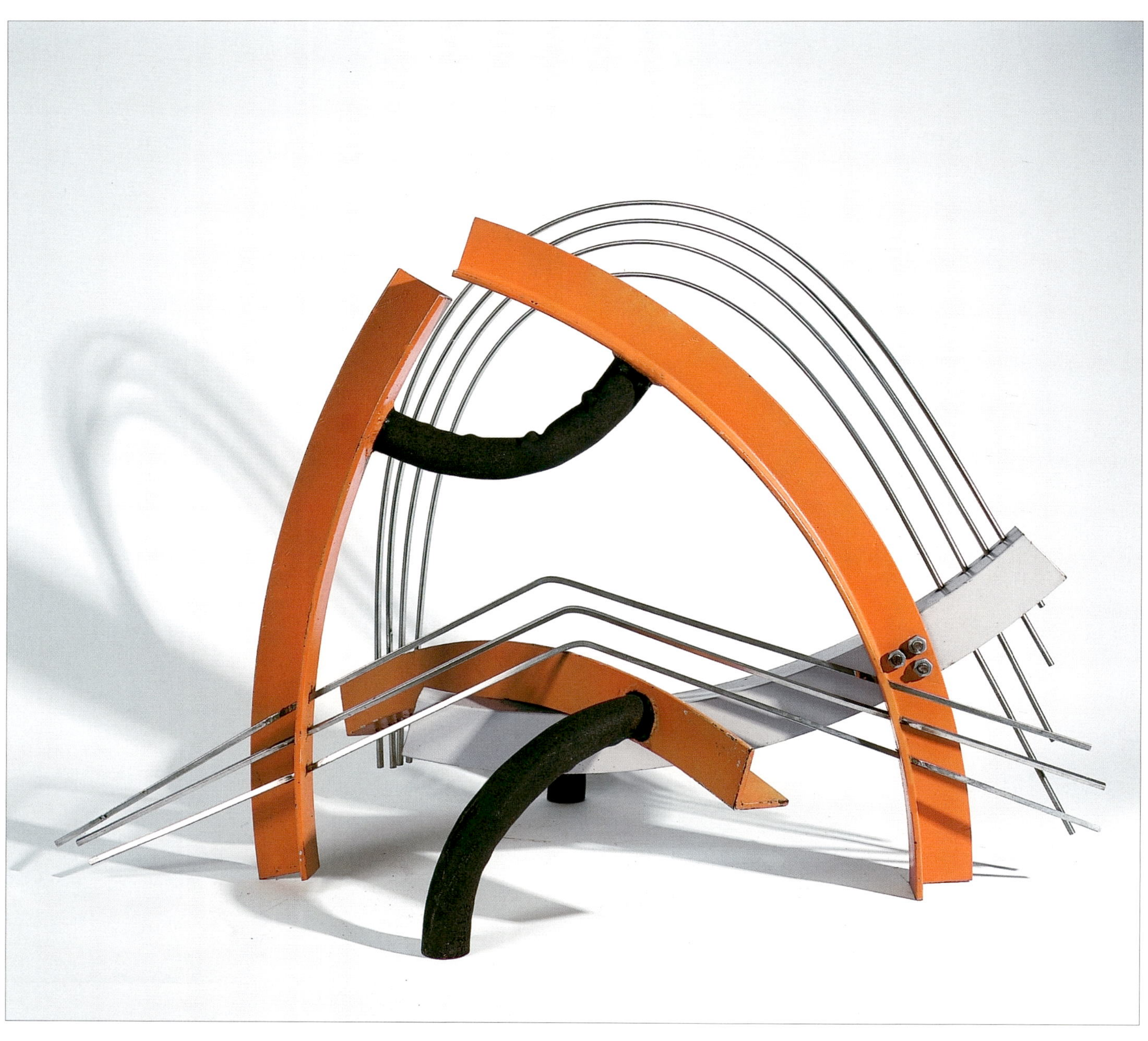

Orange.

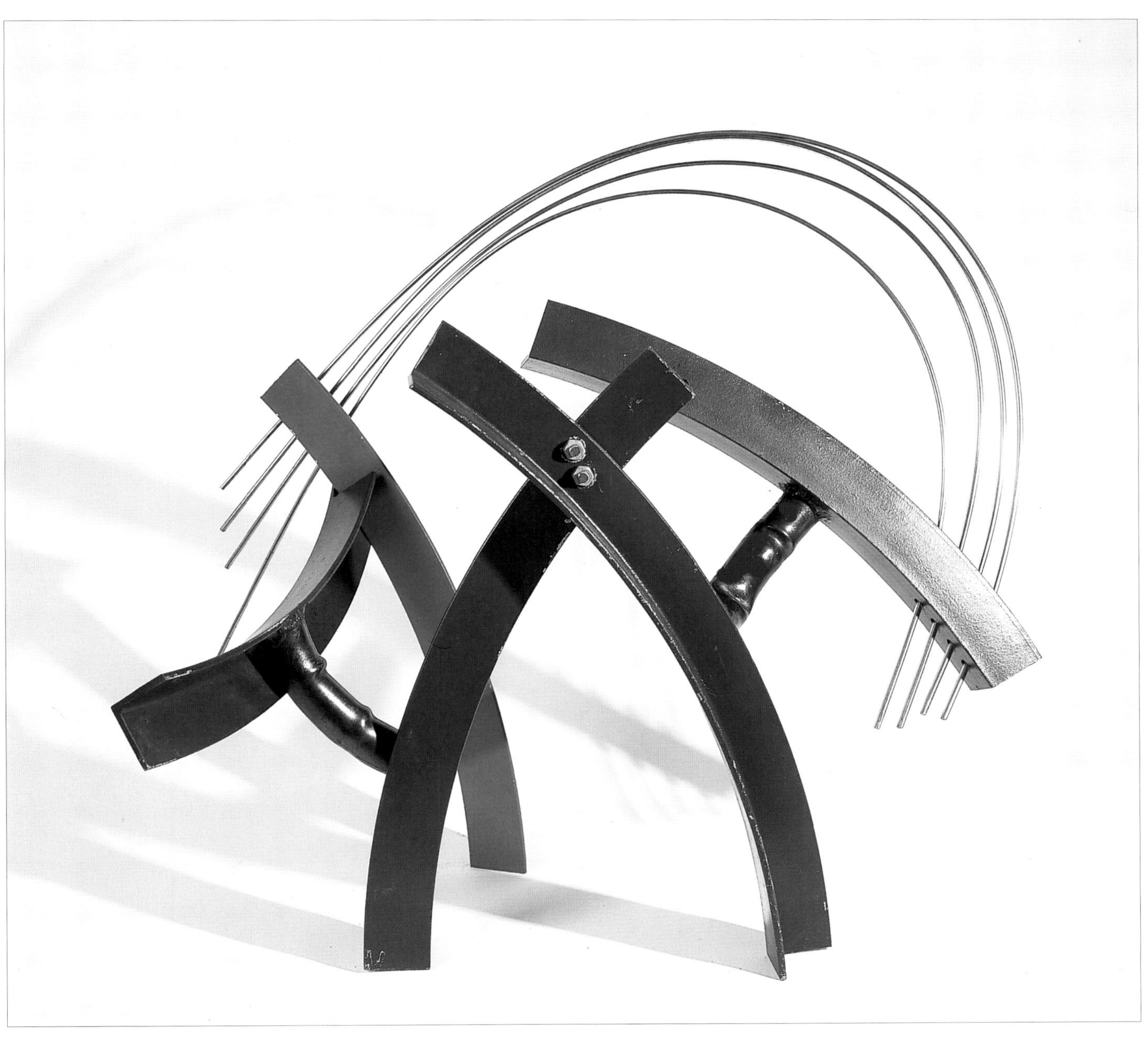

Pine Green.

SÉRIE GRISE

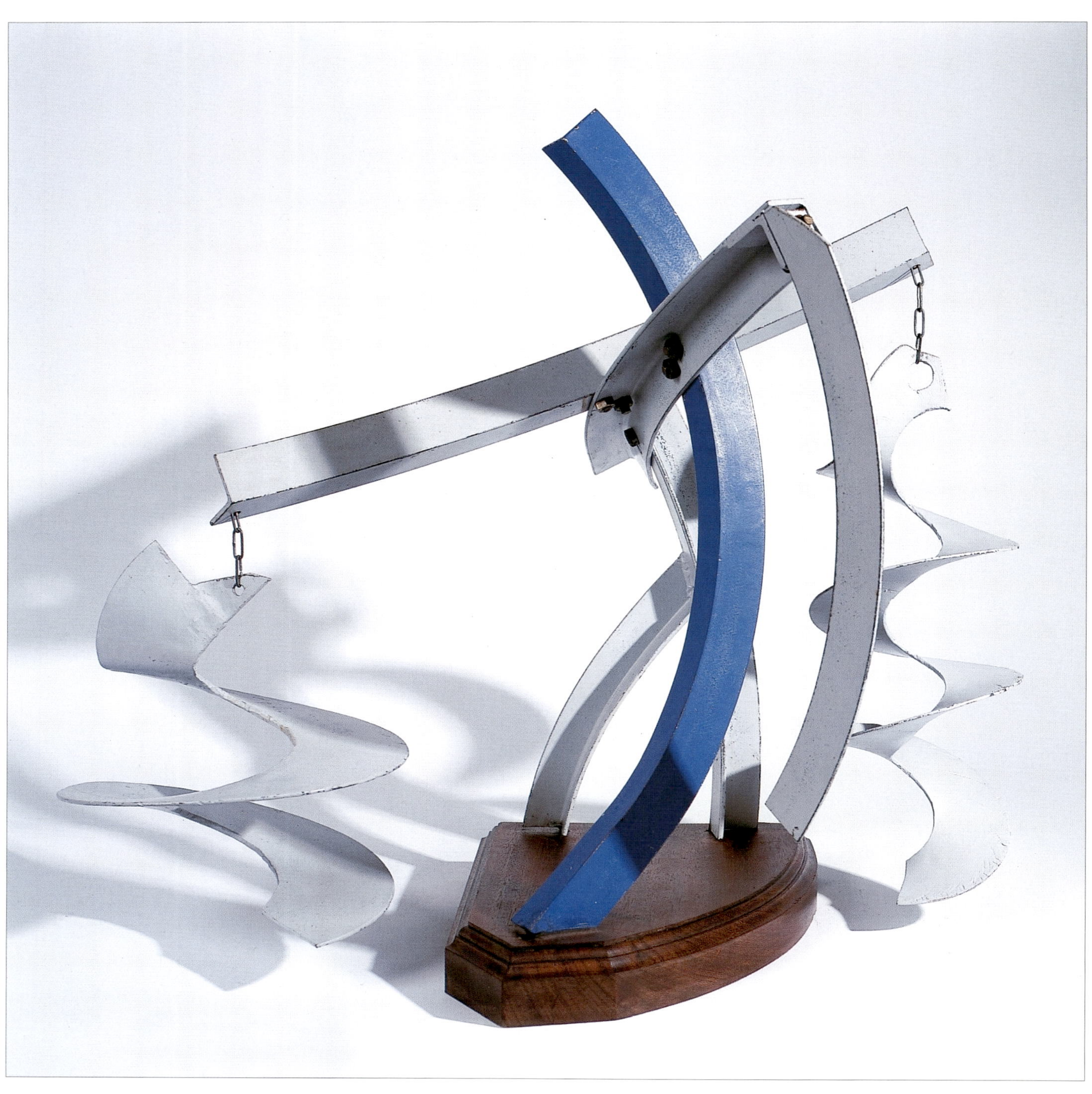

Curly Cues.

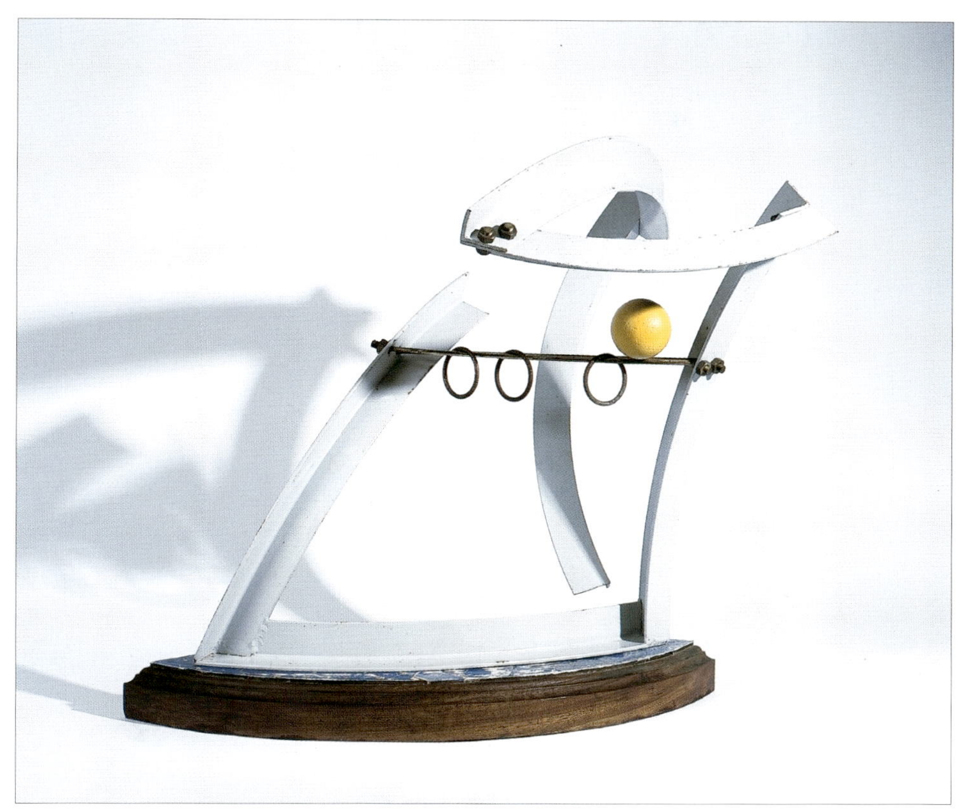

Cornell.

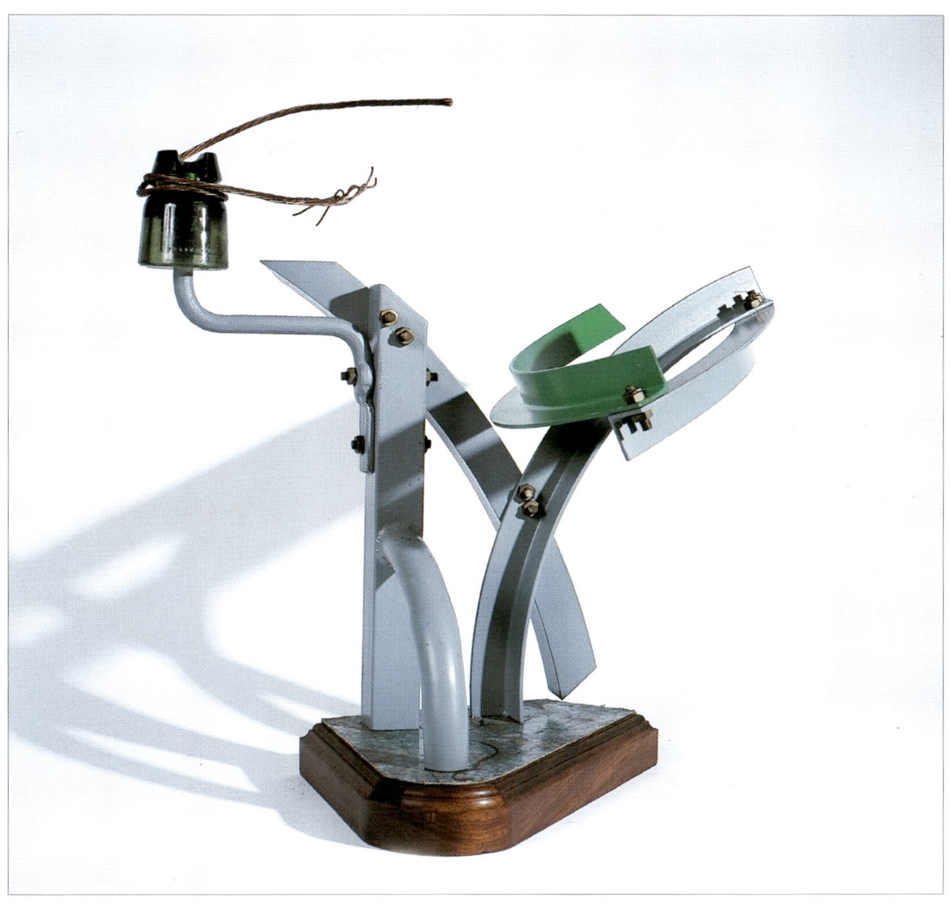

Toulouse.

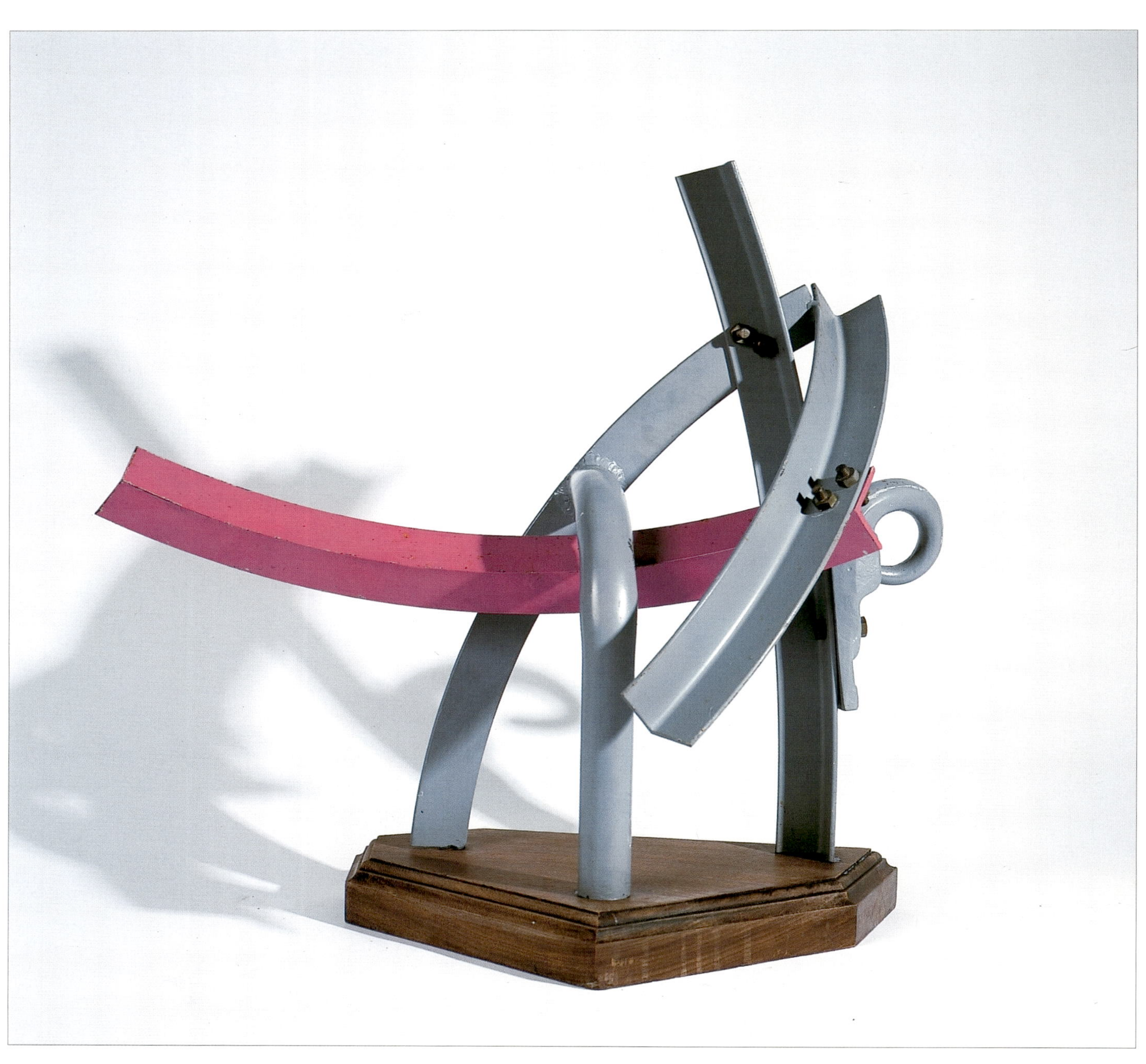

Eléphant rose.

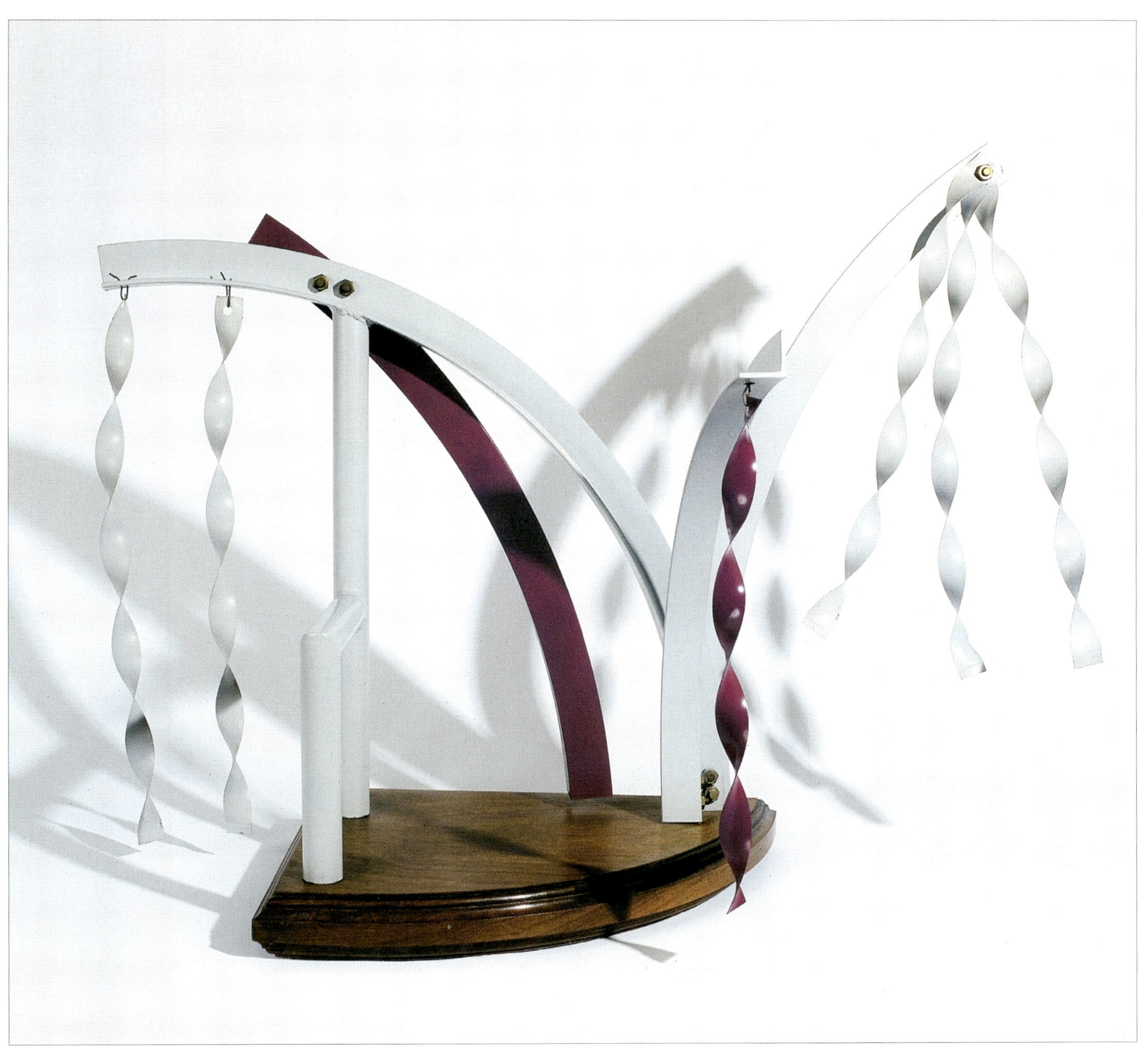

Ribbons in the air.

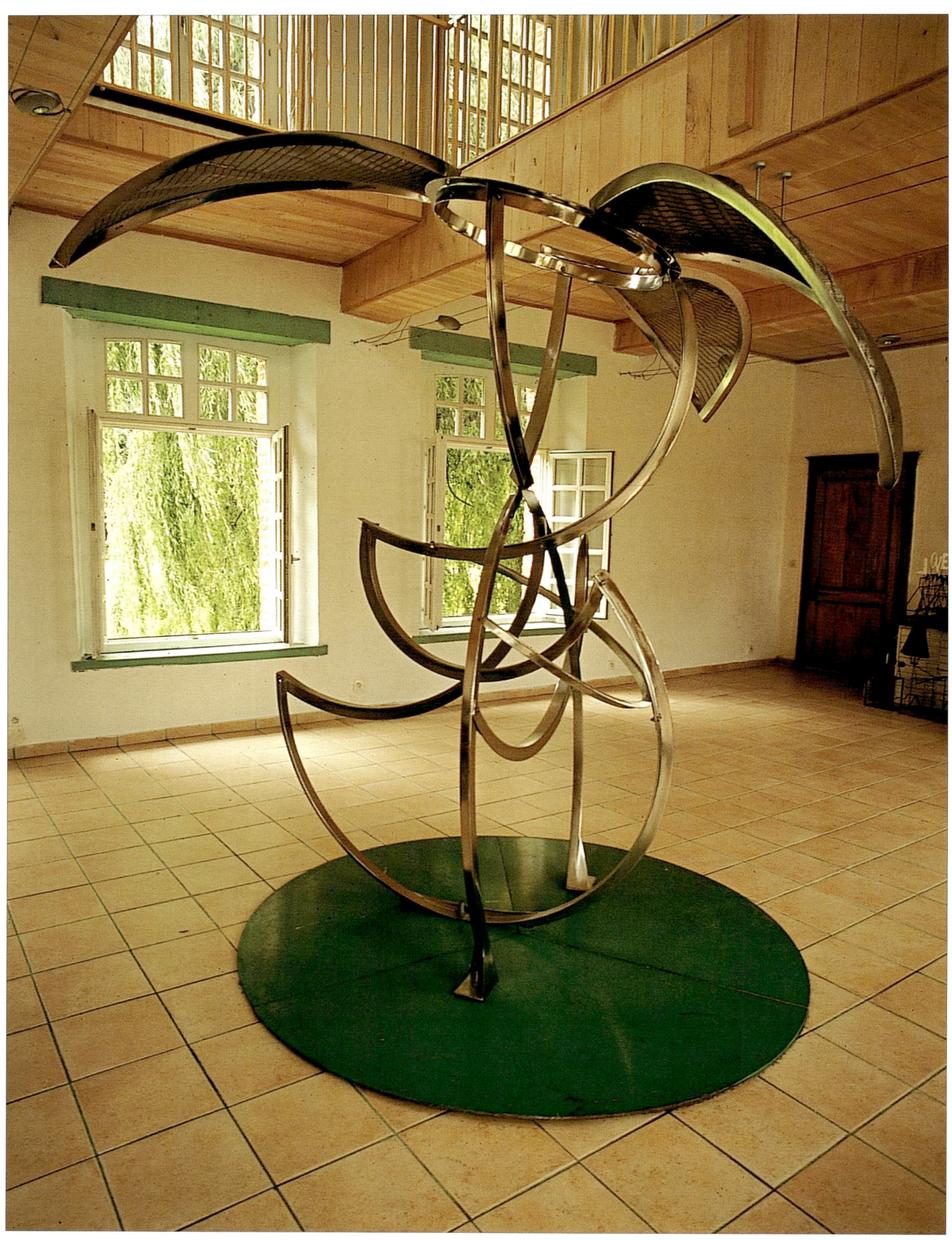

Palmier.

THE AVIARY

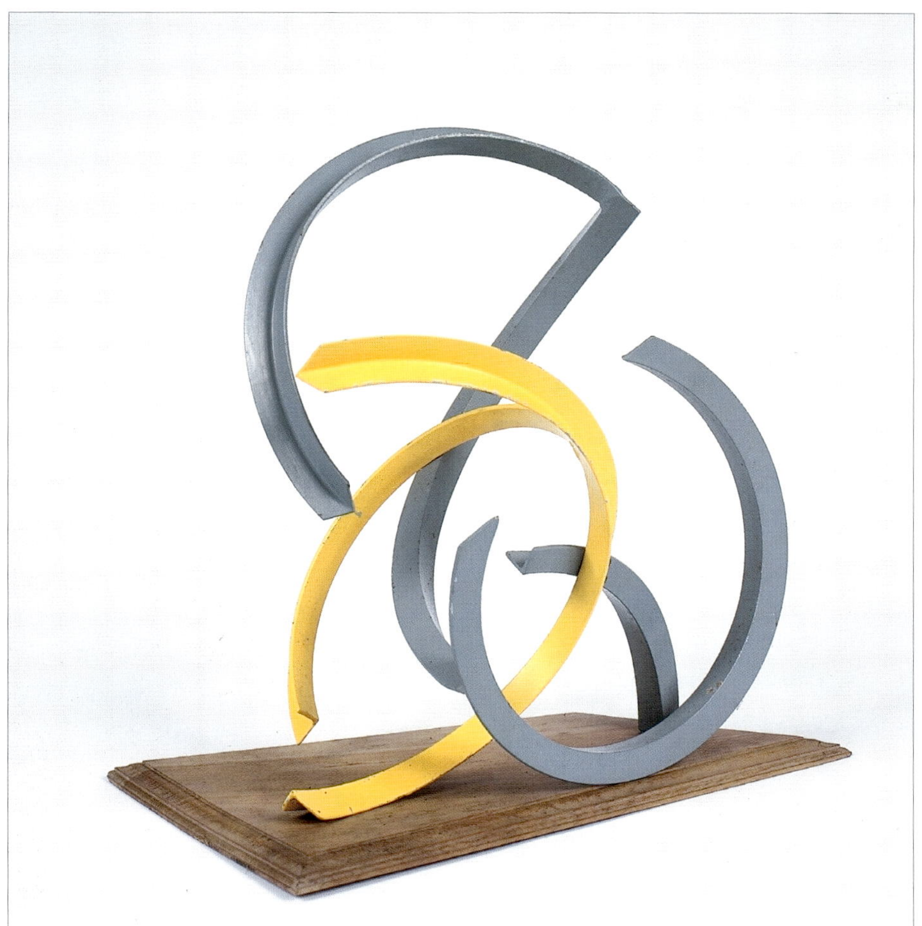

Coucou.

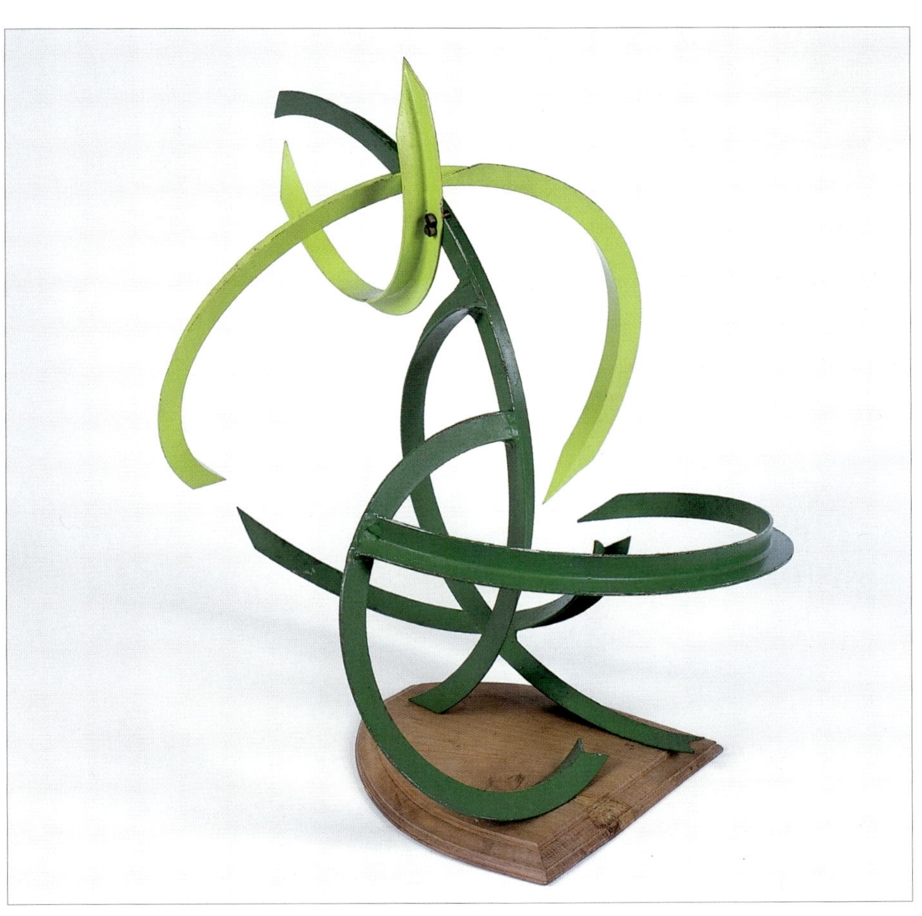

Perroquet.

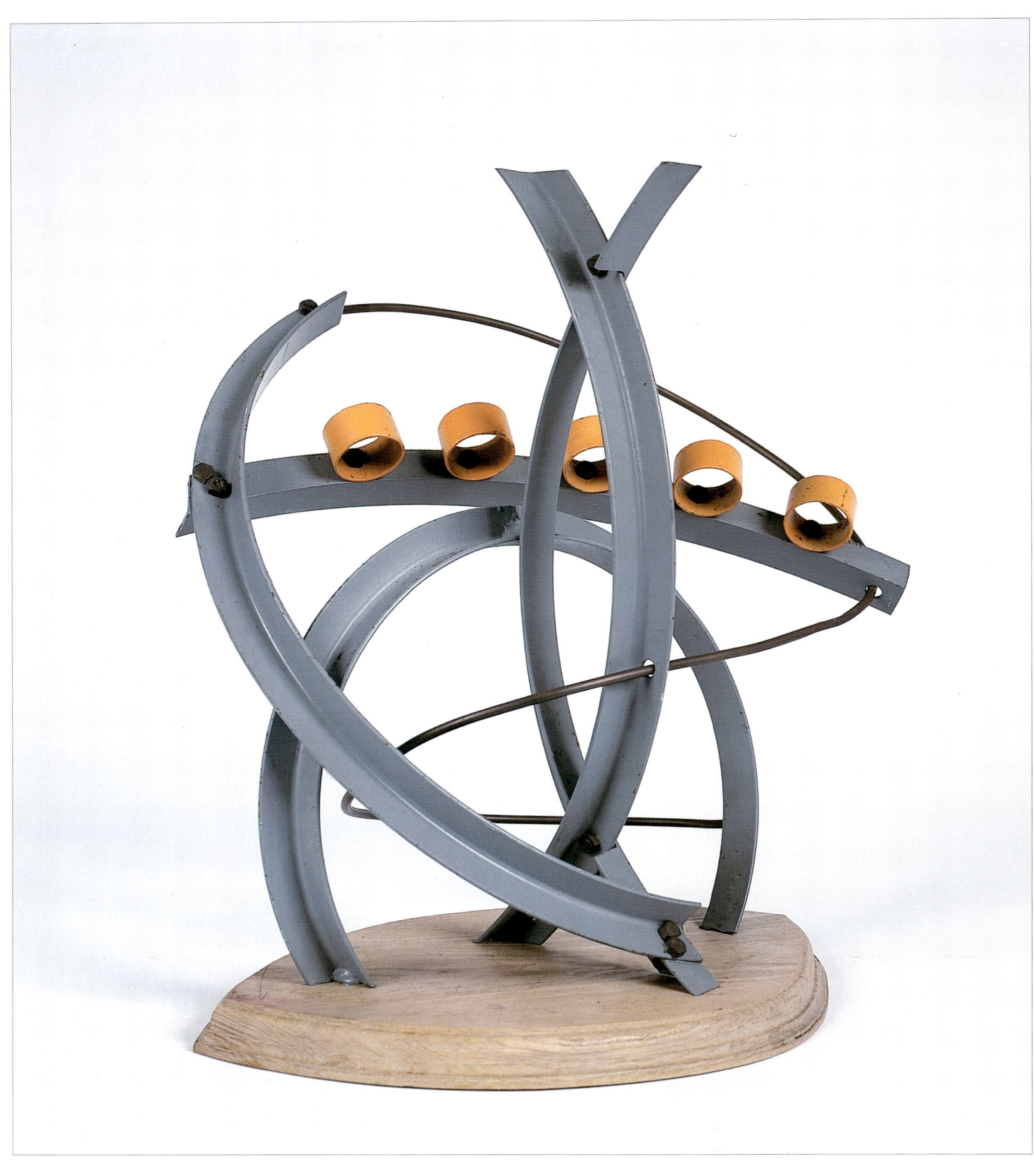

Canari.

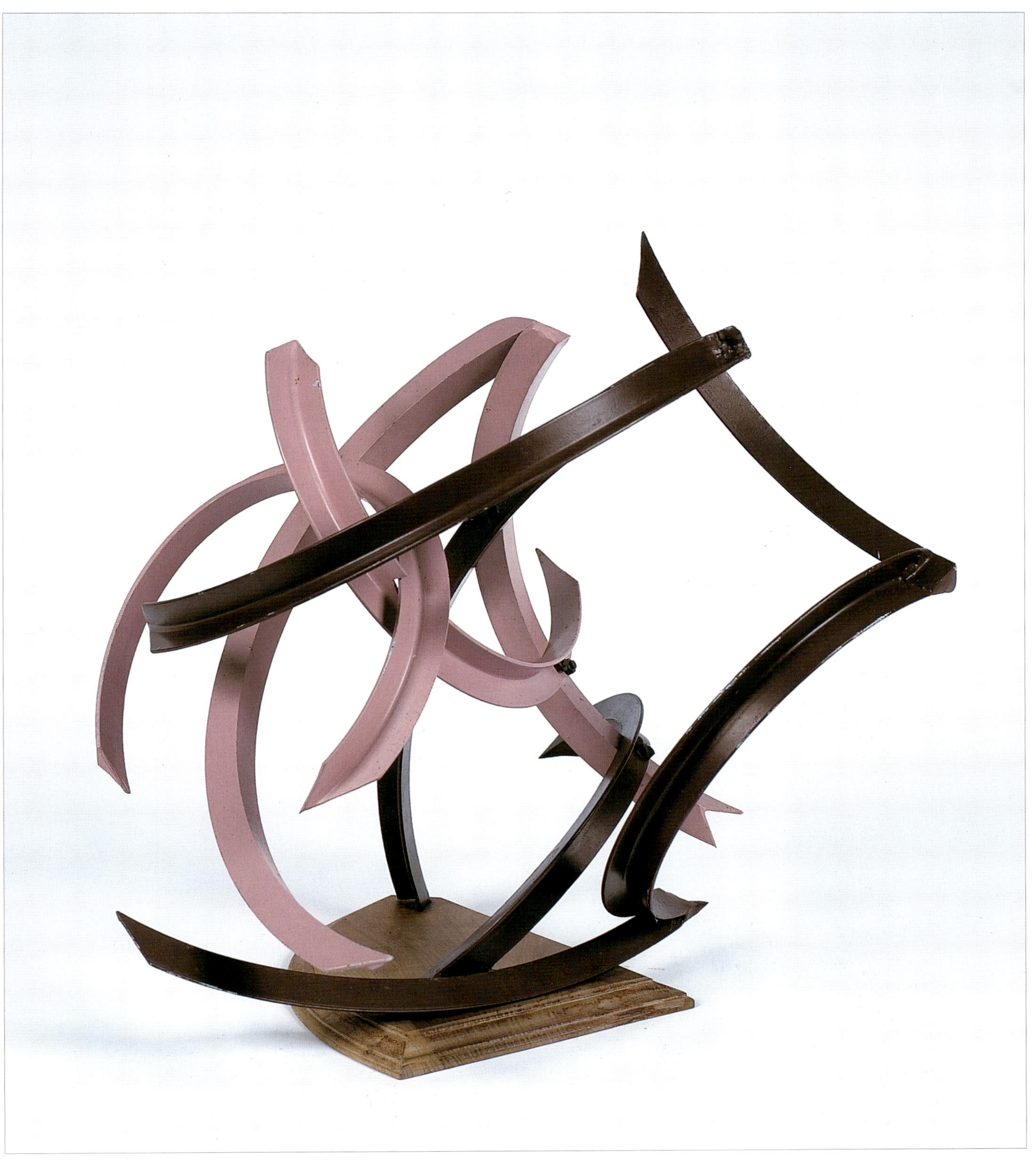

Bécasse.

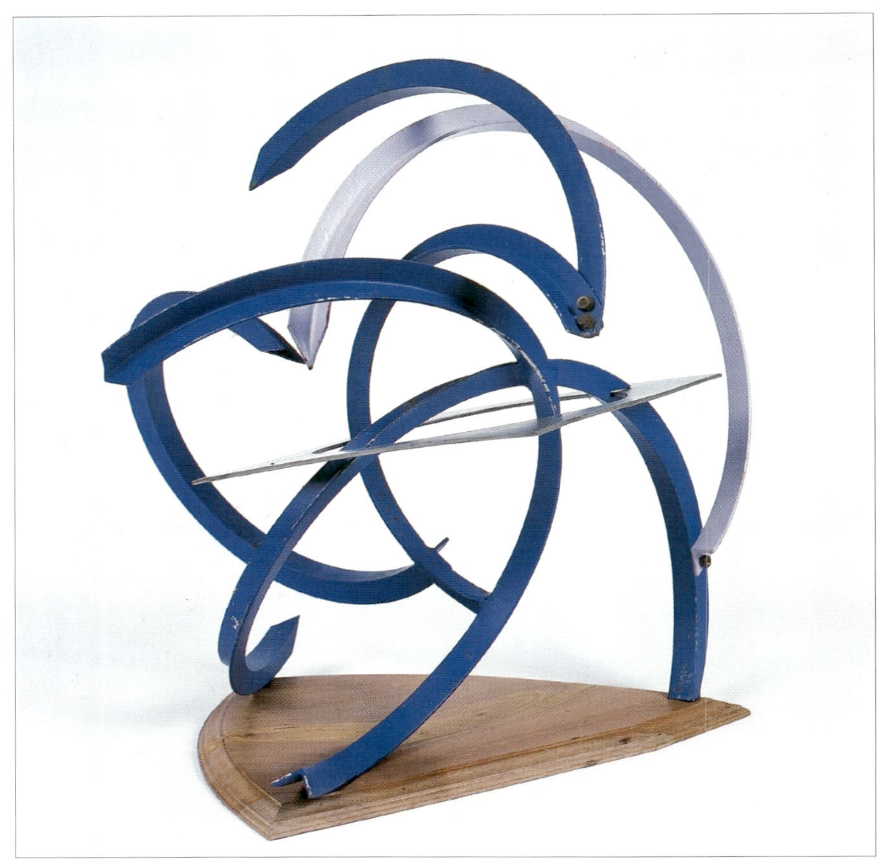

Hirondelle.

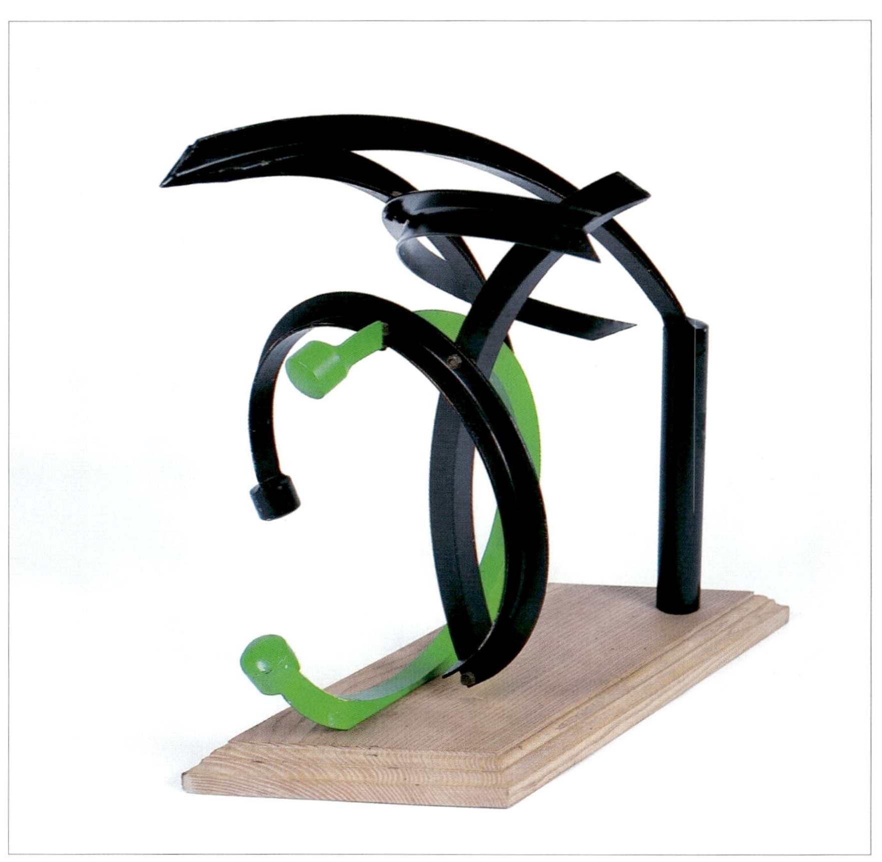

Pic Vert.

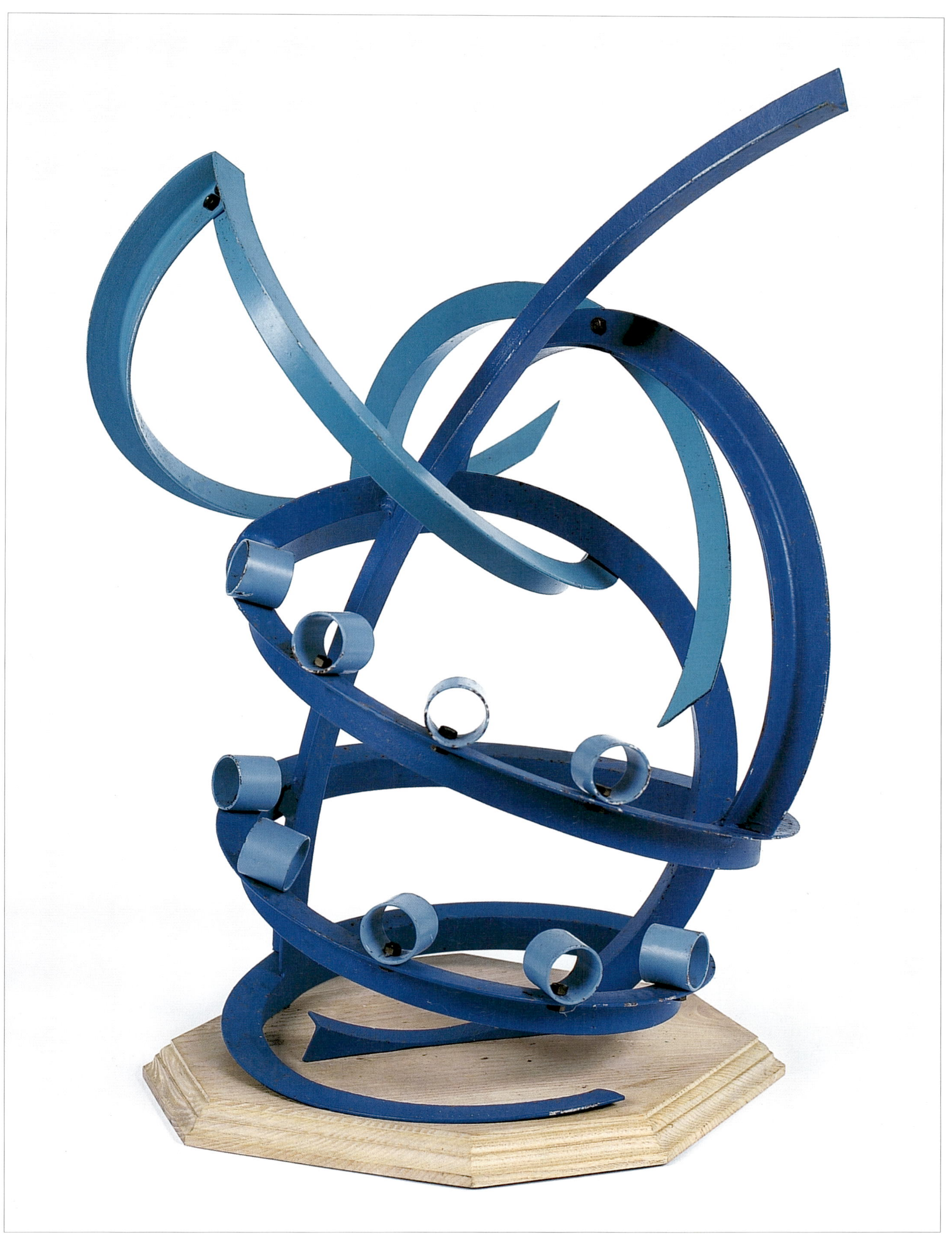

Martin Pêcheur.

THE AVIARY

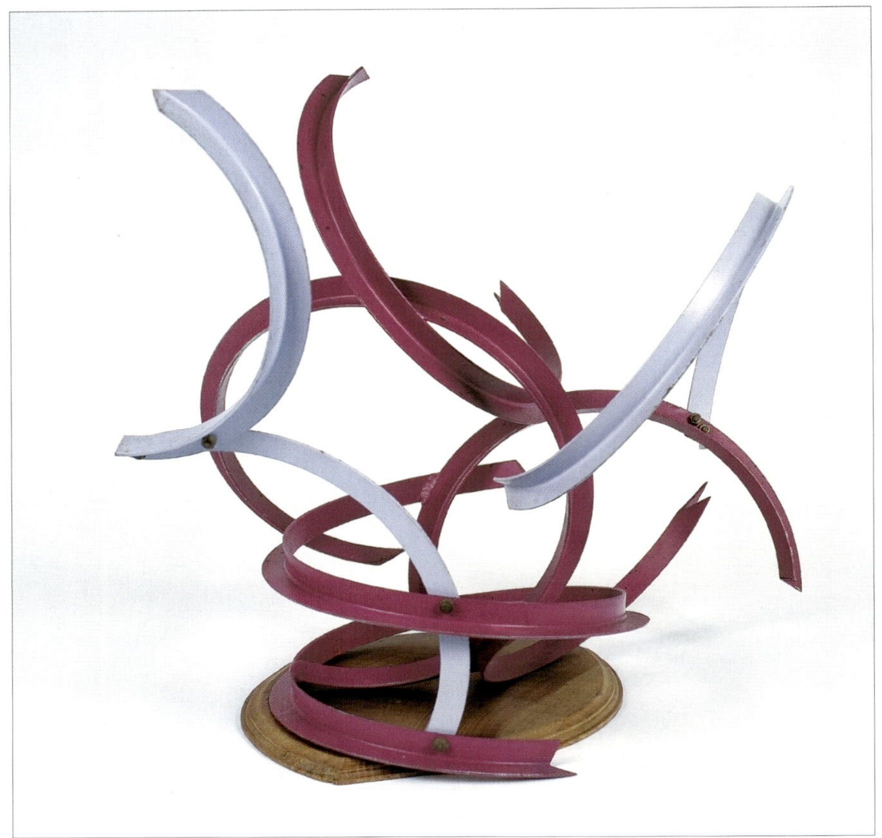

Flamant.

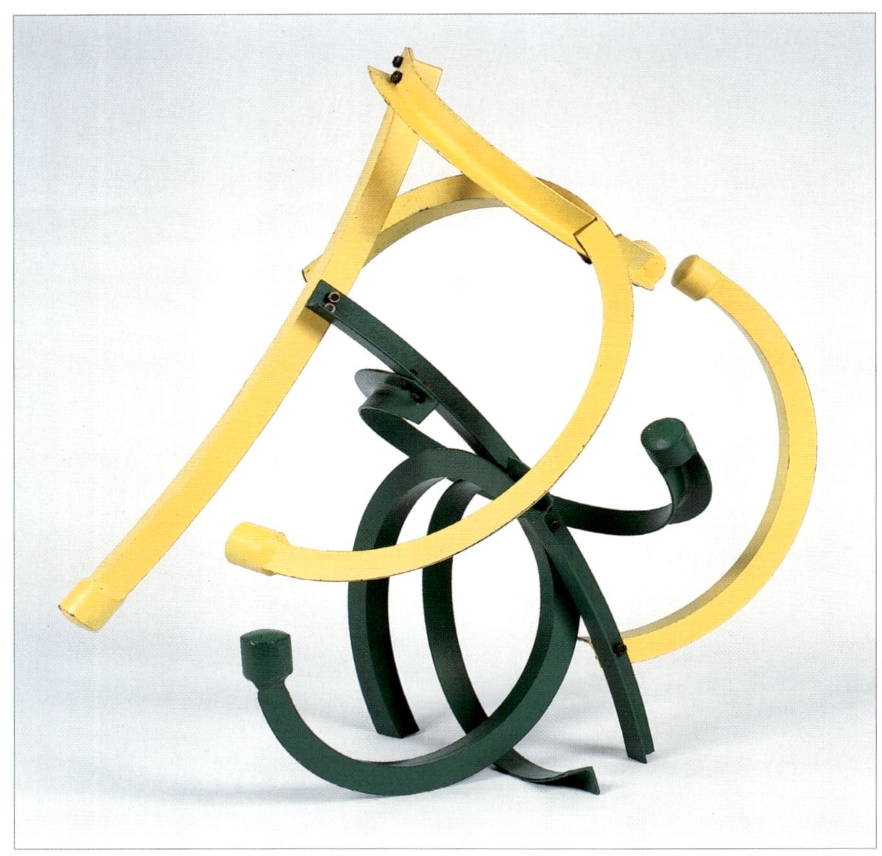

Paradisier.

HARD & SOFT

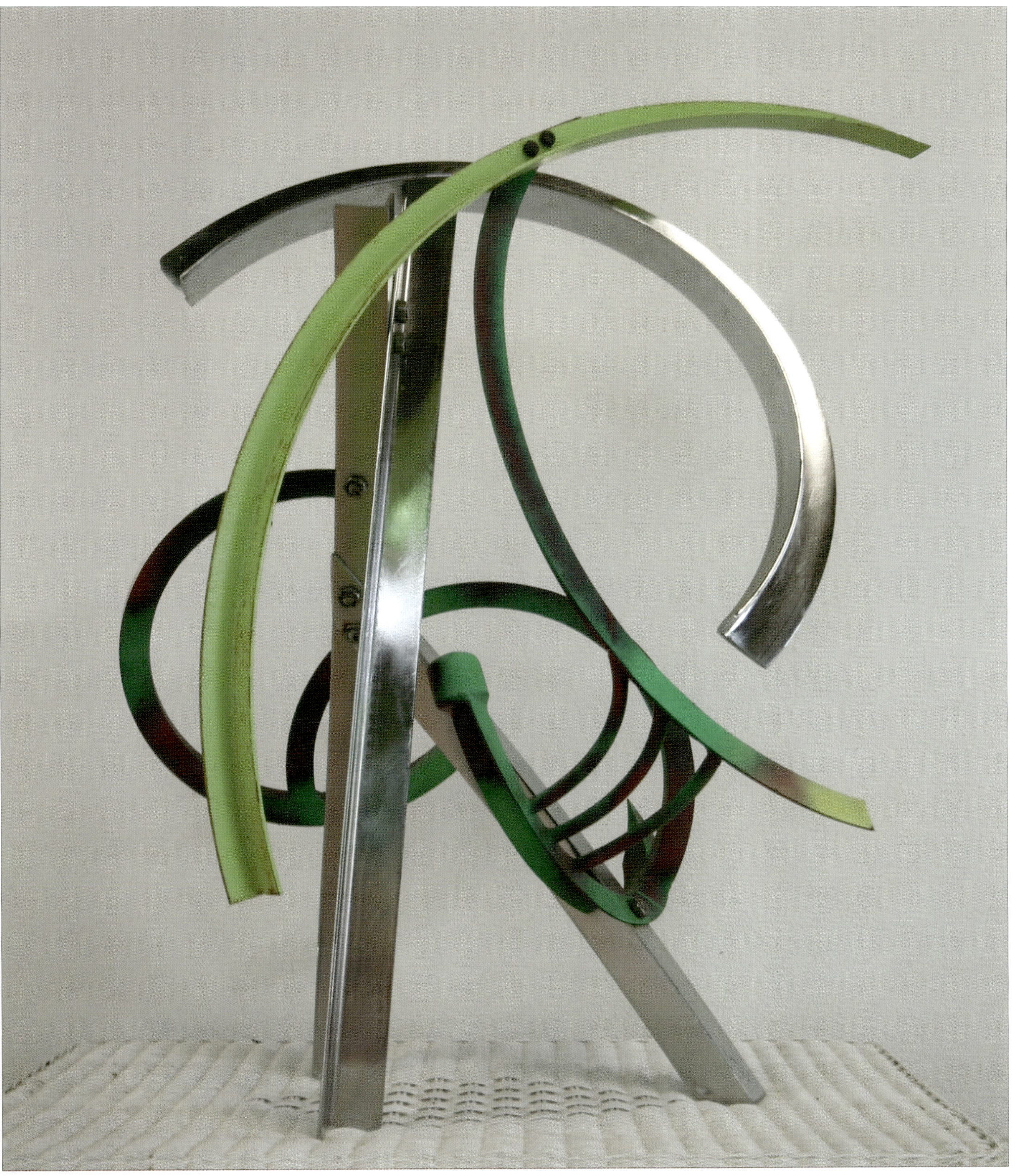

Humphrey B.

DICKON EAMES

In the manner of Oriental calligraphers, Dickon Eames expresses his personal sensitivity through a creative process based on the global and simultaneous organization of space, in which, by a play of complementary asymmetries, he seeks to establish a balance, using the system of opposing forces to achieve stability. His sculptures, like Chinese characters, are tangible units deriving from a fairly complex combination of strokes, and may be defined as three-dimensional ideograms. As such, they allow the viewer to consider them in their entirety or to deconstruct them into segments in order to apprehend the process behind their creation.

However, while the ideogram represents an idea, in Eames' work the conceptual gives way to the purely aesthetic. In the lineage of builders who think in terms of lines, weights and volumes, Dickon Eames has no use for messages and prefers to give materials their full prerogatives. Displayed in their raw simplicity or heightened by the use of color, steel and stainless steel express themselves in their own particular language, choosing to converse only with a feather, which like a pen, recounts its frivolities in playful flourishes.

But, one may say, the exhibition has a theme and the works have titles that seem to place them in the symbolic register. Since everything is "hard and soft", the rough power of virility is counterpointed by the fragile quintessence of femininity, and the emphatic tributes to departed stars of Hollywood deliberately anchor contemporary art in a mythical past. So is Dickon Eames trying to tell us something about Marlene, who, rising from the blue aura of feminine mystery, appears to us, in her sensual indolence and studied sophistication, as she really was: a delightfully perverse angel created by the fantasy world of men? Or about Garbo, who concentrates her strength like a snake coiled at the foot of steel reeds, suggesting to us that by denuding herself of all artifice and exalting her paradoxical virility, she is her own invention?

Certainly, these sculptures unveil the magic or the vanity of these unreal creatures. But let us be clear here: the reference is purely humorous. A playful wink to the spectator, inviting him simply to have fun as he discovers the logic of the humor, and placing no limits on reverie, which can take any path it chooses.

By its essence, the work can be seen to have no meaning or purpose. But it is this very gratuitousness and simplicity, reminding us at times that value must also be measured in terms of unpretentiousness, which gives the work its vitality and independence. It never exceeds its chosen domain and uses only its own instruments to conquer volume by tracing line and movement within a field of immobility. Thus the volume is the result of a very skilful architectural composition, which breaks up space in order to modify it qualitatively, and which constantly redefines relationships, so that each portion of space reverberates with all the others, allowing us to see and feel the fullness of the void.

As for movement, it is the principal quality of these metal structures, placed boldly on their tripods and seeming, at first glance, to be imprisoned in the strict fixity of frozen space-time. In an incessant play of variation and decentring, these syncopated assemblages prove to have no definite axis and can suddenly be infused with a tremendous energy that changes lines into vectors, giving the fixed form an astonishing mobility: thus in the finished building the memory of the building in progress is forever perpetuated.

Finally, since the work presents no specific angle of observation, as one moves around it one's vision is transformed, and because it comes up against interrupted trajectories and sharp edges, the visual dynamic extends from the finite to the infinite, to an utopian placelessness where the imagination can roam free. The work of Dickon Eames is therefore an invitation to travel. And we should recognize the artist for what he is: a poet of sculpture. At this point we can come to only one conclusion: he is there, not to be understood, but to be loved.

Maïté Lannes-Lacroutz

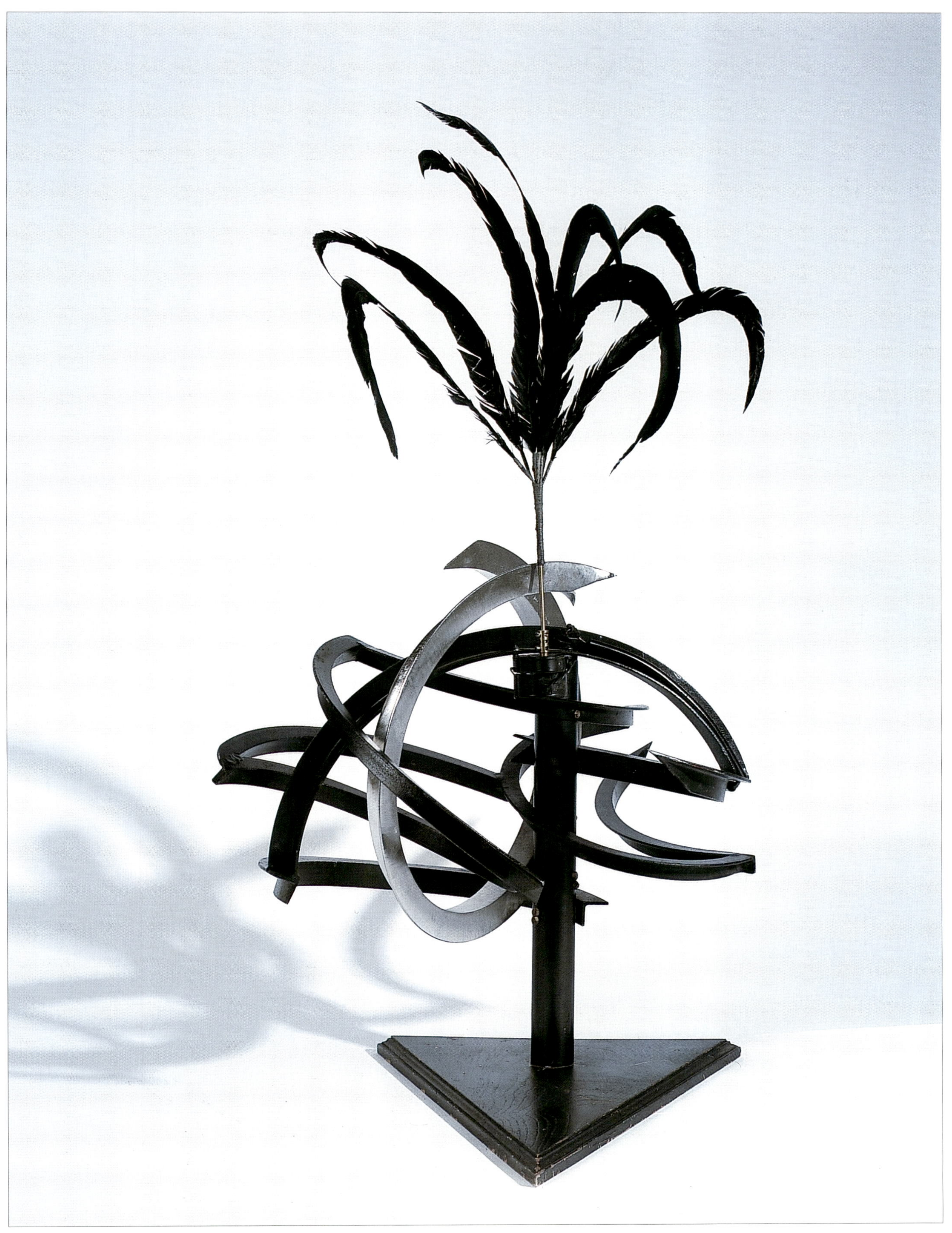

Ava G.

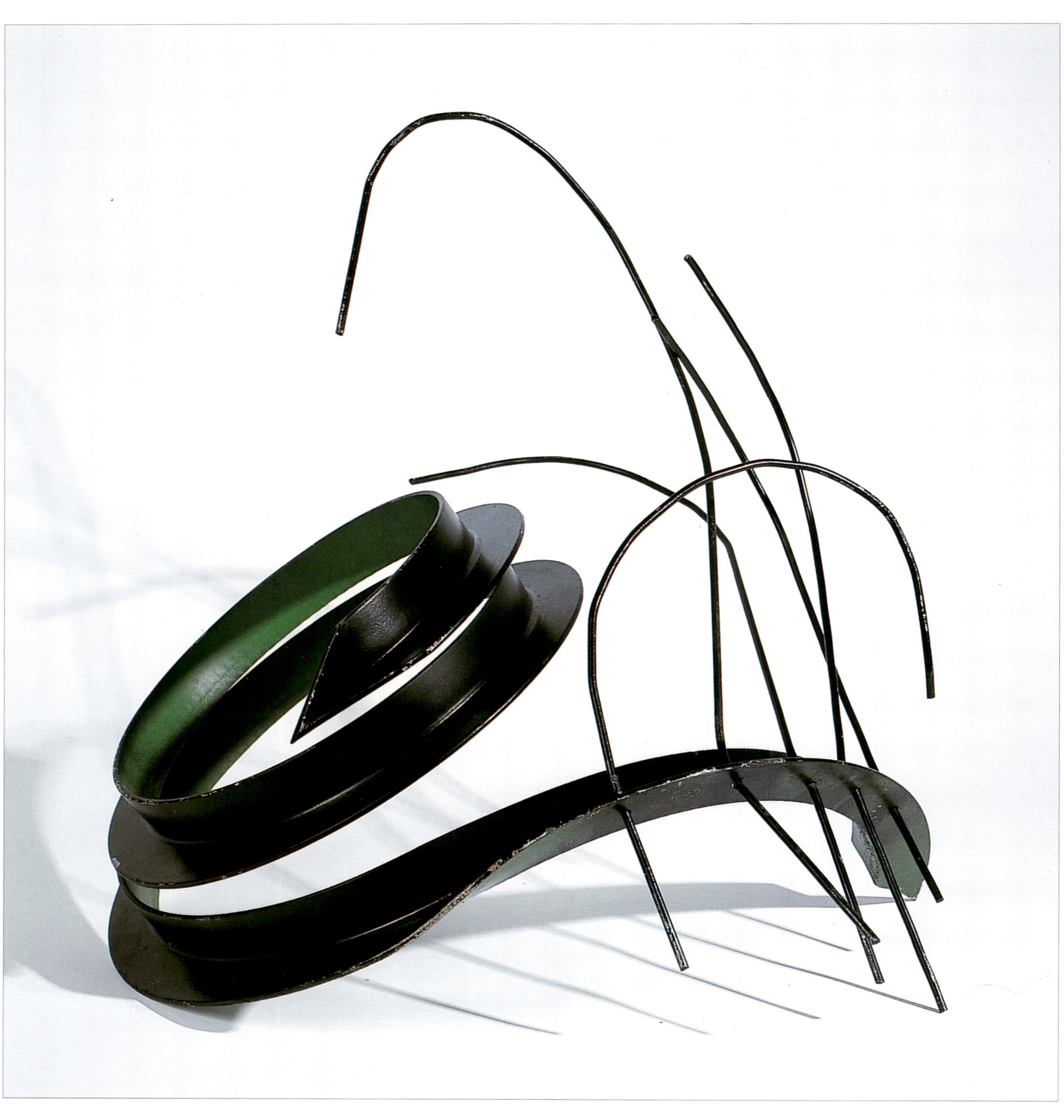

Greta G.

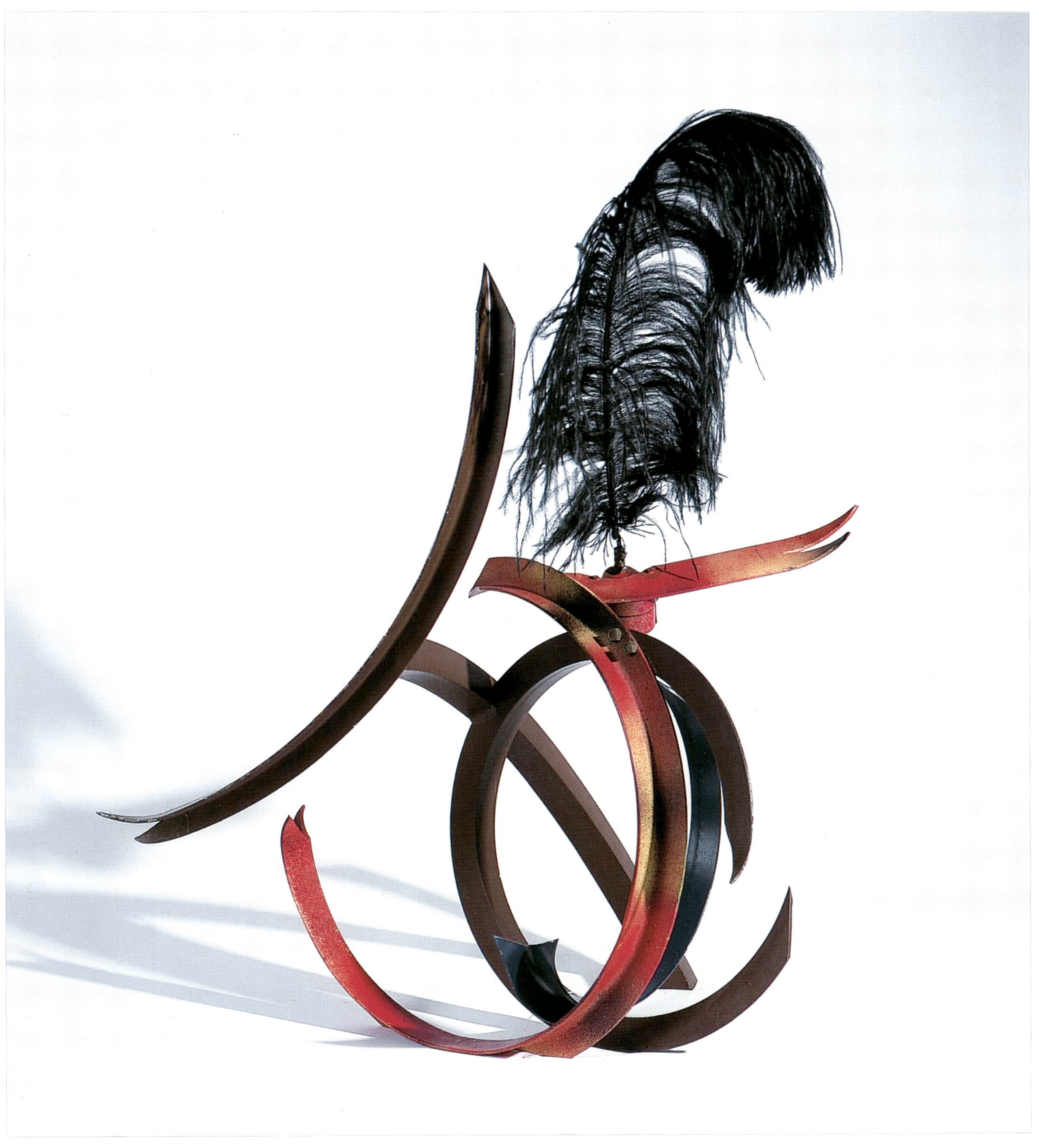

Audrey H.

HARD & SOFT

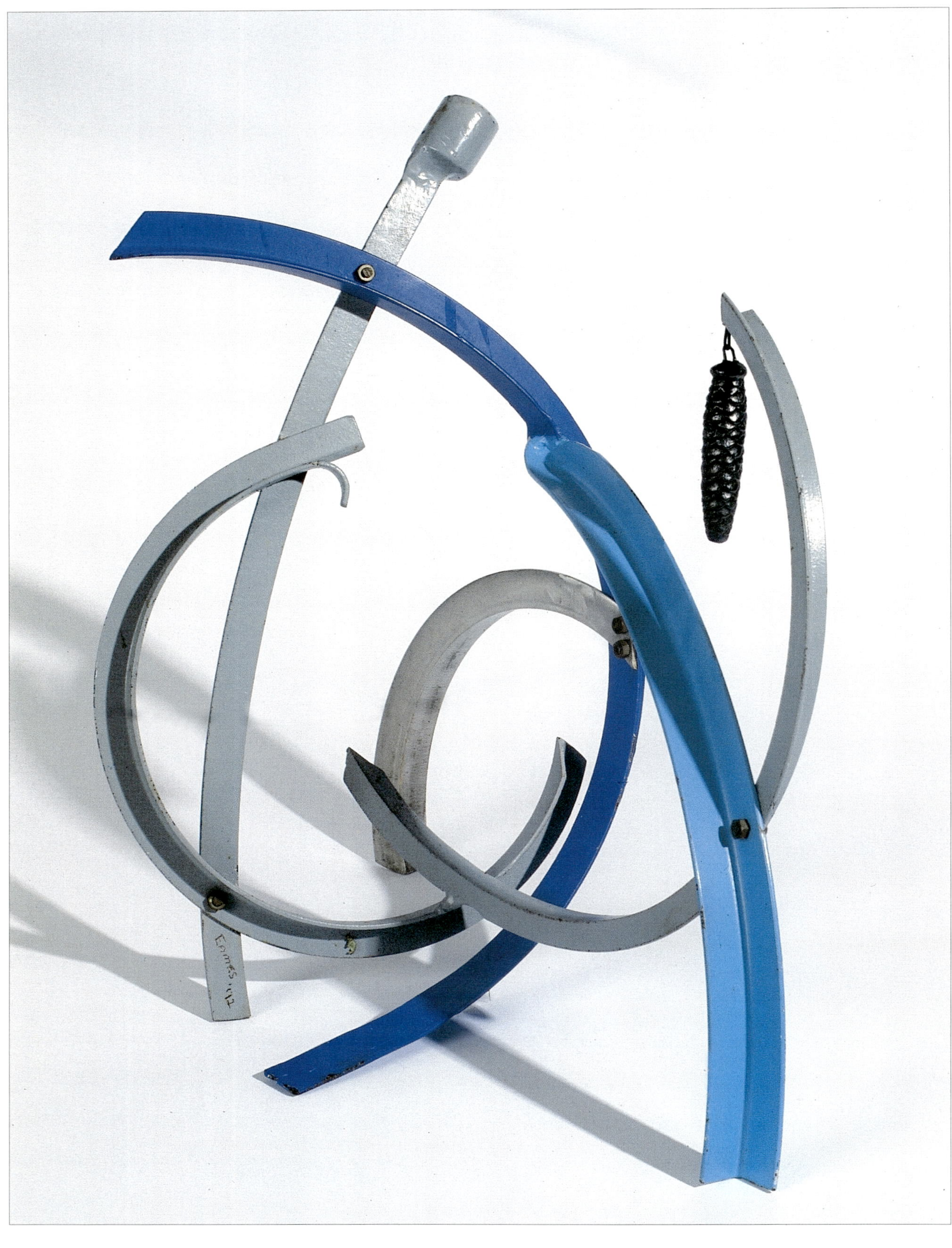

Steve M.

LES FONTAINES

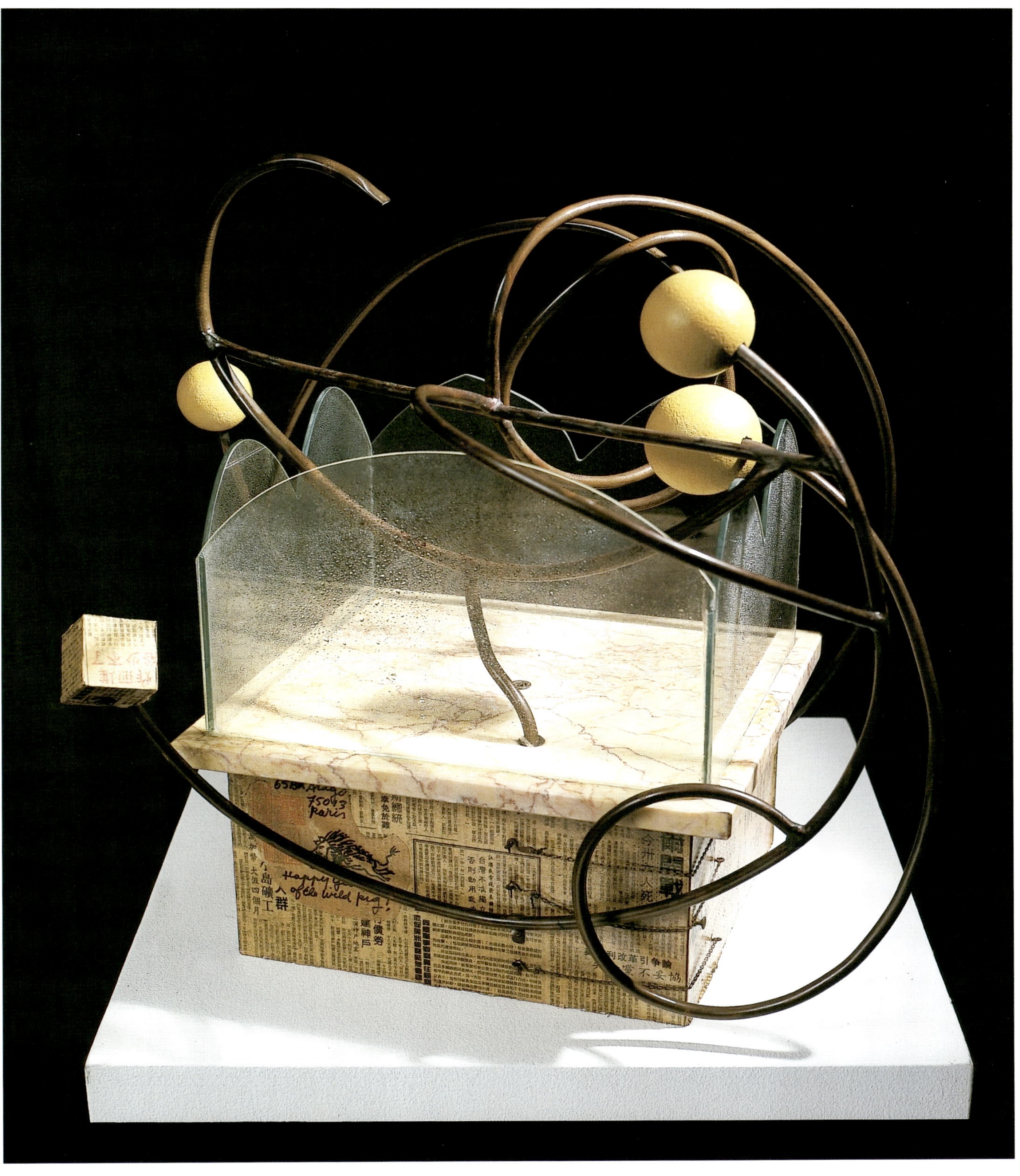

Jaune de Valence.

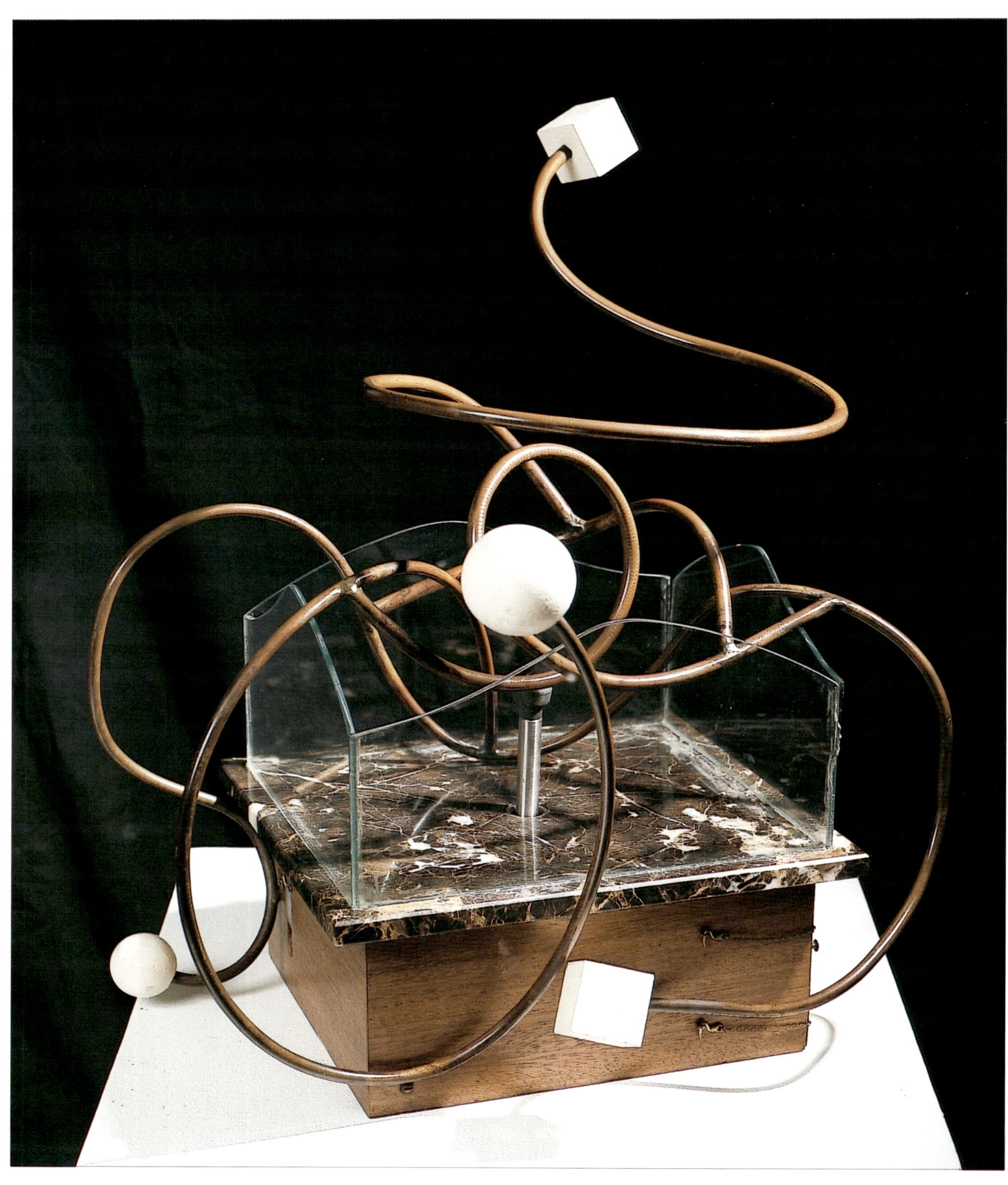

Emperador foncé.

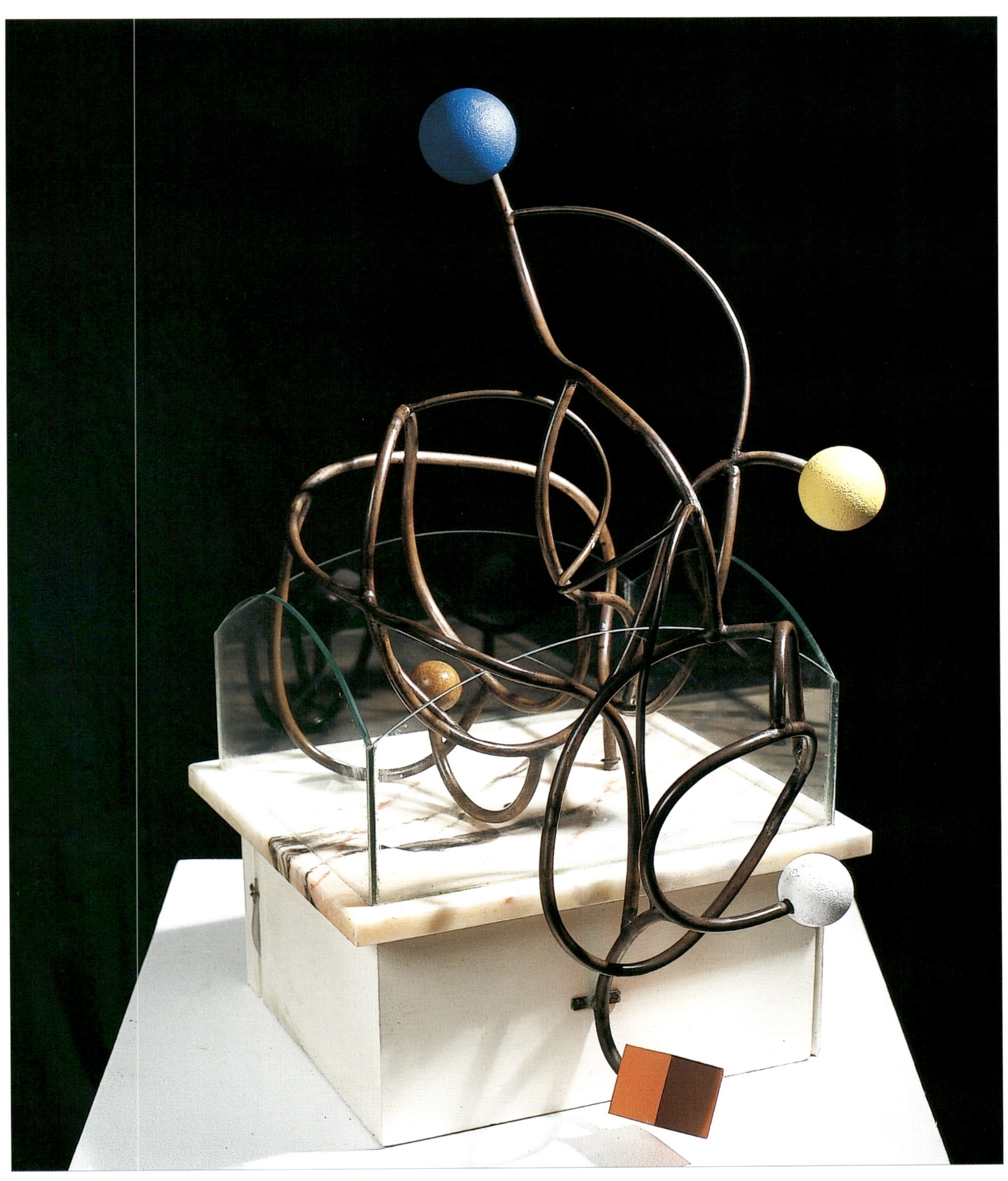

Rose veiné.

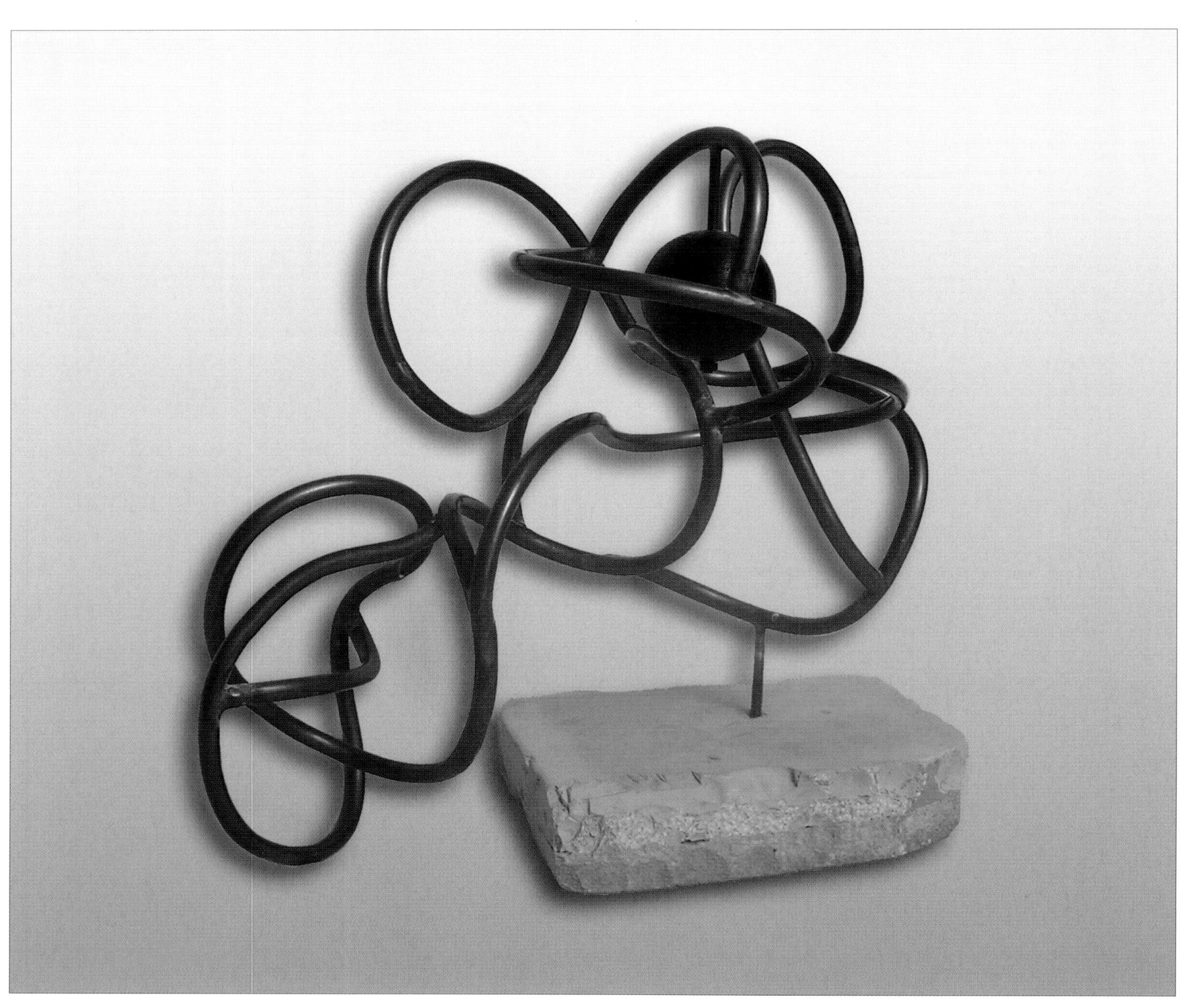

Dickon Eames' last work (untitled).

3 THE MID-ATLANTIC ARTIST

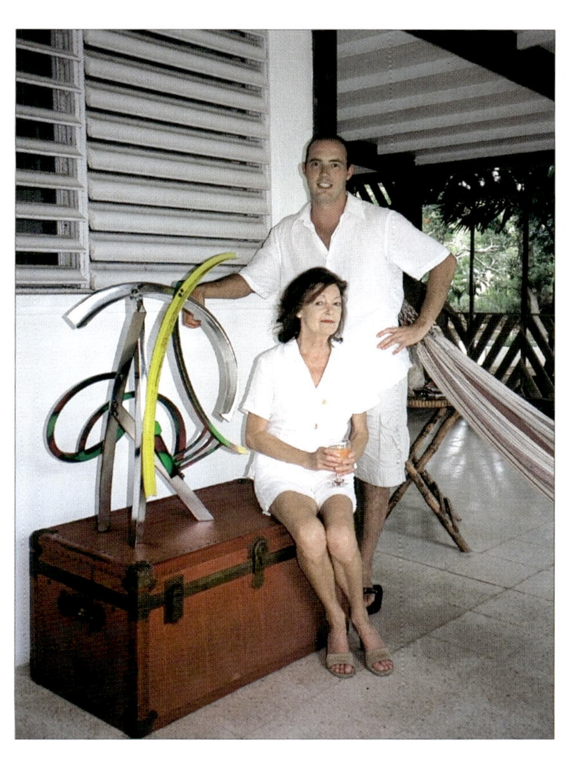

Carol and I in Puerto Rico,
with "Tribute to Humphrey B".

Today Carol lives in the Caribbean, far from the mists and the apple orchards of Normandy. But her house in the sun holds precious memories of "l'Arc en Ciel", our home in Freneuse. Whenever I am there with my mother, I like to sit at the big table that was the central feature in our Normandy kitchen. The wood has been polished to a gentle sheen by years of use, its edges softened and rounded by time. My hands run over its uneven surface. If I close my eyes my fingers can make out the names of artists and friends who have carved their signature there. I see their faces, hear their voices, and picture them sharing, each in his or her own way, exceptional moments in my parents' life.

At this table I hear once again the rise and fall of lively conversation, the clink of glasses and cutlery, the appreciative murmurs induced by my mother's excellent cooking. I hear my father's laugh and get that old feeling that all is well with the world. I remember the informal gatherings around this table - old friends, new acquaintances, neighbors who have dropped in, artists who are passing through, friends who are staying for several days. No one stands on ceremony and everyone is happy to talk or listen.

The big table is something of a visitor's book. At my father's invitation - and only at his invitation - friends might leave their mark by carving a signature into the wood. Thus our table became over the years an ever-

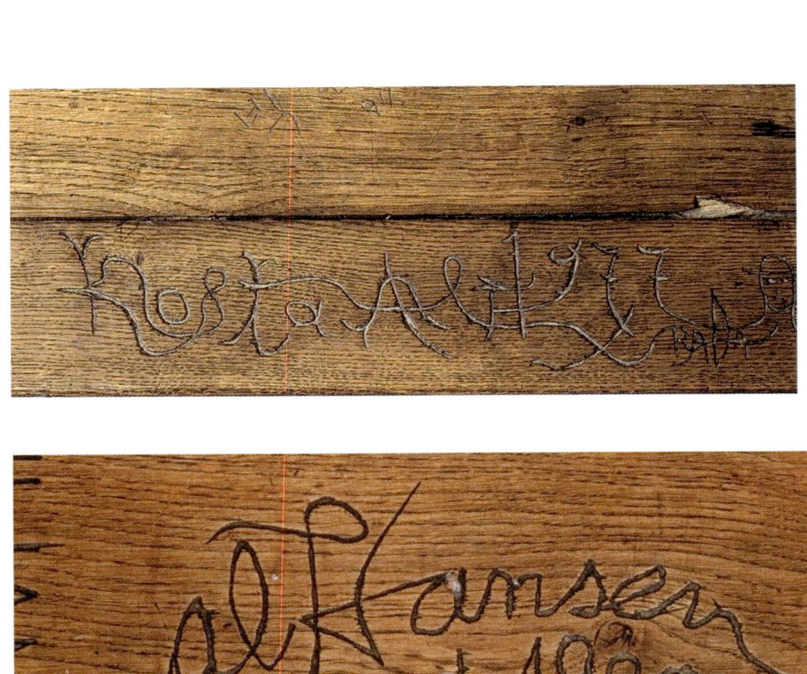
Kosta

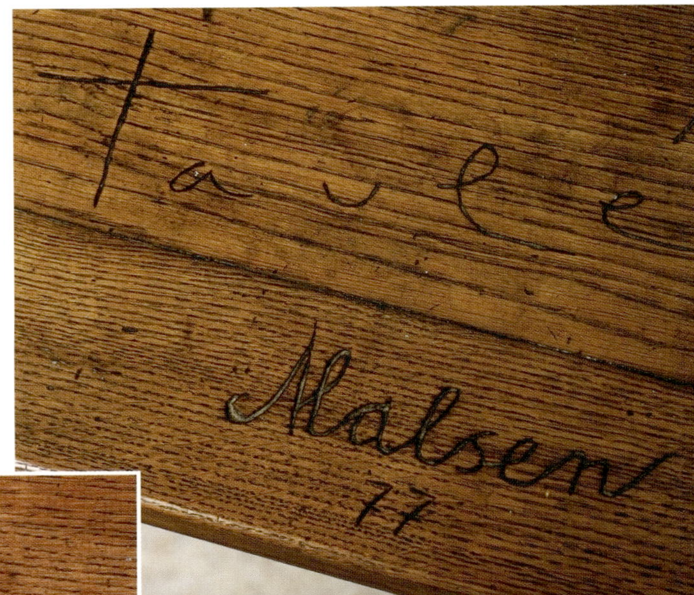
Table
Malsen
77

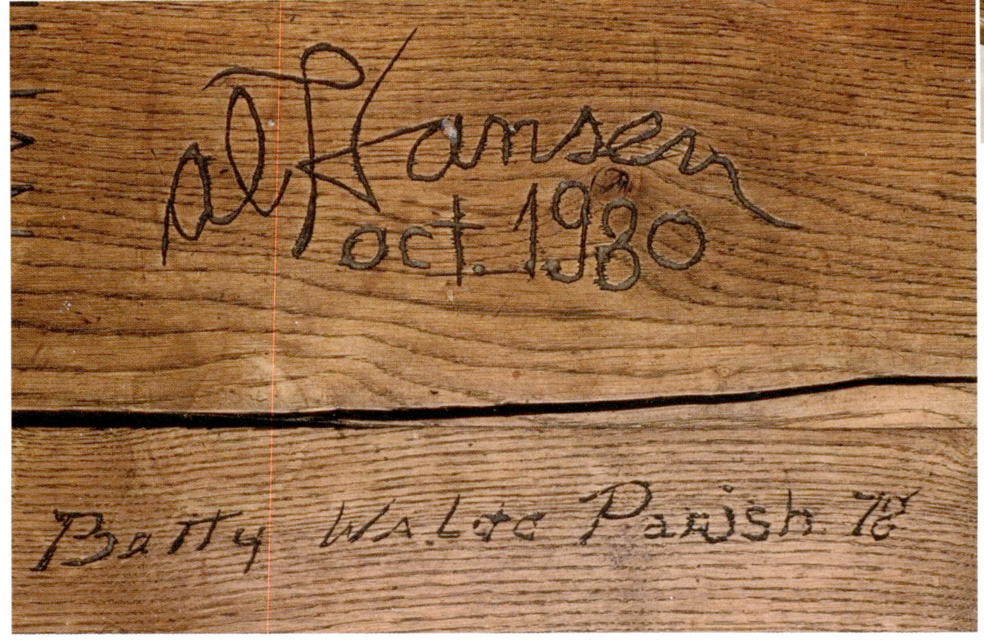
al Hansen
oct. 1980
Betty Walter Parish 76

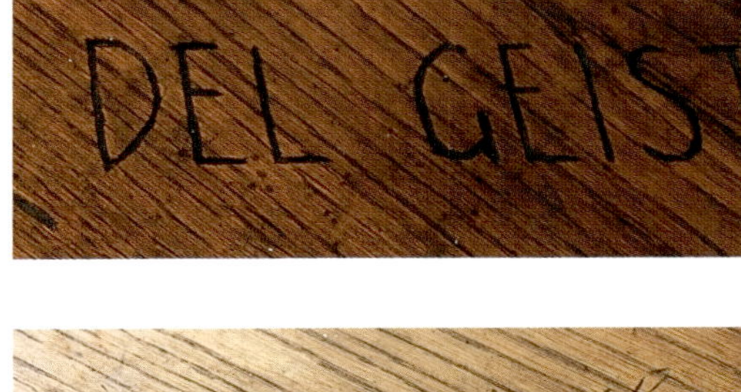
DEL GEIST

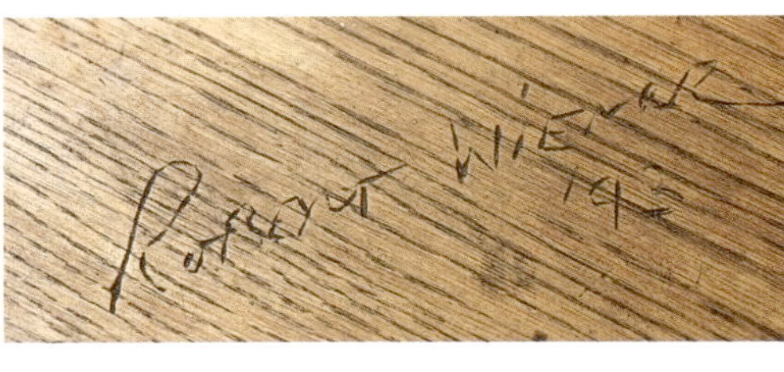

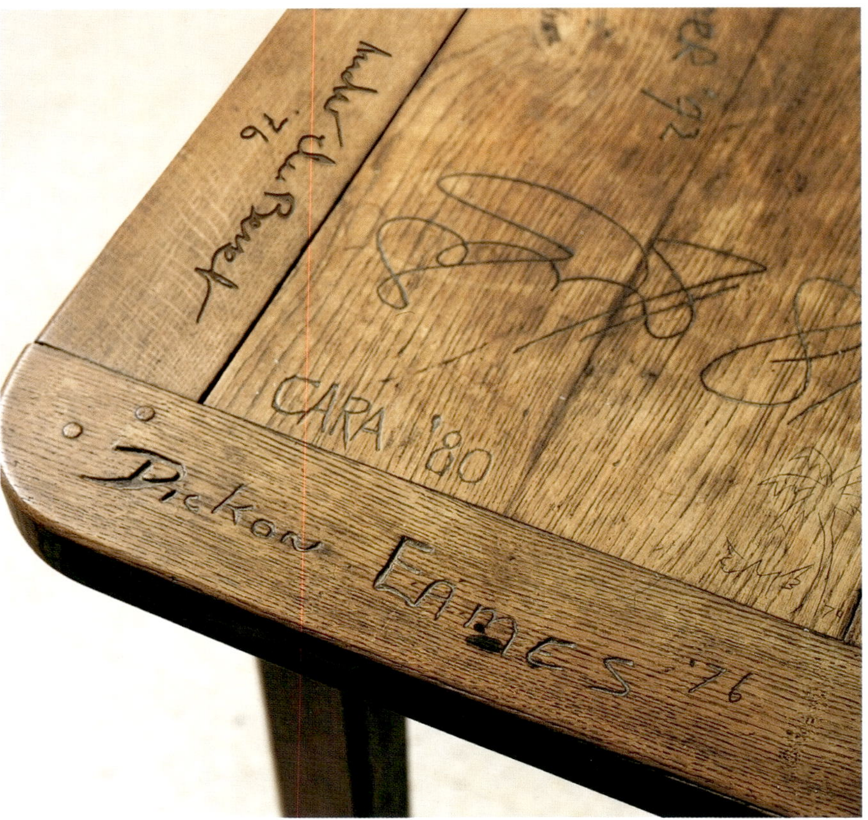
CARA '80
Dickon EAMES '76

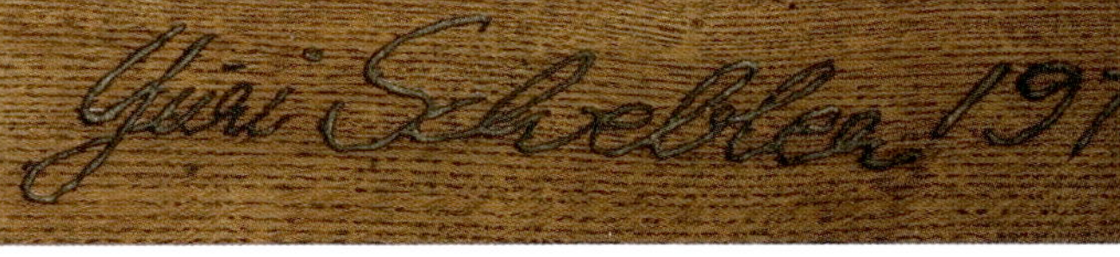

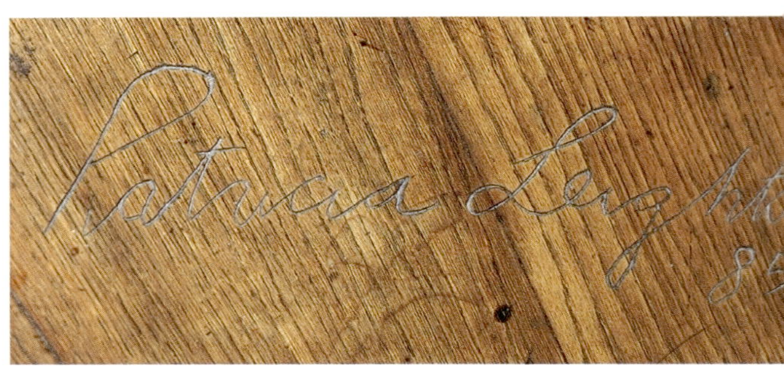

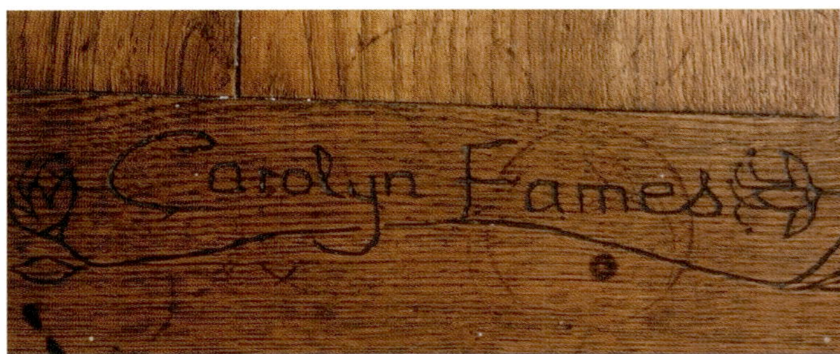
Carolyn Eames

*Dickon would ask special friends to carve
their name on the big table.
All the avant-garde of the day seems to have
passed through Freneuse-sur-Risle.*

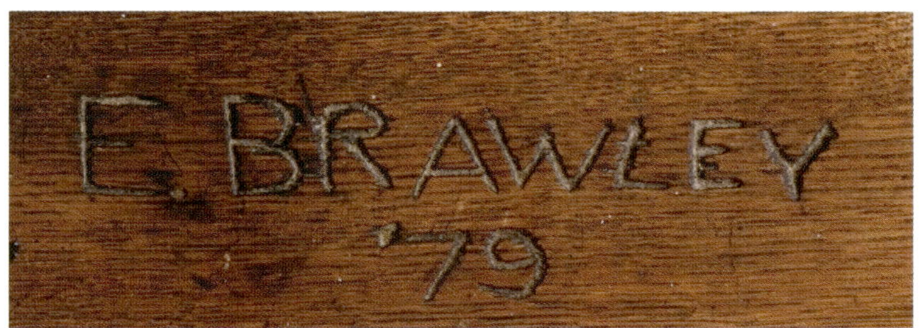

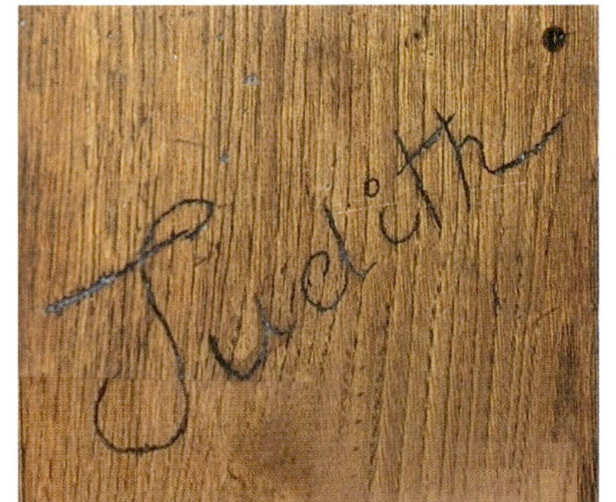

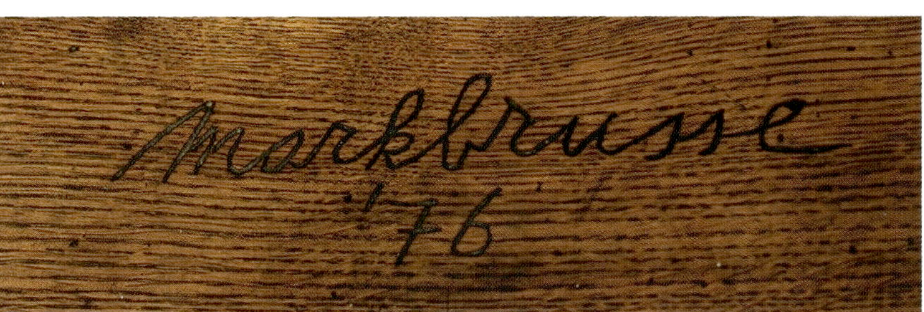

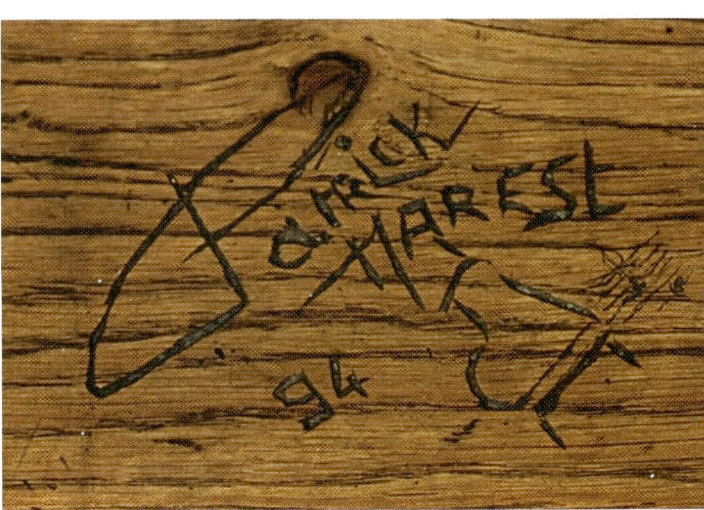

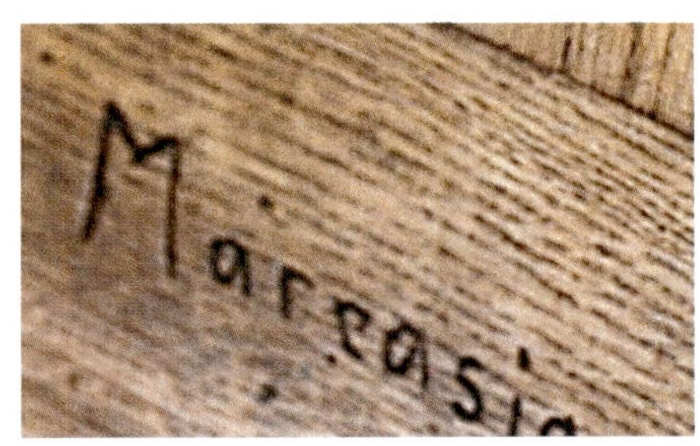

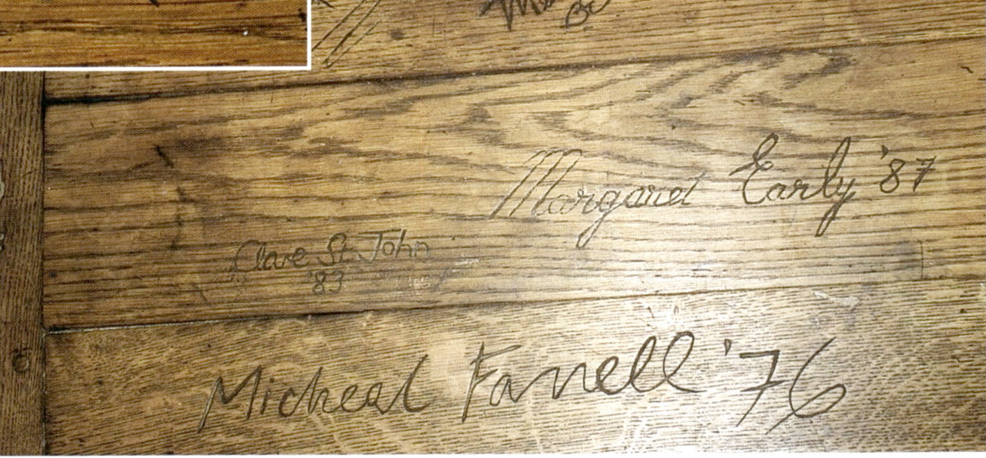

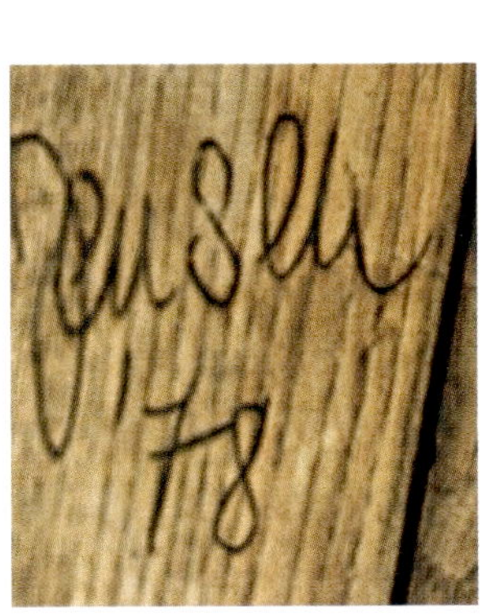

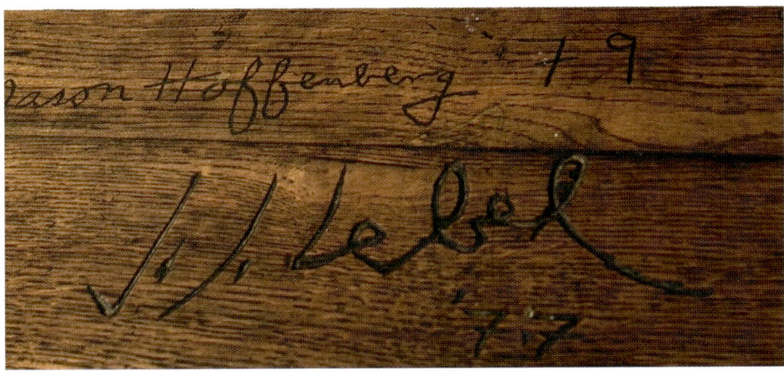

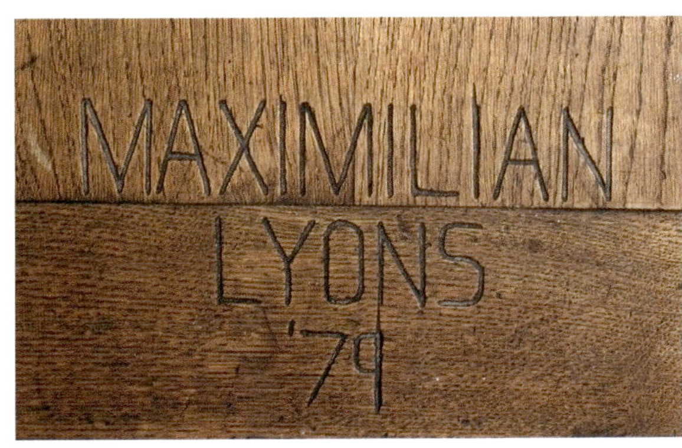

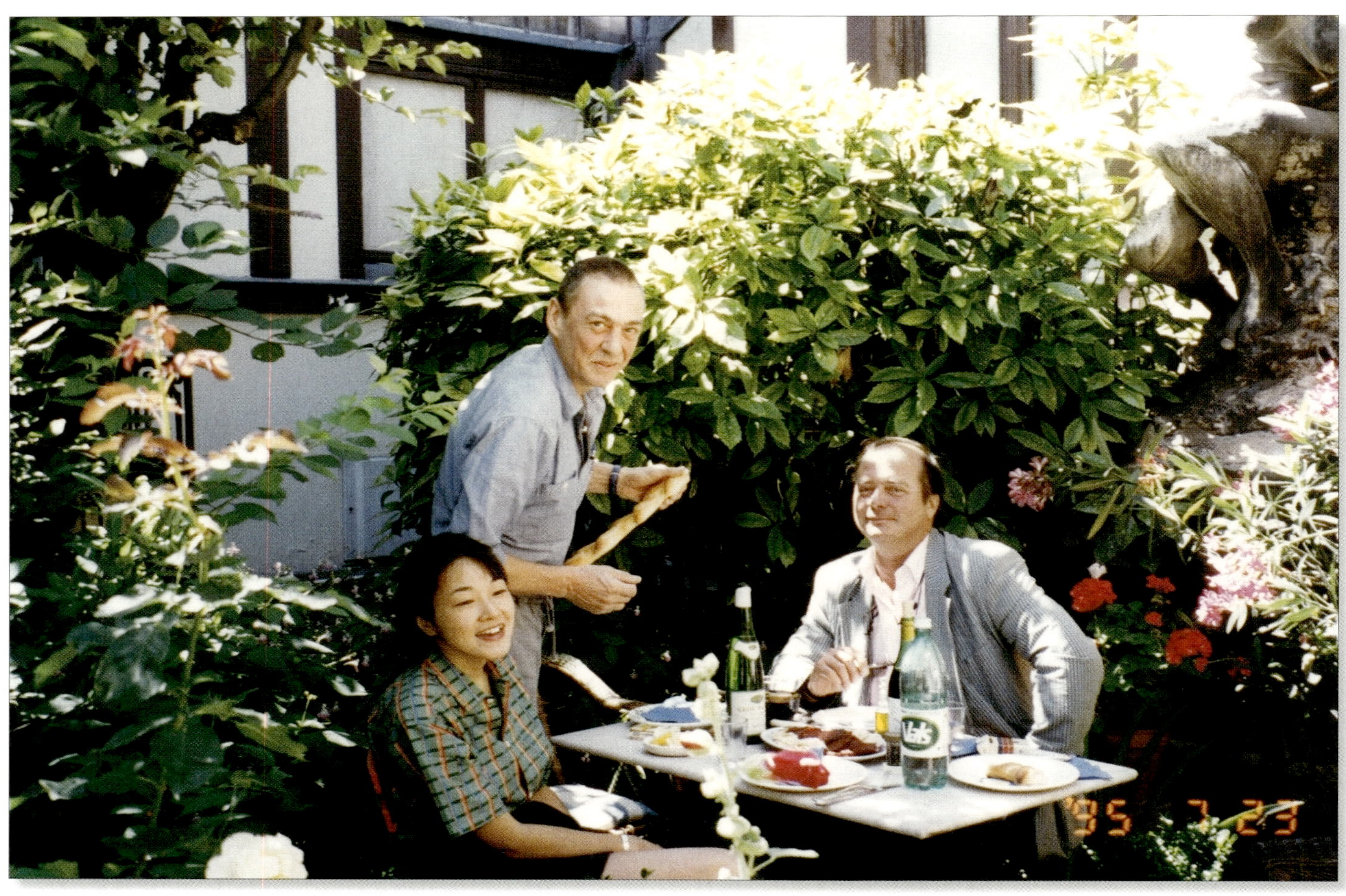

Mark Brusse and his wife, Nobuko, with Dickon in Paris.

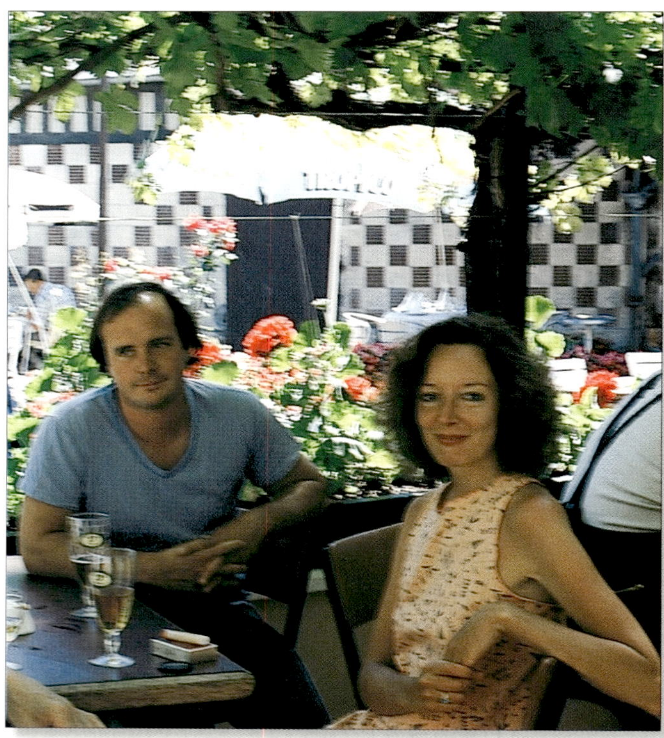

Dickon Eames with Patricia Leighton.

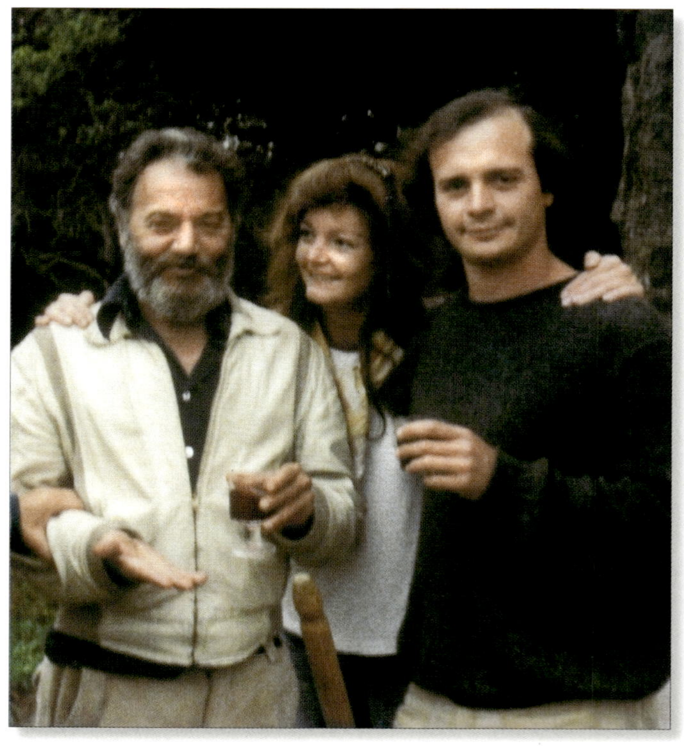

Mason Hoffenberg with Carol and Dickon Eames.
Freneuse, August 1979.

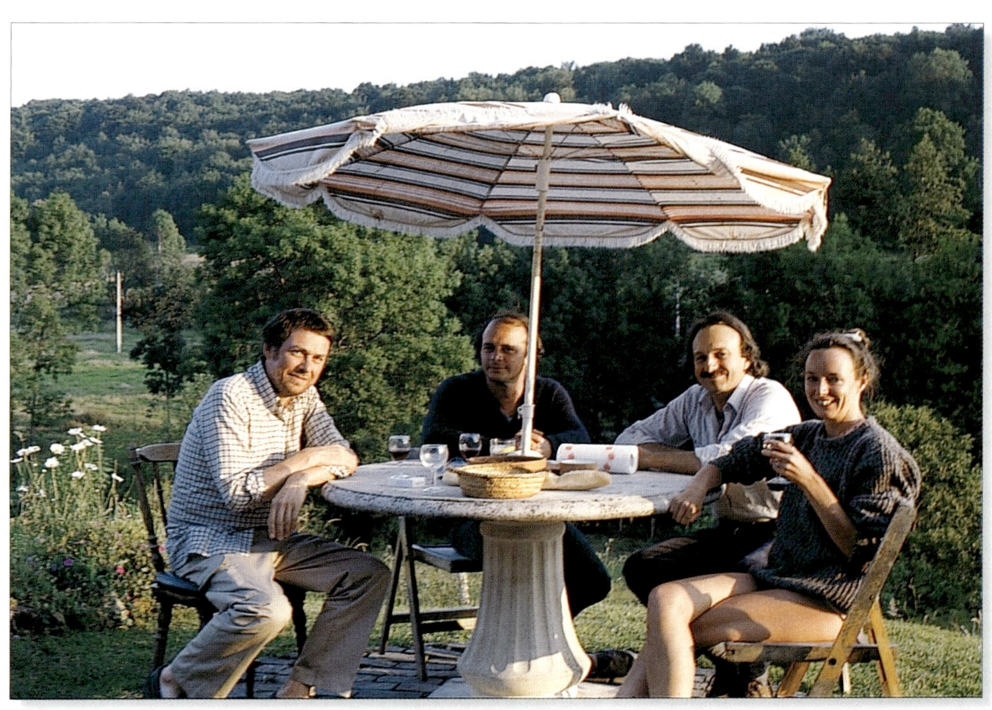

Mark Brusse, Dickon Eames, Del Geist, Patricia Leighton.

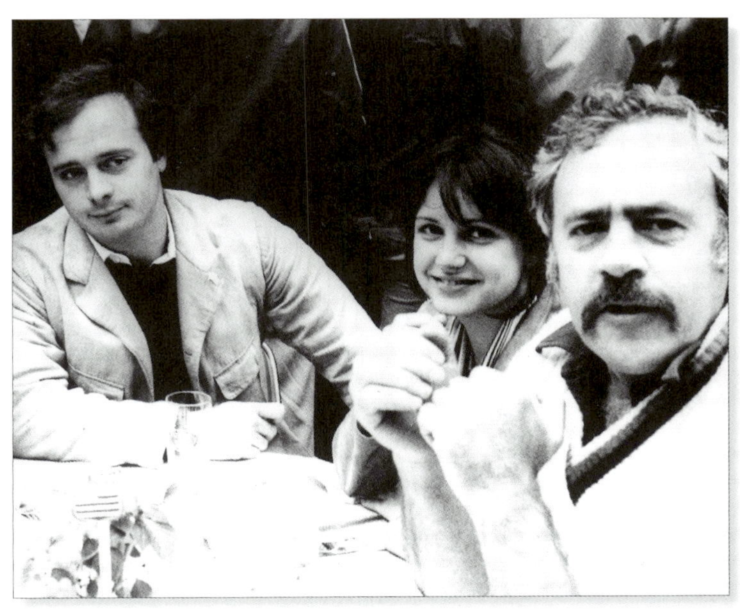

Independence Day at Mother Earth's, in Paris.
Dickon Eames with Sean O'Neil. 4 July, 1978.

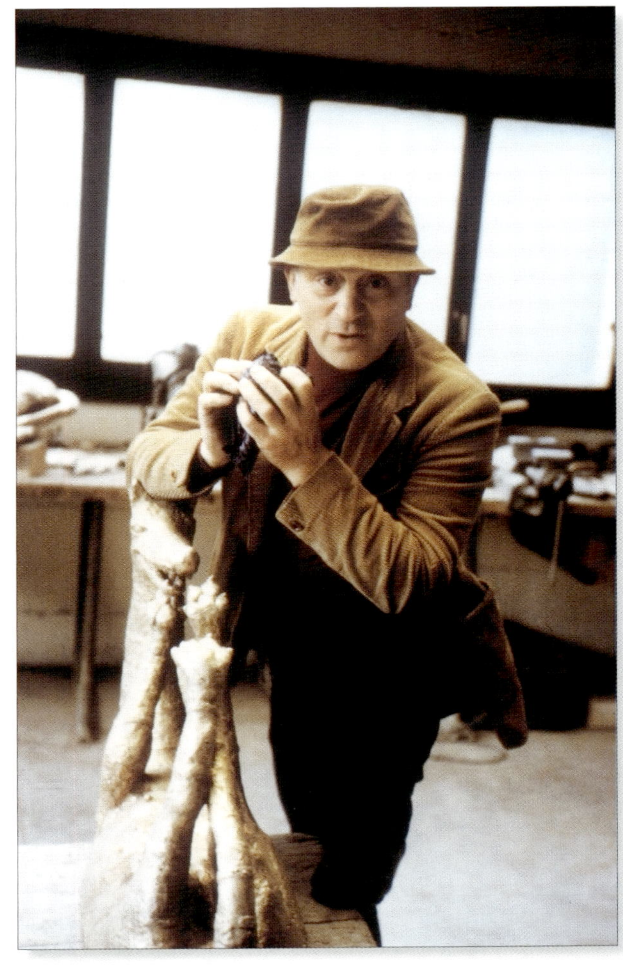

Kosta Alex, a sculptor and one of Dickon's
oldest friends. 1986.

growing testimonial to friendship and celebration. It is also a graphic record of some of the most innovative artists and intellectuals of the Seventies and Eighties.

Among the avant-garde that sat at our table, many have been kind enough to think back to this period and complement my memories with their own recollections. From our meetings and exchanges, I have been able to gather their spoken or written impressions of what my father's name means for them personally.

I asked Del Geist and his wife Patricia Leighton what memories they had of my father and his art. Del Geist was one of my father's oldest friends, while Patricia knew him for almost as long. Both are artists I greatly admire, so their contribution has a special significance for me. Their response was all I hoped for - and more. Del Geist has written:

"[…] The art climate into which Dickon was born was of the earlier Ashcan School, just then coming to a close, in the mid-1940's. That tradition was a form of social realism, which looked to the inner city for its source of inspiration. The Ashcan artists had rejected European modernism, instead stressing pathos and the underdog. The area of 14th Street, with its hustle and bustle, had become its center and the home for the Art Students League.

[…] I met Dickon in the sixties when I first arrived in New York.

[…] He was a trans-Atlantic artist (his term was mid-Atlantic). Returning to New York several times a year, to involve himself here, sometimes he brought his young son, Matthew, along. During Dickon's entire life he was surrounded by artists.

[…] We had many philosophical discussions about how to 'see' and develop sculpture. At one point Clement Greenberg, the art critic, claimed that multi-color sculpture worked against itself,

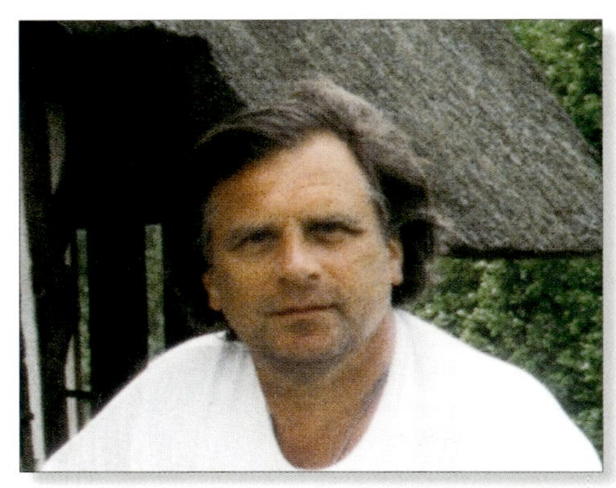

Painter and writer Jan Cremer.
Photo taken during
his stay in Freneuse.

and could not be done successfully. Dickon, with his artist's curiosity and independent nature, then developed a polychrome series, which I find to be significant and absolutely wonderful.

[…] He developed a number of distinct series, or cycles, often working on several pieces simultaneously, moving the ideas back and forth. His works with moving parts offered up words or glyphs, […] often infused with humor. His stationary steel and painted steel works could be very serious formal sculptures, which were 'of structure'. Or, sometimes alluding to a situation, or an object, they could be fantasy structures, somewhat anthropomorphic.

*It is clear that his artwork makes a significant contribution, speaking with its own unique voice. It is strong. It is clear. Dickon Eames bridged cultures, fused concepts, and then developed his own vision […]"**

Patricia Leighton, on the other hand, has provided more impressionistic memories, and her account brings to life very vividly, for me, the atmosphere of our Normandy home:

"The house was a wonderful place with echoes of the past, and bohemia.

In Normandy there was space to make art; space for Carol to breed her Dale ponies; space for Matthew to explore. We spent many happy times there filled with fun and laughter. And, of course, the inevitable heated art discussions around the infamous artist's table.

One day Dickon, Del and I went out to replenish the supply of cider and Calvados. Instead of heading towards the village we made our way to Le Bec Hellouin Abbey in the Eure. 'This is where I get my Calvados and have my best conversations,' says Dickon."

**The full version of this contribution is reproduced in the Appendix.*

I asked another important figure in my father's life, Mark Brusse, to recall as freely as possible his memories of times spent in Dickon's company. Mark is more discreet, perhaps because it is difficult to express certain feelings in words. This would appear to be the case judging by the only text he has written - to my knowledge - about my father. This letter was written in 1977.

"Some months ago, Dickon asked me to write something in the catalogue for the show at your gallery, and I really would like to do so. The only problem is that it is absolutely impossible for me to write something objective about Dickon's work. We are too close.

When I come to his farm in Normandy I always stay for about half an hour in his big studio to look at and to play with his new objects. After that, we mostly meet in the kitchen [...] and we talk about my experience of that last half hour. Those half hours are always the best half hours I can imagine. So relaxing, so happy. Well, you know what I mean 'cause otherwise you wouldn't have asked him to bring his pieces to your gallery."

But not all Dickon's friends are here to share their memories. Kosta Alex, the American sculptor of Greek origin who lived mostly in Switzerland, is no longer here to amuse us with his "men in hats", those Cycladic heads in modern guise. Maryam Ansari-Rodari, who ran the Galerie Georges Moos in Geneva, has spoken to me at length about his friendship with Dickon, dating from the Corfu days and the first exhibitions in Europe.

Another famous "signature" is that of Al Hansen, student of John Cage, leading member of the Fluxus movement and iconoclastic master of "happenings", such as the "Yoko Ono Piano Drop" from one of New York's high buildings.

Willem van Malsen, the painter and illustrator, a constant, close presence in the life of my father, has also left us.

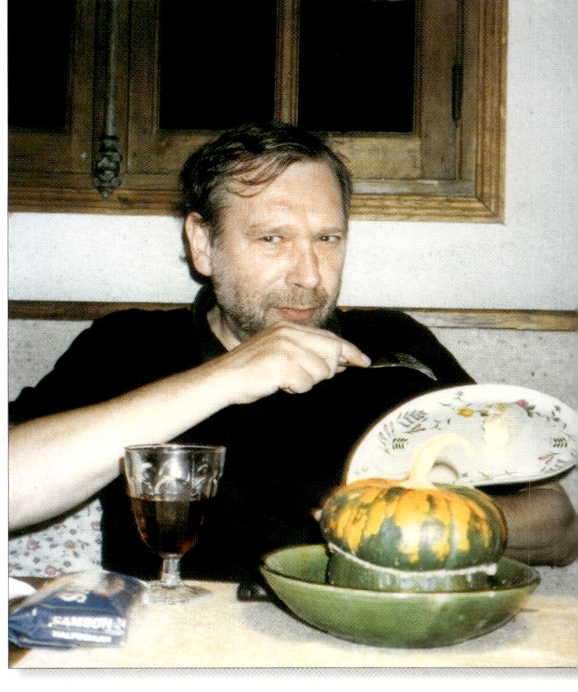

Willem van Malsen, the painter, graphic artist and illustrator, was one of Dickon Eames' close friends. Here we see him in the kitchen in Freneuse, at the famous table where he carved his name.

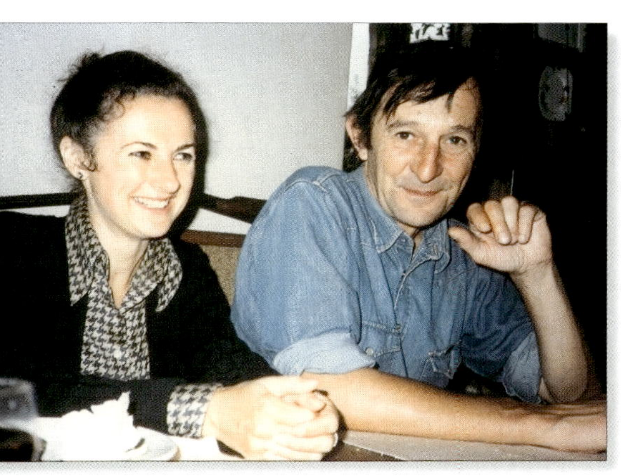

Margaret (Meg) Early
and Micheal Farrell, during one of
their trips to Freneuse,
sitting at the legendary table.

Mason Hoffenberg, who scandalized Europe when, with Terry Southern, he wrote the erotically-charged novel "Candy", went through life - and incidentally many evenings around the table in Freneuse - like a shooting star, illuminating the scene with flashes of his notorious wit.

Micheal Farrell, the Irish artist, and his wife, the artist and writer Margaret Early, also known as Meg, were close friends of my parents. I well remember going with my parents to stay at their house in the South of France one summer. Meg, who now lives part of the year in Australia, has sent me this remembrance of our friendship:

"[…] Micheal used to stay a night or two in the house in Normandy, on his way to catch the ferry to Ireland. I did this with him a couple of times too. It was on one of these occasions that I carved my signature into the famous table.

*[…] I remember the 'adult toys' Dickon made early in his life. They were like huge cages with ping pong balls inside, and they were rather wonderful. Very original and whimsical, so I think Micheal was disappointed when Dickon moved on to doing the steel sculptures … but this is a subjective approach. […]"**

The names and the memories come in a constant flow. I did not know all my parents' friends. Some of them came into our lives before I was born, or when I was very young. For example, there was Peter Woodd, who played such a large role in my father's hologram period. He remembers meeting me when I was just a small child. While I can't recall this event, I distinctly remember the fun my father had creating these mysterious pieces. I asked Peter to describe this period for me:

"[…] Dickon's work fascinated me as it was both dimensional and ironic. I introduced Dickon to Anton Furst, who was then creative director for Holoco and later creative director for Stanley Kubrick on several of his movies. Anton and Dickon became great friends.

[…] In 1981, I moved on from Holoco and launched Light Fantastic, my own hologram gallery. I continued to work with Dickon and Anton Furst and in 1982-3 we brought out a limited edition range of 8" x 10" glass plate holograms entitled 'Light Fantastic Series'. Dickon must have created some 15 to 20 designs. These were very popular and sold to other hologram galleries, museums and private collectors.

*He also created a limited edition print, entitled Red Balloon, which was a wedding present to my wife and me. […]"**

Another artist who came to Freneuse and signed the table was André du Besset. I am grateful to him for these memories and impressions:

"[…] When Dickon came back from Corfu, we would spend long evenings arguing about conceptual art, the minimalists, land art, etc. Dickon was a very sensitive artist, acutely receptive to emotions, and also very charismatic, a bon vivant who could be very funny.

*[…] He was an artist in the noblest sense: fiercely independent in his approach, passionate about contemporary sculpture, but refusing to be part of any movement or trend. He had an innate gravity, and an innate playfulness. As I see it, all his work is a marvelous play on the concept of gravity and gravitation: everything that goes up must come down. That's what struck me about his work, for example his Ping Pong Ball Machine. […]"**

The Glaizot family are also an inseparable part of Dickon's story. Their familiar presence, warm hospitality and unfailing friendship have played a major role in our lives, and perhaps even more so in mine. It is true that among my parents' friends, I especially remember those who had children of my age or thereabouts. For example, our "Franco-American" friends Anthony and Liliane Stone were often in Freneuse, where Liliane's family had their own weekend home. The

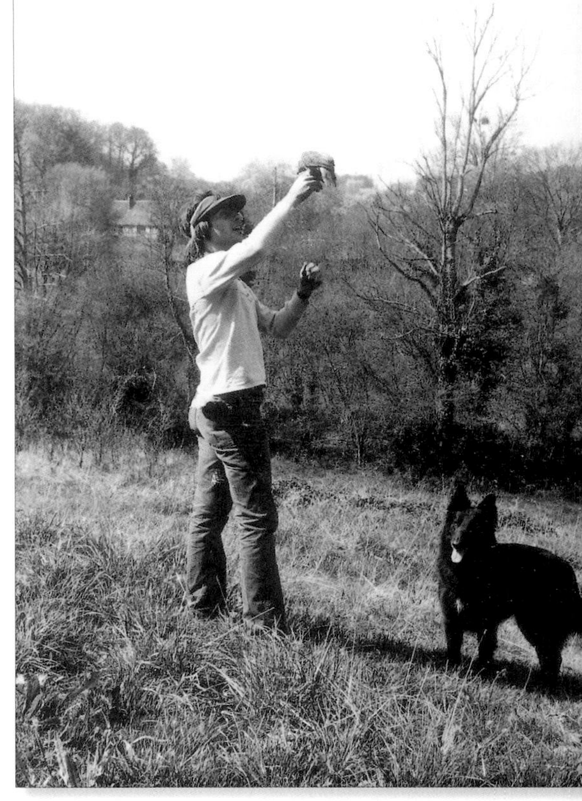

André du Besset playing with his parrot Rocco on the lawn in Freneuse while one of Dickon's dogs keeps watch.

Glaizot family, the Stone family, the American journalist Robert Wiener and his wife Elaine ... they have all shared moments with my parents that are rich in emotion. The lines they have written for me are affectionate testimonies:

*"As a friend and neighbor, Dickon was a very vibrant presence, and his way of looking at life made a big impression on our family. [...] When you look at his work you get a feeling of freedom and independence."**

Henri Glaizot, Paris

"[...] Although Dickon and his family lived in a secluded place, their many friends and admirers were always welcome, and, as far as I could judge, made much of the Eames' hospitality. Since my family and I would usually drive to Normandy most weekends of the year, I would often drop by for a drink or a chat and never failed to meet up with an international mixture from every social class imaginable: from royals to tramps, from movie stars to scientists, Carol and Dickon would be entertaining them with great ease. But - and this was another fascinating side of Dickon - he could always (whether tired of the crowd, or because he had an inspiration, I do not know) suddenly disappear into his workshop and fully concentrate on his latest work of art.

*It was a blow to me and my family to suddenly lose such a fine friend."**

Anthony Stone, Berlin.

"Dickon Eames was my buddy from the mid-seventies when we first met in Paris until his premature death at the age of 52.

[...] In the spring of 1975, after I returned from covering the end of the Vietnam war, I headed for Normandy where Dickon and Carol opened their home and their hearts to me. It was neither the first nor the last time this kindness was extended, but after the traumatic experience of Vietnam, I needed

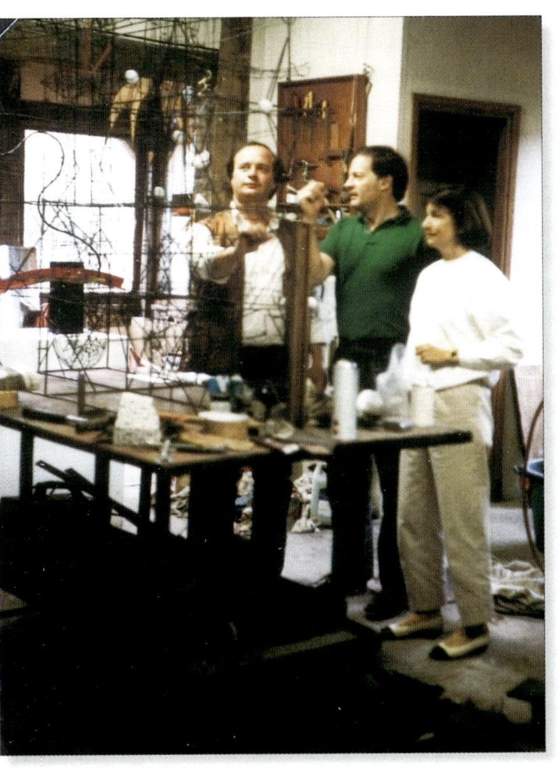

Our friends and neighbors,
Liliane and Anthony Stone,
in Dickon's studio.

a quiet place to unwind, take stock, and put pen to paper.

[…] I still visit Normandy from time to time and when I do, I think about the old days. The simple thought of Dickon brings a special feeling to my heart. It is nice to be remembered so fondly."

Robert Wiener, Paris

The painter Peter Marcasiano, long-time friend of Dickon and loving father of little Colombe, has also departed. Denise Marcasiano has recalled for me the trips to Corfu, the stays in Freneuse, the Paris vernissages. In the text that Dickon wrote for the catalogue of the exhibition "To fly - a dream" at the Museum der Stadt in Recklinghausen, my father gives pride of place to the views of his very good friend:

"Paris, spring 1977. Peter Marcasiano and I were walking along the quais of the Seine among the stands selling flowers and livestock. I was checking out the roosters. I needed a new rooster for my hens because the old one died last winter. Peter fancied a Rhode Island Red but I preferred a beautiful, very colorful one, which I bought. We put the rooster in a box and went to a bistrot for a drink. I told Peter about the work I was doing, how I would be taking part in an exhibition at the Ruhr Festival in Recklinghausen. I told him they expected me to produce a text for the catalogue and that I hadn't the faintest idea what to write. When you are totally immersed in your work as I am right now, you don't have the necessary distance to write about it. 'Yes,' said Peter, 'but that kind of text is very important, because an exhibition is like a stage play: it's not just the individual players but a complete work.'

I told Peter that the exhibition was called 'To fly - a dream', a theme I've been working on for some time.

'To fly,' said Peter, 'is to seek endless expansion, to surpass yourself. The Faustian man. The Germans must love this theme because they are so very Faustian. You should talk about Christ,

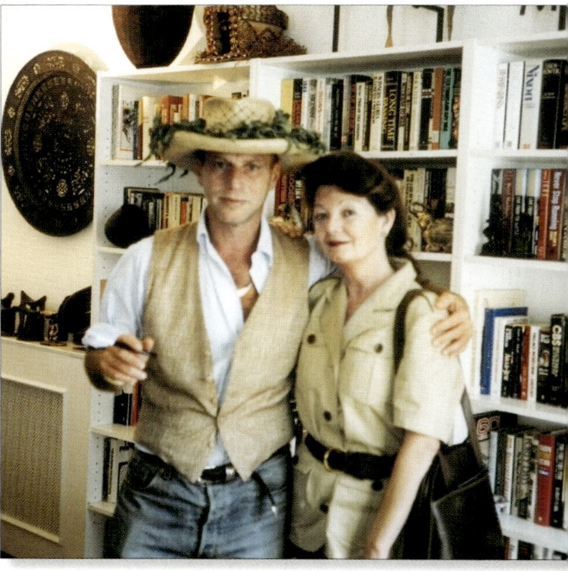

Carol with Robert Wiener, the well-known journalist and war correspondent.

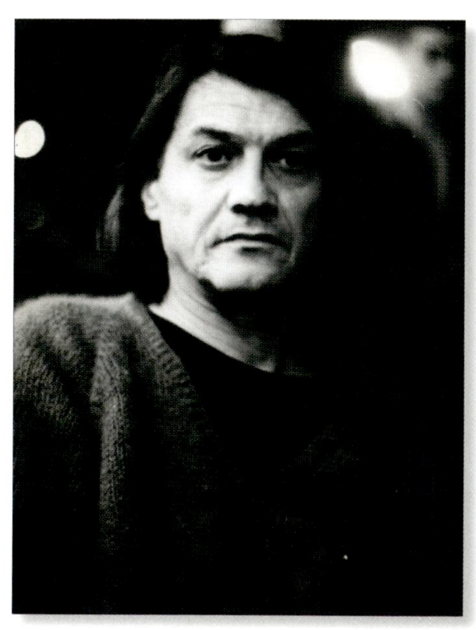

Peter Marcasiano, a very close friend, quoted at length by Dickon in a text written for the catalogue of the exhibition "To fly - a dream".

the bird, the Apollonian dream. It is important to say that your flying machines are not meant for flying. I mean the finality of art is not to fall into the trap of creating useful objects. Art should exist only to express our most secret longings. The Apollonian dream is to float up into infinity. Look at your balloons! They are flying objects that suggest this dream, this dream of flying into infinity. You must read Nietzsche: Apollo is the embodiment of the dream of flying. Dionysos is the juice that flows from the earth, the practical man. Put the Apollonian and the Dionysiac together and what do you get? The Faustian, with his link to the infinite, do you see?' I nodded - which seemed to me at the time the most intelligent reply I could give. 'You have to write something that instantly captivates the reader,' said Peter. 'You have to think of something fantastic - for instance that you dreamed you couldn't buy anything with money anymore. I hope you'll get an idea like that for your text.' We got up and continued walking along the river, Peter, myself and the rooster."

Finally, I tracked down the author of an article on Dickon Eames that appeared in the 1999 edition of the Bénézit Dictionary of Artists. Behind the initials "C.D." I found Christophe Dorny, editor-in-chief of this famous reference work. When I told him about my project, he agreed very readily to discuss my father's work from an art critic's viewpoint. His contribution is, in my opinion, a first important step in the furtherance of my project, which is to give the work of Dickon Eames its rightful place in contemporary art and art history. So I think it is very fitting that he should have the last word in this book.

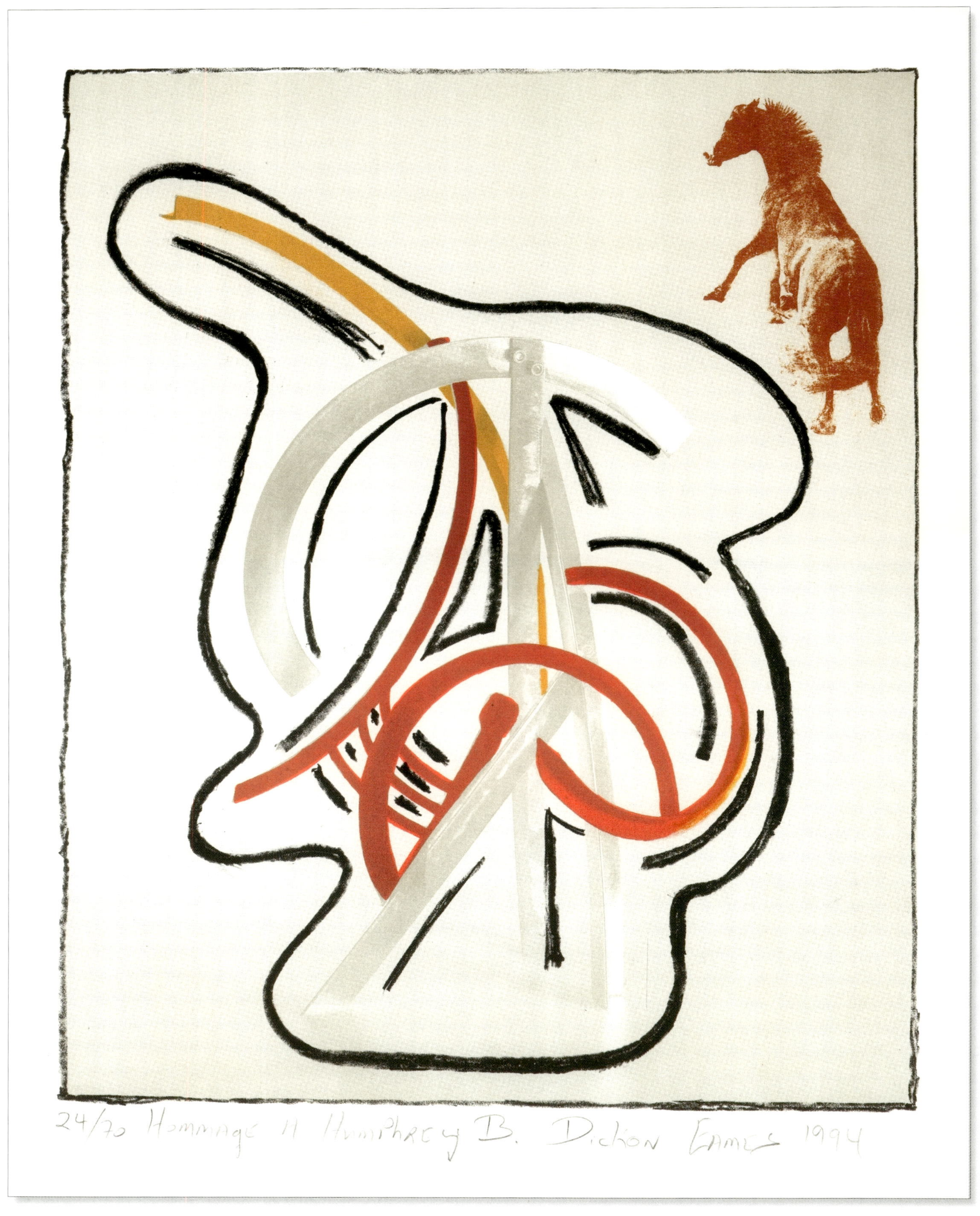

In the same lithograph, Dickon Eames brings together his reportedly favorite sculpture,
"Humphrey B" and his favorite horse, the stallion Star.

DICKON EAMES,
ENGINEER OF DREAMS

by Christophe Dorny

As a contributor to several special-ized publications and more especially to the Bénézit Dictionary of Artists, it has been my habit to make the rounds of the Paris galleries. I came across the work of Eames in 1992-1993 at the Galerie Riedel. I recall my keen interest in the "Série Grise" sculptures and my determination to include Dickon Eames in the next edition of the dictionary, due to appear in 1999. I sat down and wrote a corresponding entry that was inevitably incomplete since I had little information to draw on - only a couple of exhibition catalogues. I clearly remember writing that entry - which, I confess, cannot be said for all the many entries I have written - and taking home the catalogues rather than filing them. I had done what I intended, for one of the important aspects of this independent dictionary is to contribute to the recognition of an artist's work, regardless of current trends and market conditions. The Bénézit is a source of information for art lovers and historians, who can, in this way, come across the names of artists such as Eames and find a written record of given moments in the history of art.

My involvement with the dictionary has given me the opportunity, some ten years later, to look more deeply into the work of Dickon Eames. It has been exciting to explore its sources, stages and periods. I sensed it before, but now the multiplicity of this artist's vision is patently evident. His "Série Grise", described in the Bénézit, allowed me to deduce some specific characteristics, such as his preoccupation with structure. Today, a broader view of his output has allowed me to trace a direction, then another, and another - revealed, for example, through his subtle sense of humor, his attachment to color, his fascination for scale.

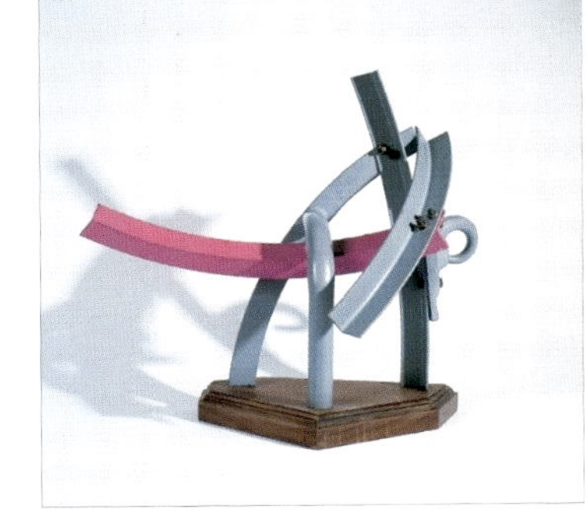

One discovers an original, inventive, cultured approach that reflects a way of being and of seeing the world. It is a pleasure I would like to share.

The earliest works of Dickon Eames were small mechanisms, intriguing yet basically simple: flying machines, mechanical birds and maze-like structures containing balls or marbles. Some of them could be set in motion by delicately turning a crank handle. Then followed a period when Eames' sculptures took on a silent, still quality, like fragments of strange machinery.

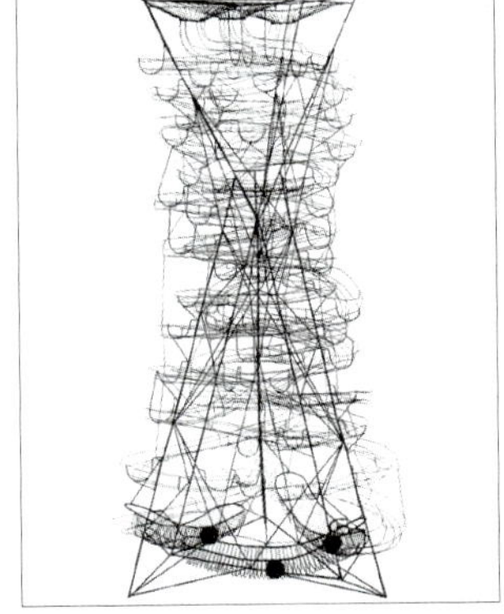

Operating outside the breakaway movements of the 70's - notably minimal and conceptual art - Eames drew on a constructive dynamic expressed through the use of metal and a fascination for machinery and rudimentary mechanics. Having shaken off the shackles of formalist dogma, the 80's was a fertile period for the plastic arts, which undoubtedly helped promote recognition of Eames' work. He had regular shows during this decade.

MACHINES THAT RECONSTRUCT REALITY

Leonardo da Vinci's flying machines were a fusion of man and artist, invention and fantasy. The machines and mechanisms of the modern world, having evolved into objects of civilization, radically transformed these relationships. They influenced all the major artistic currents of the 20th century. They inspired new visions - of magicians and demons, of instruments of progress, of esthetic renewal. They also gave sculptors, from Tinguely to Panamarenko, a means of departing from the traditional artistic canons. They were a recurrent theme of major international exhibitions: The Machine as seen at the end of the Mechanical Age at the Museum of Modern Art in New York, 1967-1968, was a seminal event.

Now let us look at machines in the creative universe of Dickon Eames. His machines are not meant to replace man. They are not finite, independent entities. Eames rejects the role of demi-god or Prometheus. He leaves it to us, as spectators, to use these "machines for seeing"

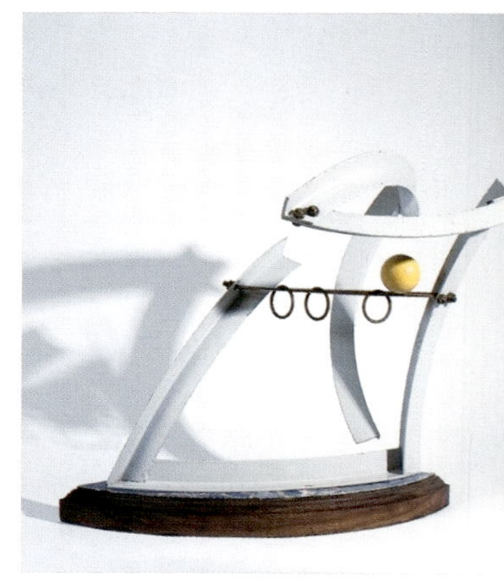

differently, as a simple extension of ourselves. In his visual approach, Eames also reveals his attraction to surrealism. Not for its darker side or its ability to create a sense of unease. Quite the reverse: the artist offers us a dreamlike fantasy world touched with a poetic candor, in the surrealistic vein of Joseph Cornell, for example, to whom he dedicated one of his sculptures "enclosing" a few objects, in the manner of the famous boxes of this American artist.

Eames engages a balance all his own - a balance that combines his attraction for construction, for simple mechanical movements like a crank, the physical act of building and the artistic process. Therein lies the challenge - exacting, playful, modest. We are in a world of metal, angle irons, welding, nuts, bolts, and air. Air, because the present instant seems forever suspended, like his flying machines, in a perpetual movement of transfer. Invisible streams of energy, or the reassuring liquidity of water (the "Fountains

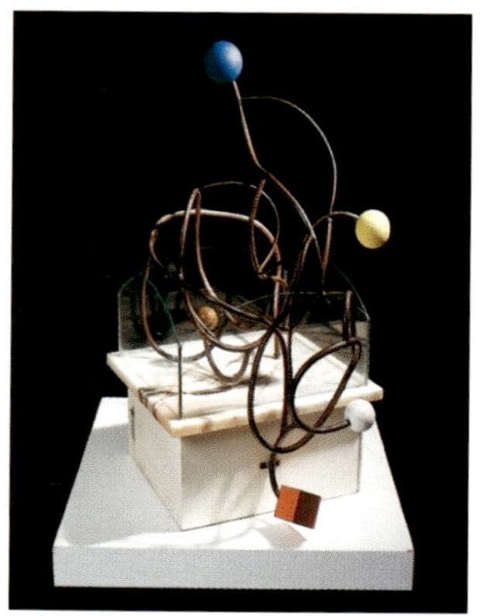

Series"), flow through axles, tubes and pipes. You might call it life itself.

Eames the artist, like an engineer of dreams, shows us how another reality can be constructed through the scale of his inventions, the humor that pervades them, and the artisanal process that created them. The fact that his approach is never subordinated to a theory, category or convention is part of its appeal.

A QUESTION OF SCALE

The physical aspect of our relationship with Eames' work is singular too. Unlike monumental pieces that impose their presence on the viewer, the scale of Eames' work goes from the all-but miniature to pieces that, with few exceptions, are no more than a meter high.

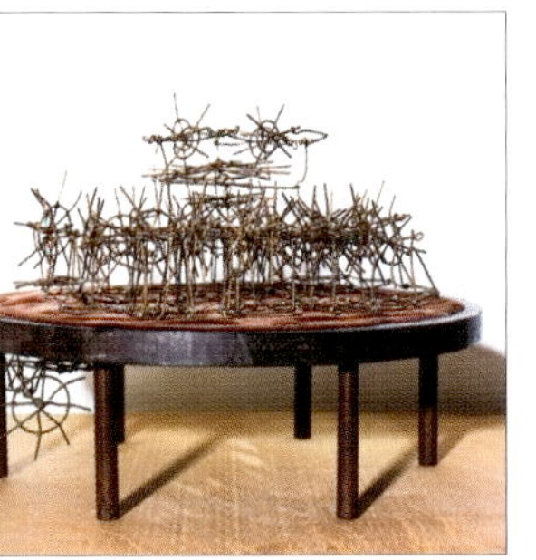

What happens to a sculpture when viewed on this small scale? Does it become an object, an objet d'art? What about this little wire mannikin? Is it a sculpture? And this miniature table, with its wheels and propellers? And this warrior - a statuette? Because they are fragile, we are not inclined to touch them. These works immediately create a distance around themselves.

And because they are also mechanical devices and machines, we tend to see these sculptures as some kind of model or maquette. But Eames' pieces never lock the spectator into a set pattern of thinking or seeing. They trigger an almost unconscious back-and-forth movement to other scales and dimensions. We are free to translate them, if we wish, into a vision of the monumental, and several pieces invite us to do so: for instance the sculptures of the 80's and the "Fountains Series" (1994). But just when we have decided that they are models, these small-scale fountains suddenly become real fountains spurting real water!

The size of his other metal sculptures, usually 70 to 80 centimeters in height, generates another form of resistance. They are too large to be picked up and held, yet they seem not entirely external to the spectator, nor do they ever overwhelm. It is a deliberately chosen distance that encourages a dialogue between equals, a circumspect exploration, a delicacy of approach.

Few contemporary sculptors have explored, as Eames did, the miniature - a dimension often relegated to the rank of cottage and folk art. Such are the boundaries of artistic recognition, which fortunately are constantly evolving. Since Eames' creations invite us to apprehend them by minute observation, by "bending over" them, they challenge our customary way of seeing. This is also true of the hologram, a technique little used by contemporary artists, and which Eames adopted with success.

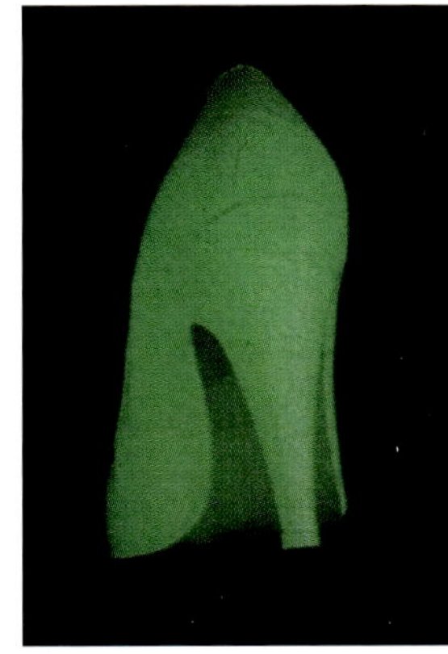

THE FUN OF FABRICATING

These machines/objects, mechanisms, sculptures - to use the titles given them in certain catalogues - these imaginary prototypes owe their existence first of all to the pure pleasure of fabricating - because Eames is "handy" in the everyday sense of the word. He uses poor or commonplace materials -

often reclaimed from the scrapyard - leaving their joints and seams clearly visible. A few strands of wire become human figures, strips of welded brass pivot on their hinges, a few bolts and screws set the tone for these constructions. Mechanical in aspect, they are nevertheless built by hand, and in the series using manufactured pieces they make no secret of their original source and function.

If there is a link with tradition (but not in the conservative sense) it goes counter-current to our culture of mass production, reflecting the chain of transmission between hand, tool and result. It is clearly not the artist's aim to achieve the "well-made", the finely crafted. Eames is not interested in what technology has to offer, especially in his early pieces: what matters is the gesture, the impulse, the raw energy. The derisory simplicity of his mechanisms turns them into a primal, fundamental experience. And this vital energy is not to be lost, as we see in the sculpture series of the 80's. More focussed on structure, they reestablish the balance between machine and man, machine and reality. A pulley, or perhaps a hook, breaks an arrangement that might otherwise be too facile. In his "Hard and Soft Series", paradoxically his most abstract, Eames adds feathers, a ball that looks strangely like a lemon, and gives his works the names of his favorite movie stars.

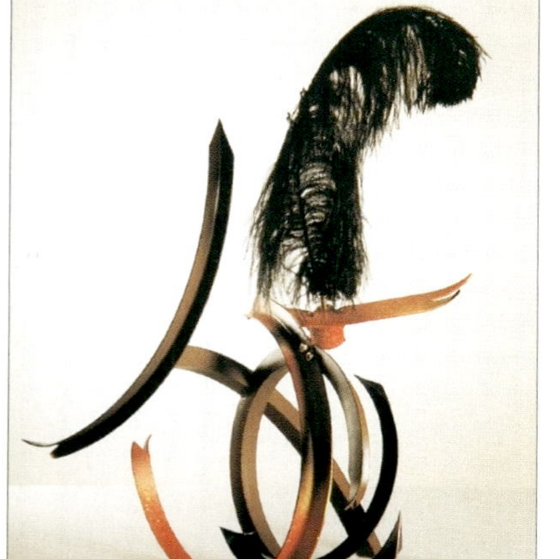

CONSTRUCTING FROM EMPTINESS

Eames' work encourages us to question our perception of sculpture. It re-poses the problems shared by sculptors working in metal at the beginning of the 20th century, like Archipenko, Gargallo and Julio Gonzalez. Gonzalez had come to realize that with metal one does not extract a solid form from its original mass. One starts from an empty space, a void. Eames, together with a number of his contemporaries, like Joel Shapiro and Anthony Caro, takes the same approach. There is no handling and fashioning of a solid mass. These artists link and combine elements. Shapiro explores primary geometric shapes with rectangles arranged in parallelepipeds; Eames, in his 1980s series, uses mainly curvilinear elements that he

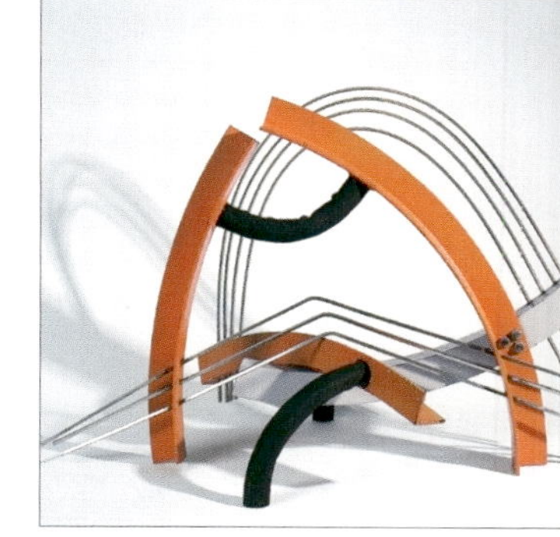

screws together. One artist thinks in straight lines, the other in curves.

For Eames, the work is visualized and constructed in terms of fluidity of line: linear perspective and tension are created by the juxtaposition and linkage of elements. This fluidity is present from his very first pieces made of wire, and reaches maturity in the series created at the end of the 1980s. The addition of spheres, of undulating wire, of circles and rings gives these constructions an almost baroque appearance. Movement is suggested rather than real. Even when his sculpture is less built than assembled - black or yellow balls immobilized in space, a pulley suspended in air, helicoids - the same relationship of movement and balance dominates the whole.

Whereas the sculptures of Shapiro and Caro are part of the framework of a history (the history of forms) - in other words, sculpture descended from modernism and abstraction, linked to mankind and the human body - Eames, the fabricator, has simply come across this history on his route ... and then traveled on. This allows him to do with it as he pleases: adhere, not adhere, create diversions, amuse himself, free himself ... while at the same time paying tribute to the forms that provide his means of expression. How else can we interpret these sculptures that are a kind of constructivist "game" in the third dimension: pulleys, rings, suspended spheres - forms that the first constructivists of the 1920s "manipulated" on canvas, these metallic curves that recall the spirals of the constructivist Vladimir Tatlin and the Moholy-Nagy movement?

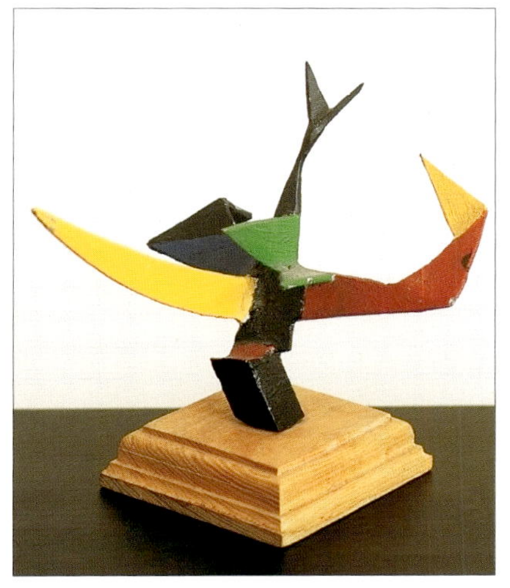

A SCULPTOR OF COLOR

In sculpture there can be no color without form. Eames' use of color exactly reflects his way of creating relationships between elements. Color is their link, their escape from uniformity, their breath. There is always a color counterpoint, even in his "Grey Series". Color shares fully in the dynamic of movement. Warm, contrasting colors or graduated tones of faded, matt colors afford balance and even grace. Color, immaterial though it may be, becomes the flesh of these pieces and enlightens us on the pictorial dimension of Eames' work. Sculpture, painting ... the genre matters little. One quickly realizes that the structure is never an end in itself, that the metal is not used merely for its material effects. Structure and material are only valid if they allow us to see differently, beyond the conventional limits.

OFFBEAT HUMOR

Humor is an integral part of Eames' artistic approach. Many artists have used it, almost unconsciously, to live and work in the so-called post-modern era. With Eames, attracted by surrealism and the appeal of the object, it represents a refusal to be locked into any rigid or formalistic system of thought. His humor is quirky, surprising, offbeat, ironic, but never bitter or morbid. Once his poetic "system" is in motion, like a kaleidoscope the bolts fly open, the shapes and meanings overlap in the simplest of ways. The process is reminiscent of children's play, which at its best engenders real invention and rich discoveries full of meaning. It is not surprising that Eames delighted in creating his numerous holograms, an almost magical technique allowing the artist to superimpose light images in the third dimension. In his sculptures, when he is manipulating shapes favored by the constructivist and abstract artists, he does not draw, as they do, on the world of ideas and concepts. He has nothing to prove or demonstrate. In his structures he boldly inserts objects of everyday use - curtain rings, disks, flywheels, cable hooks, etc. With his humor and love of independence, he pierces the sacred aura of art with the playfulness of his mechanisms. Take, for instance, his portable machine with a manual crankshaft that, when turned, sets colored cut-outs in motion, reminiscent of Calder's monumental mobiles.

This quirky ambivalence can be verbal as well as visual. The artist encourages us to name these object or shapes - as he clearly does in the titles of his works - in order to inject them with a genuine reality and closeness. Thumbing his nose at the concept of art's absolute autonomy, Eames is always happiest working at the outpost. What more natural, therefore, than to use names as subjects for his sculptures? They too are part of a "mechanism". More interested in poetry than concepts, faithful to his own phantasmagoria, he takes pleasure in deconstructing names and then re-creating them under our gaze, as in the "Crankshaft Series". Where there is language, there is necessarily structure and also play ... wordplay! The letters of words ("the crankshaft", "no statements", "cheap thrills") are threaded together and animated by a crank handle. In the case of "the crankshaft", when the handle is turned the letters rise and fall alternately, illustrating their own meaning in the third dimension, just as Apollinaire's calligrammes are "shape poems" illustrating their own titles. In other pieces, the crankshaft system mischievously inverts two letters or adds another, so that "art" becomes "rat", "money" becomes "monkey". Is this mere visual punning and wordplay? We know that the world of art and money is often the butt of jokes,

parody and caricature. So beware: the artist always has the last word! His work and his style are part of the great, derisive guffaw of the art world's dadaists.

LIGHTING THE SPARK OF LIFE

Eames' sense of fun exerts an irresistible draw on the spectator. He plays on the edge of a certain artistic world. With no declared agenda, he lights the sparks of life. In Eames we find echoes of that grand project of the 60's - to link art and life. Its leaders were the American and European artists known as the neo-dadaists. It was a multiform project - constantly re-kindled, re-thought, renewed, thwarted - which reflects a state of mind as much as a way of being. One thinks of Yves Klein, to whom Eames pays tribute in one of his pieces, the sculptor of emptiness who sought to apprehend reality differently. One also thinks of Rauschenberg, with whom Eames might easily have concurred when he said that his own art had everything to do with life and absolutely nothing to do with Art (capital A). By shortcircuiting our habits of seeing and thinking, by his salutary humor, Eames also wants to test the border between life and the thing we call art. Behind this apparent simplicity - disconcerting at times - his work is transgressive and fundamentally meaningful. It takes us, quietly and without fuss, toward poetic territories that are close to ourselves.

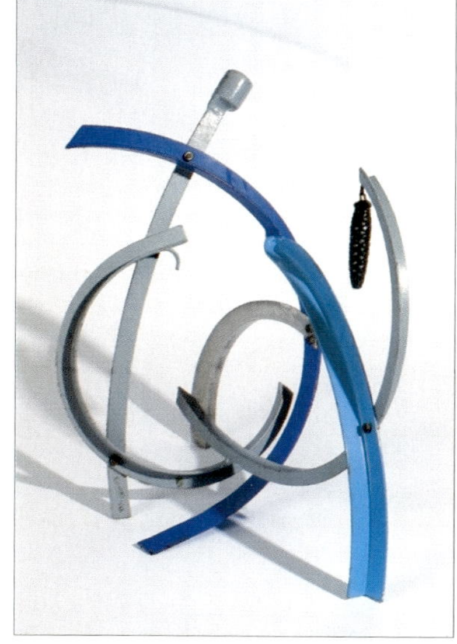

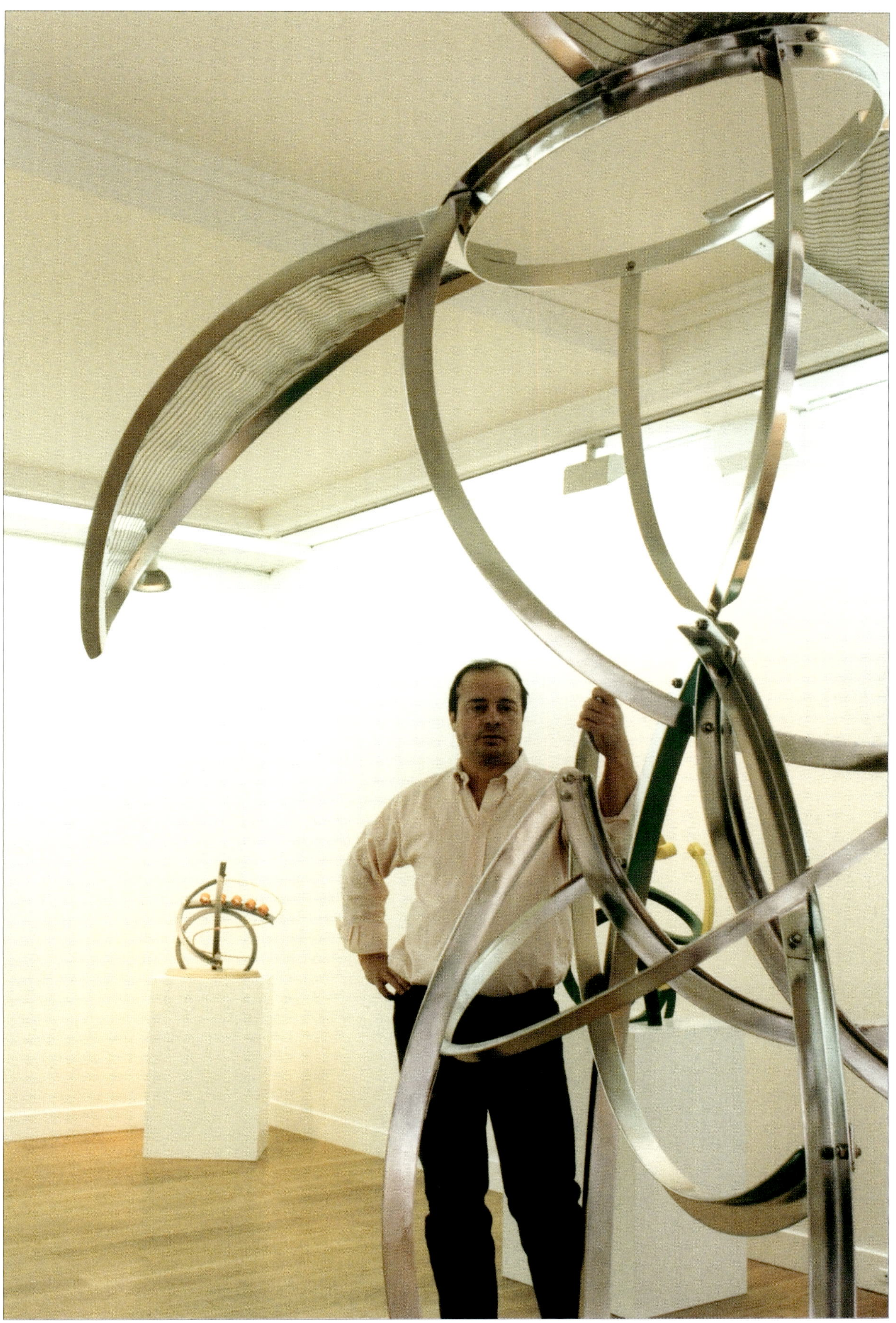

This "palm tree" in stainless steel, undoubtedly a key work in Dickon's output, is a study in technical complexity and artistic license. Dickon was rightly proud of this piece, as the photograph suggests.

RECOLLECTIONS

Paris, Spring 1977. Peter Marcasiano and I were walking along the quais of the Seine among the stands selling flowers and livestock. I was checking out the roosters. I needed a new rooster for my hens because the old one died last winter. Peter fancied a Rhode Island Red but I preferred a beautiful, very colorful one, which I bought. We put the rooster in a box and went to a bistrot for a drink. I told Peter about the work I was doing, how I would be taking part in an exhibition at the Ruhr Festival in Recklinghausen. I told him they expected me to produce a text for the catalogue and that I hadn't the faintest idea what to write. When you are totally immersed in your work as I am right now, you don't have the necessary distance to write about it. 'Yes,' said Peter, 'but that kind of text is very important, because an exhibition is like a stage play: it's not just the individual players but a complete work.'

I told Peter that the exhibition was called "To fly - a dream", a theme I've been working on for some time.

'To fly,' said Peter, 'is to seek endless expansion, to surpass yourself. The Faustian man. The Germans must love this theme because they are so very Faustian. You should talk about Christ, the bird, the Apollonian dream. It is important to say that your flying machines are not meant for flying. I mean the finality of art is not to fall into the trap of creating useful objects. Art should exist only to express our most secret longings. The Apollonian dream is to float up into infinity. Look at your balloons! They are flying objects that suggest this dream, this dream of flying into infinity. You must read Nietzsche: Apollo is the embodiment of the dream of flying. Dionysos is the juice that flows from the earth, the practical man. Put the Apollonian and the Dionysiac together and what do you get? The Faustian, with his link to the infinite, do you see?' I nodded - which seemed to me at the time the most intelligent reply I could give. 'You have to write something that instantly captivates the reader,' said Peter. 'You have to think of something fantastic - for instance that you dreamed you couldn't buy anything with money anymore. I hope you'll get an idea like that for your text.'

We got up and continued walking along the river, Peter, myself and the rooster.

Text written by Dickon Eames for the catalogue "To fly - a dream".

Micheal's friendship with Dickon went back many years. I can't say exactly when or where they met. I believe Micheal spent a Christmas or two with Dickon and family before I shared his life.

For my own part, I met Dickon's family several times, in our own house in the south of France, and in Normandy, in Dickon's home in Freneuse. Micheal used to stay a night or two in that house, on his way to catch the ferry to Ireland. I did this with him a couple of times too. It was on one of these occasions that I carved my signature into the famous table.

When we first bought our house near Nîmes in southern France, Dickon and his family came to stay with us for a few days. That was in 1988. Micheal was busy working on the house over the summer, mixing cement, etc. Dickon helped with this and the two of them had lots of laughs and enjoyed each other's company. They were both glad to have something to do. Amongst all the drinking and joking between them, they got quite a bit done as well.

I remember the 'adult toys' Dickon made early in his life. They were like huge cages with ping pong balls inside and they were rather wonderful. Very original and whimsical, so I think Micheal was disappointed when Dickon moved on to doing the steel sculptures … but this is a subjective approach.

Matthew was something of an artist, too. When he was in my house, he did a painting of a ship and a castle on a rock. I kept it because I really liked it, and I still have it. I hope Matthew is carrying on with his art, in the steps of his gifted father.

Meg Early, Painter and Writer, Nîmes

One day I saw some artworks by Dickon Eames in the Parisian studio of an artist friend. I was instantly struck by the humor, joy and inventiveness that must have gone into their making. When Dickon heard about my enthusiasm, he wrote to me proposing we meet to discuss an exhibition in Amsterdam. This we did, and soon afterwards Dickon had his first show at my gallery.

The Galerie d'Theeboom was located in an old warehouse dating from 1701, in the days when ships docked in the town center bearing tea and exotic spices from the Indies. Standing on a corner, it was flooded with daylight on two sides and provided the perfect setting for Dickon's "Crankshaft Series".

It was a joyful and spirited exhibition that had people walking all around the pieces to discover their many surprising facets. Some even had a handle you could turn to see the object change and deliver a message, often spelled out in letters.

This first exhibition was followed by others, always a source of fascination and delight .

Cathy Hemmer, Galerie d'Theeboom, Amsterdam

In 1975, when I first visited my parents-in-law's weekend house in Freneuse-sur-Risle (Normandy), a village of certainly less than 300 inhabitants, one of the first things I was told was: "There is another American who lives in this village!" Since Freneuse could be called far off the beaten track, I was curious enough to look up this "another American" and drove up a narrow road, as indicated, past small decrepit farmhouses, for about one mile. Suddenly, to the right hand side of the road, slightly lower down, I saw this most magnificent "Hansel and Gretel" house, directly out of a fairy-tale: a typical Normandy house, but everything about it was bigger, more opulent, in other words, a huge Normandy thatched roof home with more emphasis to every detail. The American mailbox at the driveway told me that this was the place Dickon was in, and not being a shy person, he immediately invited me in for a drink, presented me to his beautiful and charming English wife Carol, showed me around his fantastic house - I will leave it up to more talented people to describe it - and naturally, his atelier with his incredible pieces of art. This was the beginning of a long friendship.

If I were to sum up in a few lines this long friendship and how I experienced Dickon, I would begin by saying how open and kind-hearted Dickon was. Very humble, always helpful, always smiling, always a funny story handy. The next remarkable point about Dickon was his limitless imagination which went far beyond his work. One day he would turn up with a dog-cart he had built, which was pulled by his beloved Belgian Shepherd "Blackhawk", with his son Matthew proudly as coachman - to take my children for a ride. The next day he would show me a seat he had designed for truckdrivers which would revolutionize truckdrivers seats, and so on.

Although Dickon and his family lived in a secluded place, their many friends and admirers were always welcome and, as far as I could judge, made much of the Eames' hospitality. Since my family and I would usually drive to Normandy most weekends of the year, I would often drop by for a drink or a chat and never failed to meet up with an international mixture from every social class imaginable: from royals to tramps, from movie stars to scientists, Carol and Dickon would be entertaining them with great ease. But - and this was another fascinating side of Dickon - he could always (whether tired of the crowd, or because he had an inspiration, I do not know) suddenly disappear into his workshop and fully concentrate on his latest work of art.

It was a blow to me and my family to suddenly lose such a fine friend.

Anthony Stone, Paris, Berlin

Dickon sought clarity through abstraction, achieving an aesthetic expression that stirs the emotions and stimulates insight. His sculpture constantly provokes the eye and the imagination.

Christophe von Hohenberg, Photographer, New York

Dear Debbie,

Some months ago, Dickon asked me to write something in the catalogue for the show at your gallery, and I really would like to do so. The only problem is that it is absolutely impossible for me to write something objective about Dickon's work. We are too close.

When I come to his farm in Normandy I always stay for about half an hour in his big studio to look at and to play with his new objects. After that session, we mostly meet in the kitchen for some vodka tonics and we talk about my experience of that last half hour. Those half hours are always the best half hours I can imagine. So relaxing, so happy. Well, you know what I mean 'cause otherwise you wouldn't have asked him to bring his pieces to your gallery.

Please, Debbie, be so friendly and explain to Dickon, when you see him, that I really would like to write something about his work, but that because of our great friendship it is not possible.

Yours,

Mark Brusse, Painter and Sculptor, Paris

When I think of Dickon Eames, my mind goes back to a period full of enthusiasm, high spirits and shared artistic passion. In a way it's like reliving the 70s, because we first met at the beginning of the decade in Corfu, and then lost track of each other at the onset of the 80s, when I left France to live abroad.

When Dickon came back from Corfu, we would spend long evenings arguing about conceptual art, the minimalists, land art, etc. Dickon was a very sensitive artist, acutely receptive to emotions, and also very charismatic, a bon vivant who could be very funny.

This love of fun was contagious. I remember our epic trip to Amsterdam in my van, in the company of Mark Brusse. We were taking Dickon's Crankshaft Series to a vernissage. It was one of those unfor-gettable journeys, a bit like a Jacques Tati film with an extra dose of craziness thrown in.

Dickon was an artist in the noblest sense: fiercely independent in his approach, passionate about contemporary sculpture, but refusing to be part of any movement or trend. He had an innate gravity, and an innate playfulness. As I see it, all his work is a marvelous play on the concept of gravity and gravitation: everything that goes up must come down. That's what struck me about his work, for example his Ping Pong Ball Machine.

The 70s were intensely vibrant years, full of remarkable and unusual people, among whom Dickon stands out in my memory. There is still much to discover about his art and the importance of his work.

André du Besset, Painter, Présilly, France

Some notes on Dickon Eames.

In 1983 I was working for Light Fantastic, one of the first hologram galleries, set up by Peter Woodd and located in London's Covent Garden. The holograms were made in our lab in Loughborough, Leicestershire. At that time it was just me and David Hamson, a brilliant man and one of the unsung heroes of holography. David and I were by no means artists, and looking back on some of the images we made in those days, I have to smile a little. Clearly, we needed some creative input to generate interesting ideas. That's where Dickon came in. As soon as I saw some of his subjects for holograms, I could see that he knew what the process required. Making a hologram is a complex operation, involving the production of perfectly formed sculptures that are very stable. His understanding of the art enabled us to make quick progress because his sculptures were made to the strict technical requirements of holography, yet without placing constraints on the creative content. You see, holography is a very unforgiving medium. What you see is what you get. If there are small flaws on the sculpture, they will show up as huge faults under the powerful gaze of the laser. Dickon's attention to technical perfection as well as to the design aspect made the whole process work.

Dickon used to come over from Normandy by train and I would pick him up at the station. He would be wearing a long dark coat and carrying a heavy holdall that would clank as he loaded it into the back of the car. David and I never knew what subjects Dickon would bring and he always surprised us. We would set up the first hologram in the morning and then go to the local fish and chip shop for lunch! We had a great time working together. I think Dickon enjoyed these visits because David and I showed no mercy in our jokes about his efforts. I still have some of the original holograms we made. My personal favourites are the interlocking metal stars, the little starfish in a welded steel cube and the one we called "Cashcade", which is a hologram of money pouring out of a purse.

I used to feel quite proud when we saw the finished pieces in our Covent Garden gallery. Now, many years later, I can fully appreciate the major contribution Dickon made to holography.

Patrick Flynn, Technical Director, London

As a friend and neighbor, Dickon was a very vibrant presence, and his way of looking at life made a big impression on our family. We children loved to be around him. When you look at his work you get a feeling of freedom and independence. The lithograph that has pride of place in my living room is a constant reminder of Dickon as an artist and a much valued friend.

Henri Glaizot, Rouen, Paris

I met Dickon when I was living in Paris in the late 70's. Soon after that I returned to England to run Holoco, a special effects company which also specialized in holography and was financed by The Who.

Dickon's work fascinated me as it was both dimensional and ironic. I introduced Dickon to Anton Furst, who was then creative director for Holoco and later creative director for Stanley Kubrick on several of his movies. Anton and Dickon became great friends.

They went on to explore pseudoscopic imagery with large format plates. Dickon was deeply interested in illusion. He and Anton produced a coffee table design around the concept of integrating reality and the reality of illusion. I bought the sketch of this project from Dickon. We also experimented with Dickon's wire structure based on the tesseract, or hypercube. Because of its dimensionality and parallax it was an ideal subject for a hologram.

This was the "pioneer" period of holographic art. It was an exciting, vibrant scene and the artists working in the medium all knew each other. Matthias Lauk, who set up the first hologram museum in Germany, loved Dickon's work and acquired several pieces.

In 1981 I moved on from Holoco and launched Light Fantastic, my own hologram gallery. I continued to work with Dickon and Anton Furst and in 1982-3 we brought out a limited editon range of 8" x 10" glass plate holograms entitled "Light Fantastic Series". Dickon must have created some 15 to 20 designs. These were very popular and sold to other hologram galleries, museums and private collectors.

He also created a limited edition print, entitled Red Balloon, which was a wedding present to my wife and me.

These are some of my memories of Dickon. The last time I saw him was at his house in Normandy. He was a great guy and I was sad to hear he had died.

Peter Woodd, Light Fantastic, London

Dickon was a fascinating and interesting character who brought to his sculpture a unique eye for shape and form. He was the husband of my oldest friend which was how I first knew him, and during my many visits to Freneuse, Normandy I became an ardent admirer not only of his work but also of his warm and generous personality. After his death, Carol gave me his last sculpture which has pride of place at my home in Devon.

Judith Dale, Photographer, Devon, UK

Fond memories

The house was a wonderful place with echoes of the past, and bohemia.

In Normandy there was space to make art; space for Carol to breed her Dale ponies; space for Matthew to explore. We spent many happy times there filled with fun and laughter. And, of course, the inevitable heated art discussions around the infamous artist's table.

Dickon, Del and I went out to replenish the supply of cider and Calvados. Instead of heading towards the village we made our way to the Abbey Le Bec Hellouin in the Eure. "This is where I get my Calvados and have my best conversations", says Dickon.

Patricia Leighton, Artist, New York

Dickon Eames was my buddy from the mid-seventies when we first met in Paris until his premature death at the age of 52. We started off as drinking partners but our relationship evolved into much more. We shared confidences about our respective work, he as an artist, me as a journalist and would-be book writer. We shared stories about travel, romance, and the ups and downs of our bohemian lives.

In the spring of 1975, after I returned from covering the end of the Vietnam war, I headed for Normandy where Dickon and Carol opened their home and hearts to me. It was neither the first nor the last time this kindness was extended, but after the traumatic experience of Vietnam I needed a quiet place to unwind, take stock, and put pen to paper. All this, I heartily add, while Miss Carol prepared her famous gastronomic delights and Dickon and I made sure the larder was full of vodka and Schweppes.

Later on, Elaine and I had a lavish apartment in Paris where Mr. and Mrs. Eames often stayed when they visited the capital. I was then making a good buck and happy to extend to Dickon and Carol the hospitality they had shown me when I was struggling.

I was on assignment in South Africa when I learned that Dickon has passed and I toasted him that night in a Cape Town bar.

I still visit Normandy from time to time and when I do, I think about the old days. The simple thought of Dickon brings a special feeling to my heart. It is nice to be remembered so fondly.

Robert Wiener, Journalist and Producer, Paris

I made the acquaintance of Dickon through the best of intermediaries: through his work.

One evening in 1993 when I happened to be strolling in Paris' Left Bank, I decided to drop in on a gallery owner I knew. He gave me a quick tour of the exhibition area, and then did me the honor of taking me into his "cabinet des merveilles" - a fabulous jumble of periods and styles where works by painters, sculptors, illustrators and designers jostled for space. It was then that I saw her: a superb iron lady with strangely voluptuous curves and a feathery plume that twitched mischievously as I passed, as if to distract my attention from everything else and draw me into a realm of gloriously free, untrammeled signs.

I was immediately won over and asked to meet the artist. I think I expected him to reveal a mystery I felt incapable of penetrating. But in fact, at that decisive first meeting, Dickon had absolutely nothing to say for himself! I swiftly came to the conclusion that he was an artist who could only express himself through his art, protected by an impenetrable shell of silence.

So it was I who started talking, with the result that Dickon immediately recovered the power of speech. He responded in such a simple, warm and genuine way that he implicitly answered all the questions I hadn't been able to ask. For example, a chance remark about his contemporaries, a few picturesque words describing his house in Normandy or a frank confession about his little weaknesses told me infinitely more than any lofty pronouncement could do.

Like all generous souls, he had given much without knowing it, and even better, by releasing me from my academic scruples, he enabled me to write with total freedom. From then on, our relationship was based on a perfect spontaneity. And so it was that we met again for his vernissage.

On this occasion, I found Dickon absolutely true to the image of his sculptures: light-hearted, informal, luminous, content to be himself, entirely indifferent to the interests at stake. Between what was spoken and what remained unsaid, I sensed a growing recognition and complicity that promised to develop into real friendship.

When I left, I little suspected I would never see Dickon again, but time and obligations intervened, and when I finally got in touch it was too late: Dickon was dead.

From those meetings with Dickon - brief sparks of life with neither a past nor a future - there remains the vague feeling of a missed opportunity, as if some kind of existential accident let everything slip away before I could tell Dickon why he had touched me so deeply.

Perhaps that is what I am trying to do today. Too late, as is often the case. But then ... who knows?

Maïté Lannes-Lacroutz, Writer, Paris

My friend Dickon

Dickon Eames was born and raised in Greenwich Village, at a time when the village was a bohemian enclave of artists and writers in New York. He was steeped in the arts in his everyday life, and then studied at the Art Students League.

The art climate into which Dickon was born was of the earlier Ashcan School, just then coming to a close, in the mid-1940's. That tradition was a form of social realism, which looked to the inner city for their source of inspiration. The Ashcan artists had rejected European modernism, instead stressing pathos and the underdog. The area of 14th Street, with its hustle and bustle, had become its center and the home for the Art Students League.

Here, Edward Hopper had developed a vision of modern city life, placing his alienated, melancholy figures in isolation, and in deserted city streets. His colors were muted, but in planes, a prelude for the later Color-field artists. On the other hand, Reginald Marsh's works were crowded with a rich profusion of human forms and exuberant girls, life in all its vitality, highly colorful.

Betty Parish, Dickon's mother, was a painter in this social realist form, and a gifted printmaker, of mostly woodcuts and etchings. She worked from her studio on Union Square. In her youth she was also an artist's model, and appears in many of Reginald Marsh's paintings hanging in museums throughout the US.

Dickon inherited a joie de vivre, as well as Edward Hopper's paint brushes from Betty, who had received them upon Hopper's death.

In the late forties and fifties, during Dickon's youth, Abstract Expressionism was being developed in the village. David Smith used industrial materials and welded metal, drawing lines and planes in space using delicately articulated steel rods. Alexander Calder had developed mobiles, kinetic sculpture.

I met Dickon in the sixties when I first arrived in New York. I recall a snake dancer at his first wedding, only a brief marriage. Later, in 1971, he met Carol in Corfu, who became the love of his life.

In the sixties he moved to Paris to explore a passion for other cultures and to participate in the European arts. Attracted to the Left Bank, he became involved with a group of European artists. Mark Brusse and Mike Farrell, as well as Willem Van Malsen and Peter Marcasiano, were close friends. They later carved their signatures into his large artists' oak dining table in Normandy.

He was a trans-Atlantic artist (his term was mid-Atlantic). Returning to New York several times a year, to involve himself here, sometimes he brought his young son, Matthew, along. During Dickon's entire life he was surrounded by artists. In Paris he had also been exposed to Julio Gonzalez' pioneering works of welded sculpture.

In New York, among his friends were, author, Ernest Brawley, and sculptors, Patricia Leighton, Ed McGowin and Claudia DeMonte. Here, he looked at works of Anthony Caro, Willard Boepple, and Robert Morris.

We had many philosophical discussions about how to "see" and develop sculpture. At one point Clement Greenberg, the art critic, claimed that multi-color sculpture worked against itself, and could not be done successfully. Dickon, with his artist's curiosity, and independent nature, then developed a polychrome series, which I find to be significant and absolutely wonderful.

Once, when I was visiting Dickon and Carol in Normandy, we went to a country fair. As we walked in a field at a slight distance, Dickon pointed out a visual overview of the lights and movement of the fair. There he saw Betty's somewhat romantic painterly images in the scene. I saw Dickon's sculpture of movement and messages there.

He developed a number of distinct series, or cycles, often working on several pieces simultaneously, moving the ideas back and forth. His works with moving parts offered up words and glyphs, often infused with humor. His stationary steel and painted steel works could be very serious formal sculptures, which were 'of structure'. Or, sometimes alluding to a situation, or an object, they could be fantasy structures, somewhat anthropomorphic.

It is clear that his artwork makes a significant contribution, speaking with its own unique voice. It is strong. It is clear. Dickon Eames bridged cultures, fused concepts, and then developed his own vision.

I miss those conversations and great times.

Del Geist, Sculptor, New York

To all who helped me travel back in time to the events and the friendships that marked my father's life, I offer heartfelt thanks. Without their patience and generosity, their personal recollections and the documents they placed at my disposal, this book could never have been written.

I would like to give special thanks to
Maryam Ansari- Rodari, Galerie Georges Moos, Geneva
Claude Bernard, Galerie Claude Bernard, Paris
Mark Brusse, Painter and Sculptor, Paris
Patrick Cramer, Galerie Patrick Cramer, Geneva
Judith Dale, Photographer, Devon, UK
Christophe Dorny, Editor of the Bénézit Dictionary of Artists, Paris
André du Besset, Painter, Présilly, France
Meg Early, Painter and Writer, Nîmes
Leena Fernando, Tabor Academy, Massachusetts
Patrick Flynn, Technical Director, London
Del Geist, Sculptor, New York
Robin Gibson, Robin Gibson Gallery, Australia
The Glaizot family, Rouen, Paris
Cathy Hemmer, Galerie d'Theeboom, Amsterdam
Michiel Hennus, Wetering Galerie, Amsterdam
Christophe von Hohenberg, Photographer, New York
Maïté Lannes-Lacroutz, Writer, Paris
Matthias Lauk, Collector, Cologne
Patricia Leighton, Artist, New York
Maximilian Lyons, Architect, London
Denise and Colombe Marcasiano, Paris
Andy Pepper, Art Director, London
Erik Pott, Artist, Amsterdam
Eve Ritscher, Creative Director, London
Jonathan Ross, Jonathan Ross Hologram Collection/Gallery 286, London
Olav Skipnes, Collector, Hamar, Norway
Anthony and Liliane Stone, Paris, Berlin
Robert Wiener, Journalist and Producer, Paris
Deborah Wolf-Campert, Galerie Balans, Amsterdam
John Wolff, Director of Holoco, London
Peter Woodd, Light Fantastic, London

My thanks go also to the French *commune* of Freneuse, to its mayor, municipal team and local residents who helped me retrace a shared past.
Finally, I wish to express my infinite gratitude to Monika Tencer, without whom none of this could have been possible. Her determination and total commitment to this project were an unfailing support during my long months of research and writing. A brilliant orchestrator, she brought together a talented team whose contribution to this work has been considerable. Sincere thanks to Maguy Tager for the excellent book design, and to Joëlle Lobut and Judith Harris for their editorial insight and advice.

Photo credits:
Christophe von Hohenberg : pages 29 - 66 to 67 - 71 to 73 -
83 - 85 to 109 - 111 to 116 - 119 to 125 - 127 to 129
Cathy Hemmer : pages 58 to 59 - 66 to 69
Patrick Flynn : pages 75 to 80
Olav Skipnes : page 78
Maurice Morand : page 110
Judith Dale : page 126

Photogravure: Fotimprim, Paris

Printed and bound in Germany
by Ludwig Auer GmbH, D-86609 Donauwoerth